THE EVERYTHING RESTAURANT RECIPES COOKBOOK

Dear Reader,

Trying to create your favorite restaurant foods at home can be fun and save you a lot of money in these tough economic times. Most of us cannot afford to eat out as much as we used to, so I've been searching for ways to make foods that I enjoy the most at home and share them with you. I live in a town with no stoplights or drive-thru windows, so fast food is not readily available to me. When I get hungry for a particular type of food, my only option is to go to the grocery store and figure out what I need to make it at home. That has been the inspiration for this book; the recipes are arranged according to food cravings. If you are in the mood for Italian, you can find popular dishes on the menu at Olive Garden, Romano's Macaroni Grill, and Buca di Beppo. Want something from your favorite bar and grill? There is a nice selection of recipes from Applebee's, Chili's, and T.G.I. Friday's. Don't forget dessert. We often skip it when dining out, but now you can have your cake and eat it, too! Hope you enjoy exploring these recipes and make some great restaurant meals at home for your family and friends.

Becky Bopp

Welcome to the EVERYTHING® Series!

These handy, accessible books give you all you need to tackle a difficult project, gain a new hobby, comprehend a fascinating topic, prepare for an exam, or even brush up on something you learned back in school but have since forgotten.

You can choose to read an Everything® book from cover to cover or just pick out the information you want from our four useful boxes: e-questions, e-facts, e-alerts, and e-ssentials.

We give you everything you need to know on the subject, but throw in a lot of fun stuff along the way, too.

We now have more than 400 Everything® books in print, spanning such wide-ranging categories as weddings, pregnancy, cooking, music instruction, foreign language, crafts, pets, New Age, and so much more. When you're done reading them all, you can finally say you know Everything®!

QUESTION
Answers to common questions

FACT
Important snippets of information

ALERT
Urgent warnings

ESSENTIAL
Quick handy tips

PUBLISHER Karen Cooper
DIRECTOR OF ACQUISITIONS AND INNOVATION Paula Munier
MANAGING EDITOR, EVERYTHING® SERIES Lisa Laing
COPY CHIEF Casey Ebert
ACQUISITIONS EDITOR Lisa Laing
SENIOR DEVELOPMENT EDITOR Brett Palana-Shanahan
EDITORIAL ASSISTANT Ross Weisman
EVERYTHING® SERIES COVER DESIGNER Erin Alexander
LAYOUT DESIGNERS Colleen Cunningham, Elisabeth Lariviere, Ashley Vierra, Denise Wallace

Visit the entire Everything® series at www.everything.com

THE EVERYTHING® RESTAURANT RECIPES COOKBOOK

Copycat recipes for:
- Outback Steakhouse Bloomin' Onion • Long John Silver's Fish Tacos
- T.G.I. Friday's Dragonfly Chicken • Applebee's Baby Back Ribs
- Chili's Grill & Bar Molten Chocolate Cake . . . and hundreds more!

Becky Bopp

Avon, Massachusetts

To Jesse for helping me finish what I started.

Copyright © 2011 by F+W Media, Inc. All rights reserved.
This book, or parts thereof, may not be reproduced
in any form without permission from the publisher; exceptions
are made for brief excerpts used in published reviews.

An Everything® Series Book.
Everything® and everything.com® are registered trademarks of F+W Media, Inc.

Published by Adams Media, a division of F+W Media, Inc.
57 Littlefield Street, Avon, MA 02322 U.S.A.
www.adamsmedia.com

ISBN 10: 1-4405-1125-X
ISBN 13: 978-1-4405-1125-7
eISBN 10: 1-4405-2509-9
eISBN 13: 978-1-4405-2509-4

Printed in the United States of America.

10 9 8 7 6 5 4 3 2 1

Library of Congress Cataloging-in-Publication Data
is available from the publisher.

This publication is designed to provide accurate and authoritative information with regard to the subject matter covered. It is sold with the understanding that the publisher is not engaged in rendering legal, accounting, or other professional advice. If legal advice or other expert assistance is required, the services of a competent professional person should be sought.

—From a *Declaration of Principles* jointly adopted by a Committee of the American Bar Association and a Committee of Publishers and Associations

Many of the designations used by manufacturers and sellers to distinguish their products are claimed as trademarks, including the restaurant and recipe names used in this book. Where those designations appear and F+W Media was aware of a trademark claim, the designations have been printed with initial capital letters. All rights to these trademarks are reserved by the various corporations that own these rights.

This book is available at quantity discounts for bulk purchases.
For information, please call 1-800-289-0963.

Contents

Introduction ix

1 Creating the Restaurant Feeling at Home 1
    Become a Restaurant Detective 2
    Appliances and Cookware 2
    Stocking the Pantry 4
    Choosing Ingredients 8
    Cooking Terms and Techniques 11
    Food Presentation 13

2 Breakfast and Brunch 15

3 Appetizers 32

4 Soups, Stews, and Chilis 55

5 Salads and Sandwiches 75

6 Fast Food and Treats 93

7 Steakhouse Favorites 111

8	Bar Food..................................	125
9	Mexican..................................	145
10	Asian....................................	163
11	Italian...................................	184
12	Family Style..............................	209
13	Southern Style...........................	227
14	Desserts.................................	241
15	Signature Cocktails and Drinks............	265

Appendix A: Recipe List by Restaurant Name......... 282
Appendix B: Restaurant and Copycat Recipe Websites .. 286
Appendix C: Healthier Substitutions and Conversions... 288

Index... 290

Acknowledgments

I'd like to thank my loyal fans on hubpages for their comments and feedback through the years. Thank you to my editors at Adams Media who found me online and helped me through the writing process. Encouragement and support came from both family and friends. I am truly blessed and grateful to all.

Introduction

AMERICAN FAMILIES LOVE TO go out to eat at their favorite restaurants; however, surveys have shown that people are spending less money than ever at restaurants due to budget restrictions and a declining economy. If you are one of those people, why not surprise your family and friends with their favorite restaurant dish by making it at home in your own kitchen?

This book will pay for itself the first time you use it because you can cook at home for a fraction of the cost of dining out. You will find step-by-step instructions for all those amazing dishes that draw people into restaurants, and you will be sure that the food was cooked under hygienic conditions since you will be making it yourself.

You don't have to be a master chef to prepare these meals. All the recipes in this book use basic ingredients that can be found in any grocery store. There is no need to buy any fancy equipment, since the cooking techniques are simple.

In this book, you will find tips on how to create the restaurant feeling at home. You'll get a list of basic cookware and appliances you need to have in your kitchen as well as how to stock your pantry to prepare some amazing dishes. There will be a primer on how to choose the best and freshest ingredients. You will also learn the basic cooking terms and techniques used in this book. Other key factors to be discussed in creating a restaurant atmosphere at home are setting an inviting table and presenting the food in the most appealing way.

Another benefit of *The Everything® Restaurant Recipes Cookbook* is the ability to alter dishes to your own tastes and dietary guidelines. Restaurant foods contain more fat, salt, and sugar than we should have in our diets. You may use these recipes and make your own substitutes for a lower calorie or sugar free meal. Since you already know in advance what the dish is supposed to taste like, you know you will enjoy it before you start cooking.

Portion control is a huge issue in the restaurant industry today. Every meal is served on a giant plate with the thought that more is better. Most diet books recommend that when dining out you eat only half the portion of an entrée and put the rest in a box to go. Cooking at home allows you to control the amount of calories you consume. Plus, you can take a break from the meal and have dessert and coffee several hours later, which is something you cannot do in a restaurant.

Recipe cloning can be a fun activity in which the whole family can participate. You will be able to prepare dishes from several different restaurants in one sitting. Let the children pick an appetizer from T.G.I Friday's, Dad can choose his favorite dish from Outback Steakhouse, and Mom can choose a dessert—everyone will be happy with the meal—because this book will add a variety of restaurant recipes to your cooking repertoire.

CHAPTER 1

Creating the Restaurant Feeling at Home

Many families eat out about three times per week. If you have a large family or even a small family with big eaters, you know that the cost of this adds up quickly. With prices rising in all areas of retail, it can be a good idea to have a less costly alternative to dining out. Your family will truly appreciate the effort you make to get a restaurant-quality recipe to serve for everyday meals. In most cases, restaurant recipes have taken a lot of years to perfect, but you can have them, tried and true, to serve up piping hot to your family.

Become a Restaurant Detective

Wherever your tastes lie, it is no longer difficult to find out the ingredients in most restaurant recipes. With a little detective work and a quick visit to the local grocery store, you can be serving up a dinner that no one will be able to resist. You will be amazed at the savings you will accumulate when you use a copycat restaurant recipe instead of dining out.

If you are having a party, you can make a copycat restaurant recipe that will have your guests swearing you purchased it from the restaurant that made the dish famous. You can enjoy the attention your cooking will bring when you decide to make a copycat restaurant recipe for your next party or potluck dinner.

Just because you cook your own food doesn't mean it can't be as delicious as a five-star restaurant; all you need are a few simple tools. You don't have to be a master chef to cook like one, either. The equipment needed to prepare the recipes in this book are broken into appliances, cooking gadgets, cookware, and bakeware. You will also learn the terms and techniques needed to make a wonderful restaurant-quality meal.

Appliances and Cookware

Appliances

These appliances will provide the greatest convenience and versatility in your kitchen:

- **Electric mixer**—A portable handheld mixer will do well for all of the recipes in this book.
- **Blender**—This kitchen helper cuts time instantly by blending, chopping, and puréeing foods.
- **Deep fryer**—A small Fry Daddy is the best at regulating the temperature of the cooking oil when deep frying meats or vegetables.
- **George Foreman Indoor Grill**—This is a great time saver in the kitchen when grilling any kind of meat, since both sides cook at once.
- **Microwave oven**—As ubiquitous as they are, you can rely on them for quick thawing and heating jobs in the kitchen.

Cooking Gadgets

A good cook knows that a good-quality set of knives can accomplish more in the kitchen than any electronic device. These are the knives that you will need:

- A **chef's knife** that has a broad, tapered shape, which can easily be rocked over ingredients
- A **bread knife**, which has a serrated edge that makes it perfect for cutting through crusts
- A **paring knife** has a short blade that is used for peeling, trimming, coring, and seeding vegetables

ALERT

Cooking in the kitchen can be fun, but it is a spot for potential accidents. There are some basic safety rules you should follow to make your cooking experience more enjoyable: The kitchen is not the place to go barefoot; it is important to understand your tools and how to handle them properly; read the instructions on how to use your appliances.

Other Tools

Other tools needed in food preparation include:

- Bottle opener
- Can opener
- Colander
- Cutting board
- Grater
- Long-handled forks, spoons, and spatulas
- Meat mallet
- Pizza cutter
- Rolling pin
- Set of measuring cups

- Set of measuring spoons
- Set of mixing bowls

Cookware

You'll also need the following pieces of cookware:

- Saucepans with lids (small, medium, and large)
- Stockpot (large enough to make soup for your family)
- Cast-iron skillet (for using in the oven)
- 12" nonstick skillet

Bakeware

Don't forget these necessary pieces of bakeware:

- Baking sheets
- Casserole dishes (small, medium, and large)
- Muffin pan
- Rectangular sheet cake pan
- Roasting pan with a rack
- Pizza pan

Stocking the Pantry

Cooking is much easier when you know what you've already got on hand and aren't running to the grocery store every time you want to fix a meal. Having a well-stocked pantry is a cook's secret weapon. Here is a list of basic ingredients that should be in your pantry. Of course, you can adjust items on the list to suit your family's likes and dislikes.

Herbs and Spices

If you've spent any time in the spice aisle at the supermarket lately, you know how expensive spices are. A little bottle will set you back a couple of bucks. Therefore, it is recommended that you buy seasoning blends. Some of the most common and widely used flavors are:

- Barbecue seasoning, which contains a variety of spices that are good sprinkled onto meat before grilling, roasting or broiling.
- Cajun seasoning is a blend of red pepper, garlic, onion, salt, and pepper used to add a hot taste to any dish.
- Italian seasoning is a favorite mix of basil and oregano useful in most pasta dishes.
- Lemon pepper seasoning adds flavor to poultry and vegetables.
- Mexican seasoning contains a mixture of peppers, garlic, salt, and cumin suitable for tacos, fajitas, and enchiladas.

ESSENTIAL

A great way to stock your pantry with spices is to buy one or two new ones each time you go shopping and buy fresh herbs only when needed.

Sauces

Sauces are a great way to add flavor to your dishes. Here are some sauces you should have on hand in your kitchen:

- Barbecue sauce
- Chili sauce
- Hot pepper sauce
- Olive oil
- Packages of dried onion soup mix
- Packages of salad dressing mix
- Soy sauce
- Soups in a can (cream of mushroom, chicken, celery)
- Steak sauce
- Sweet and sour sauce
- Teriyaki sauce
- Vinegar (red, rice, and balsamic)
- Wine (red and white suitable, for drinking)
- Worcestershire sauce

Basic Grocery Items

You also need some essential grocery items, things you will find yourself using over and over in myriad recipes. These kitchen basics include:

- Beans (a variety of canned and dried)
- Bread crumbs
- Bullion cubes and powders
- Cooking oil
- Crackers (a variety)
- Croutons
- Meats (canned tuna, chicken, crab, and clams)
- Olives (black and green)
- Pastas (a mixed variety)
- Rice (white, long grain, wild, brown)
- Salsa
- Tomatoes (a variety of canned)
- Tomato paste
- Tomato sauce

Baking Items

To bake like the best restaurants, you need to keep some baking basics in your pantry, including:

- Baking mix
- Baking powder
- Baking soda
- Brown sugar
- Confectioners' sugar
- Cocoa powder
- Cornstarch
- Flavored chips (chocolate, peanut butter, caramel)
- Flour
- Honey
- Nuts (a variety)
- Pancake mix

- Sugar
- Sweetened condensed milk
- Vegetable shortening
- Yeast

For Desserts

To create many restaurant-inspired desserts, you should have the following on hand:

- Applesauce
- Canned fruits
- Cake mixes, brownies, and frostings
- Fixings for ice cream sundaes
- Puddings

In the Refrigerator

Keep these items handy in the fridge so you can whip up your favorite copycat recipes without having to run out to the store. Make sure to have:

- Butter or margarine
- Cheeses (a good variety)
- Cream
- Eggs
- Ketchup
- Milk
- Mayonnaise
- Mustard
- Salad dressings
- Salad fixings (a variety of fresh vegetables)
- Sour cream

In the Freezer

There are a few items that, while you won't use them every day, you'll still want to keep stocked in your freezer. They include:

- Baguettes
- Boneless, skinless chicken breasts
- Bread and pizza dough
- Ground beef
- Steaks
- Stew meat
- Vegetables (broccoli, spinach, sliced green peppers)

With all these things on hand, you can put together a tasty and beautifully presented restaurant copycat meal in just a few minutes. The only thing you'll have to worry about is which recipe you want to try next.

Choosing Ingredients

Cooking from scratch always tastes better. Restaurant chefs seek out the freshest ingredients they can find and so should you. Skip the prepackaged items whenever you can. Generic brands may offer a lower price, but be careful to check out the quality and flavor—you may not be satisfied with the final taste of the dish. By upgrading your choices, you can turn an ordinary meal into something special. For example, instead of using plain iceberg lettuce try romaine or a spring mix, and don't settle for boring American cheese. Experiment and try new flavors.

Meats

Red meats should have a rosy bloom and poultry should look plump and moist. Meat packages should be firmly wrapped, with no leaking or excess moisture. Check expiration dates and package labeling to make sure that the meat is fresh and has been handled properly. Refrigerate meats as soon as they are purchased. Price is not always a reflection of quality; don't assume that the most expensive meat is the best.

Chicken

You can buy a whole chicken or in any variety of precut packages. The key to cooking with chicken is to be careful to avoid cross contamination and the risk of salmonella. Wash your hands and the chicken before cooking.

Keep the uncooked chicken away from everything else on the kitchen counter. Use a separate cutting board and knife just for the uncooked chicken and do not use those same utensils for anything else. Clean anything the chicken touches thoroughly. If you follow these precautions, cooking with chicken is perfectly safe.

Beef

According to the USDA, ground beef cannot contain more than 30 percent fat by weight, so all of the packages will state their fat content. Get to know your butcher, and when London Broil or other roasts go on sale, have him grind it up for you to get premium ground beef at a reduced price.

How do you tell a great steak from a regular steak? The things to look for when buying a steak are the grade and the cut. Grade refers to the age of the animal and the marbling of the meat. The USDA grades the best steaks as prime, followed by choice and select. When selecting a steak, always take a look at the marbling or streaks of fat running through the meat. You want thin streaks that produce the best flavor. Cuts of steak are taken from different sections of the animal: The rib produces rib roast, back ribs, and rib eye steaks; the short loin produces the tastiest steaks like the T-bone, Porterhouse, New York Strip, and the best cut of tenderloin.

Always thaw meat in the refrigerator for maximum safety. Also, look for the safe handling label on packages of raw meat. It will tell you how to safely store, handle, and prepare meat and poultry.

Pork

All pork found in retail stores is inspected by the USDA. When buying pork, look for cuts with a relatively small amount of fat over the outside and with meat that is firm and grayish pink in color. For the best flavor, the meat should have a small amount of marbling. There are four basic cuts into which all other cuts are separated: the leg, side, loin, and shoulder. From those cuts, you get the bacon, ground pork for sausage, ribs, roasts, chops, and ham.

Fish

Knowing how to choose fresh fish is a skill all cooks should have. A fresh fish should smell like clean water. The eyes of the fish should be bright and clear and the gills should be a rich bright red. If it smells bad or looks discolored, don't buy it.

Fruits

Look for tenderness, plumpness, and bright color when choosing your fruit. Fruits should be heavy for their size and free of bruises, cuts, mildew, mold, or any other blemishes.

- Bananas are sold in any stage of ripeness and should be stored at room temperature.
- Berries should separate easily from their stems. Keep them refrigerated.
- Melons that have a sweet aromatic scent should be chosen. A strong smell indicates that they are overripe.
- Oranges, grapefruits, and lemons are sold when they are ripe. You may store them in the refrigerator for 2–3 weeks.

Vegetables

Take the time to inspect each vegetable before you buy. Look for crisp, plump, and brightly colored vegetables. Avoid the ones that are shriveled, bruised, moldy, or blemished.

- Asparagus should have straight stalks that are compact, with closed tips.
- Beans that are brightly colored and crisp are the best to select.
- Broccoli heads that are light green and yellowing should be avoided.
- Cabbage should have bright leaves without brown spots.
- Cauliflower with withered leaves and brown spots should not be chosen.
- Celery stalks should have firm crisp ribs.
- Cucumbers should be firm and not have soft spots.

- Mushrooms are fresh when they are firm, plump, and without bruises.
- Peas that are shriveled or have brown spots should be avoided.
- Peppers that are crisp and bright colored should be chosen.
- Spinach leaves should be crisp and free of moisture.

ESSENTIAL

Take the time to talk to the people in the produce department at the supermarket. They will be able to tell you when the trucks come to the store so that you will know when the freshest products are put out on the shelves.

Cooking Terms and Techniques

Success in the kitchen starts with an understanding of cooking vocabulary, and good technique is the key to cooking a great restaurant-quality meal.

Most ingredients are cut into smaller pieces before being used in a recipe. Sometimes you want the pieces uniform in shape and size; other times it doesn't matter. Here are the basic cutting techniques.

Chopping refers to simply cutting into smaller pieces. It's a larger cut than a dice or a mince and doesn't have to be uniform. To chop vegetables, keep the tip of the chef's knife on the cutting board and cut uniformly down through the vegetable with a rocking motion. Feed the item being chopped toward the blade, keeping your fingers curled tight.

Dicing is a cube that is usually ¼"–¾" square. To dice something, cut it into panels in the thickness you want your dice to be. Stack the panels and cut uniform matchsticks in the width you want your dice to be. Then line your sticks and cut them into a dice.

Mincing is a very thin cut of food. To mince, chop it roughly on a cutting board. Gather up the pieces in a pile. Position your knife above the pile. Keeping the tip touching the cutting board, repeatedly raise and lower the length of the blade down through whatever you're mincing, moving the blade in an arc.

Grating gives food a very fine texture and can be done with a box grater or handheld grater.

Julienne simply means to cut something into long strips. This is usually done with vegetables.

Slicing is when you cut completely through an object such as meat, fruit, vegetables, cheese, or bread.

Zesting is the process of removing the outer portion of a citrus fruit peel.

Knife maintenance is a necessary skill because a sharp knife is a safe knife. It is an essential kitchen tool, which must be properly maintained in order to keep it in perfect working order. Take the time to sharpen your knives because a dull knife will slip and cause you to cut yourself.

There are various techniques for preparing meat and vegetables for cooking. Here are the basic terms you will need to know to make the recipes in this book.

- **Al dente** means "to the tooth" in Italian, and is a term for pasta indicating that it is cooked just enough to maintain a firm texture.
- **Basting** is to moisten food during cooking with pan drippings or a sauce to prevent drying and add flavor.
- **Blanching** is to slightly cook food in boiling water.
- **Braising** is the recommended cooking method for tough cuts of meat, where they are cooked slowly in a small amount of liquid.
- **Brining** is to soak food in salted water.
- **Broil** means to cook food below direct heat.
- **Butterfly** is to split foods down the middle without completely separating the halves.
- **Deep fry** is to cook food in enough hot oil to cover the food until it is crispy.
- **Marinate** means to stand food in a liquid in order to enhance the flavor and tenderize.
- **Poaching** involves cooking a food by submerging it in simmering liquid.
- **Roasting** is a method used to cook food in an oven.

- **Searing** involves browning meat quickly on high heat to seal in the juices.
- **Simmer** means to cook a food in liquid kept just below the boiling point.
- **Sauté** is to cook or brown food in a small amount of cooking oil.
- **Steaming** is the process of cooking food in the vapor given off by boiling water.
- **Stew** means to cook food in liquid in a covered pot for a long time, until tender.
- **Stir-frying** is an Asian method of quickly cooking small pieces in hot oil while stirring constantly.

Food Presentation

Whenever you go to an awesome restaurant, the vibes around that place become as important as the quality of the food served in determining whether or not you have a fulfilling experience. Remember that food presentation and table setting is of utmost value when serving a restaurant copycat meal.

Garnishes

The ingredients in the dish can pull double duty as garnishes. Save some fresh chopped herbs required in the dish to add just before plating. Use diced tomatoes or green onions on top of a dish. Shredded or shaved cheeses add a nice touch to almost any dish.

Plating

There are several types of plating techniques restaurants use, including:

- Pie style is where the plate is divided with a section for the protein, starch, and vegetables.
- The half-and-half style of plating is where the main dish is on one side of the plate with the accompaniments located on the other.
- Vertical plating is where you build the plate upward, usually with the protein on the bottom and the side dishes on top.

- Family style plating is where the food is served on large platters meant to be shared.

Soup is such an inexpensive food to make at home. Why not splurge on some fancy oven-proof soup bowls to give a meal that special restaurant feeling with melted cheese on top?

Presenting Desserts

To showcase your beautifully created restaurant desserts, serve them in individual glass drinking glasses. A small wine glass layered with cake and ice cream or fruit and yogurt makes a nice presentation. Dessert shots are all the rage in the restaurants right now. Small sweet treats is a trend that's found its way onto dessert carts all over America. Little mini parfaits, sundaes, and layered cakes in shot glasses can easily be adapted for the home cook. It is time to raid your bar and fill those shot glasses with dessert. Small juice glasses also work well serving small-sized after-dinner treats.

CHAPTER 2

Breakfast and Brunch

Bob Evans Sausage Gravy
16

Cinnabon Cinnamon Rolls
17

Cracker Barrel Apple Streusel French Toast
18

Cracker Barrel Fried Apples
19

Cracker Barrel Ham and Red Eye Gravy
19

Cracker Barrel Hash Brown Casserole
20

Denny's Country Fried Steak
21

Denny's Country Gravy
22

Denny's Pancake Puppies
23

IHOP Chicken Fajita Omelette
24

IHOP Colorado Omelette
24

IHOP Harvest Grain and Nut Pancakes
25

IHOP Loaded Country Hash Brown Potatoes
26

IHOP New York Cheesecake Pancakes
27

IHOP Stuffed French Toast
28

McDonald's Yogurt Parfait
29

McDonald's Breakfast Burrito
29

McDonald's Steak, Egg, and Cheese Bagel Sandwich
30

Starbucks Bran Muffins
31

Bob Evans Sausage Gravy

This simple milk gravy will give you all the flavors of a country breakfast, and is served with the traditional biscuits.

INGREDIENTS | SERVES 4

1 pound roll pork sausage
¼ cup flour
2 cups milk
Salt and black pepper, to taste
8 prepared biscuits

Bob Evans in the Supermarket

Bob Evans Restaurants has many great lines of grocery products in your local supermarket. If you love their farm-fresh flavor, you can now buy their signature meat and side dishes to take home and cook in your kitchen. There are refrigerated side dishes, microwaveable sandwiches, and frozen home-style entrées to choose from.

1. Crumble and cook sausage in a large skillet over medium heat until browned.
2. Stir in flour until dissolved.
3. Gradually stir in the milk.
4. Cook gravy until thick and bubbly. Cook for about 5–7 minutes stirring constantly.
5. Season with salt and pepper.
6. Serve over hot biscuits.

Cinnabon Cinnamon Rolls

These breakfast sweets are easy to make since the recipe uses prepared pizza dough. They are sure to become a family favorite.

INGREDIENTS | YIELDS 12

1 tube refrigerated pizza dough

Filling
1 cup brown sugar
2½ tablespoons ground cinnamon
⅓ cup softened butter

Icing
4 tablespoons softened butter
3 ounces cream cheese
1½ cups powdered sugar
½ teaspoon vanilla extract
⅛ teaspoon salt

1. Preheat the oven to 400°F and lightly grease a large baking dish.
2. Spread the pizza dough out on a lightly floured surface.
3. To make the filling, combine the brown sugar and cinnamon in a bowl. Set aside.
4. Spread the butter all over the dough.
5. Sprinkle the brown sugar and cinnamon mixture evenly over the surface of the dough. Roll the long side of the dough up like you would a jelly roll.
6. Cut dough into 12 even slices and line up in a baking dish. Bake rolls for 15 minutes, or until golden brown.
7. While the rolls are baking, combine the icing ingredients. Blend well with an electric mixer until fluffy. Spread the icing over the warm rolls.

Cracker Barrel Apple Streusel French Toast

This recipe is a nice variation of the basic French toast. You may use any kind of flavored fresh bread from the bakery if you do not want to make your own bread.

INGREDIENTS | YIELDS 2 SMALL LOAVES

2½ cups Bisquick baking mix
½ cup flour
2 teaspoons apple pie spice
4 beaten eggs
1 (21-ounce) can apple pie filling
1 cup apple sauce
¾ cup brown sugar
⅔ cup cooking oil
2 eggs

Cracker Barrel Anniversary

As part of its fortieth anniversary, Cracker Barrel Old Country Stores announced a special limited time only menu featuring two new breakfast items, and the Apple Streusel French Toast is one of those items.

1. Preheat oven to 350°F. Grease and flour 2 small loaf pans.

2. In a large bowl, combine baking mix, flour, and apple pie spice.

3. In another large bowl combine 4 eggs, apple pie filling, apple sauce, ½ cup of the brown sugar, and oil. Add this to flour mixture and stir until moistened.

4. Divide batter evenly between prepared pans. Top each loaf with remaining brown sugar.

5. Bake for 55–60 minutes, or until a toothpick inserted in the center comes out clean.

6. Cool in pans on wire rack for 10 minutes. Remove from pans and cool completely on wire rack. Wrap and store overnight for easier slicing.

7. In a small bowl, beat the 2 eggs. Cut the bread in thick slices.

8. Dip each slice of bread in the egg.

9. Fry on a griddle until golden brown on each side.

Cracker Barrel Fried Apples

These are a popular breakfast side dish at Cracker Barrel. The fried apples are also great with pork chops, and can be used on top of pancakes or ice cream.

INGREDIENTS | SERVES 8

8 red apples
¼ pound butter
½ cup sugar
1 teaspoon cinnamon
Dash of nutmeg

1. Do not peel the apples. Slice the apples into slices about ½" thick.
2. Melt the butter in a skillet over medium heat.
3. Add the apples and sugar to the skillet.
4. Place a lid on the skillet and cook for 20 minutes, or until the apples are tender and juicy.
5. Sprinkle with cinnamon and nutmeg before serving.

Cracker Barrel Ham and Red Eye Gravy

Cracker Barrel uses country ham. This is a lighter and less salty version of the original.

INGREDIENTS | SERVES 2

1 (¼"-thick) ham steak
2 tablespoons margarine
2 tablespoons strong black coffee
4 tablespoons water

1. Melt margarine in a skillet over medium heat.
2. Add the ham and fry for 6–8 minutes until done. Remove ham from skillet.
3. Add coffee and water to the ham juice.
4. Bring to a boil. Serve the gravy over the ham steak.

Cracker Barrel Hash Brown Casserole

This is a wonderful breakfast side dish at Cracker Barrel that can be served any time of the day. Make it ahead of time and put it in the oven an hour before you plan to eat.

INGREDIENTS | SERVES 6

1 pound frozen hash browns
¼ cup margarine
1 (10-ounce) can cream of chicken soup
½ pint sour cream
¼ cup peeled and chopped onion
1 cup grated Cheddar cheese
½ teaspoon salt
⅛ teaspoon pepper

1. Preheat oven to 350°F.
2. Spray a large baking dish with cooking spray.
3. Mix all the ingredients together in a bowl.
4. Place combined ingredients into the baking dish.
5. Bake for 45 minutes, or until brown on top.

The Cracker Barrel Chain

The Cracker Barrel restaurant chain has a southern-themed country store at each location with rocking chairs on the front porch. The menu consists of southern comfort food, and breakfast is served all day.

Denny's Country Fried Steak

Denny's serves this golden, fried chopped beef steak smothered in a rich country gravy.

INGREDIENTS | SERVES 4

1 pound beef cube steak, cut into 4 pieces
1 cup flour
1 teaspoon salt
½ teaspoon paprika
½ teaspoon pepper
½ cup buttermilk
¼ cup vegetable oil

The History of Chicken Fried Steak

The origins of chicken or country fried steak are unknown, but it is closely associated with southern cuisine and hospitality. The meat consists of a cheap cut of beef steak, which is pounded and tenderized. It is then coated with seasoned flour and pan fried in hot oil.

1. Tenderize the meat by pounding it with a mallet or the bottom of a heavy skillet.
2. Stir together the flour, salt, paprika, and pepper in a shallow dish.
3. Put the buttermilk in a separate dish.
4. Dredge steaks in the flour mixture, dip into the buttermilk, and dip again into the flour mixture.
5. Heat the oil in a large skillet over medium-high heat.
6. Cook the steaks 5 minutes on each side.
7. Serve with Denny's Country Gravy, if desired.

Denny's Country Gravy

This traditional milk gravy is made in the same skillet that the country fried steak is cooked in. The pan drippings give the gravy its unique flavor.

INGREDIENTS | YIELDS 2 CUPS

2 tablespoons vegetable oil
2 tablespoons flour
2½ cups milk
¼ teaspoon salt
½ teaspoon pepper

1. Use the same pan that you cooked the Denny's Country Fried Steak in to make the gravy.
2. Heat the oil and whisk in the flour.
3. Stir constantly for about 5 minutes, or until light brown.
4. Whisk in the milk a little at a time until the mixture thickens.
5. Salt and pepper the gravy to taste.

Denny's Pancake Puppies

If you like fresh donut holes then you will definitely like these little bite-sized pancake balls rolled in powdered sugar. Serve with a small bowl of syrup for dipping.

INGREDIENTS | SERVES 6

Vegetable oil, for frying
1 cup Aunt Jemima Original Pancake Mix
⅓ cup milk
1 egg
½ cup chopped dried blueberries
1 tablespoon finely chopped white chocolate chips
Powdered sugar, for dusting

1. Preheat oil in a deep fryer.
2. In a medium bowl, combine pancake mix, milk, and egg.
3. Add blueberries and chocolate chips and stir.
4. Let the batter sit for 10 minutes to thicken.
5. When the oil is hot, use an ice cream scoop coated with oil to make a batter ball, and drop it into the hot oil.
6. Cook for 2½–3 minutes, or until the batter is dark brown.
7. Drain on paper towels and coat with powdered sugar.

IHOP Chicken Fajita Omelette

Everywhere you look on the menu these days you see fajitas. There are fajita burritos, fajita nachos, and now fajita omelettes. This is a great recipe to use leftover fajita fixings.

INGREDIENTS | SERVES 1

2 eggs
1 teaspoon water
½ cup leftover fajitas (chicken, onions, and peppers)
½ cup Mexican cheese, shredded
¼ cup salsa

1. In a small bowl, beat eggs and water together.
2. Pour egg mixture in a medium skillet and cook over medium heat for 1–2 minutes until the egg starts to set.
3. Add the chicken, peppers, and onions.
4. Fold the omelette in half. Turn heat off.
5. Top with cheese and salsa.
6. Cover skillet with a lid and let it sit until the cheese melts.

IHOP Colorado Omelette

Although IHOP is famous for its pancakes, they offer eight different types of omelettes. The Colorado is a very meaty omelette.

INGREDIENTS | SERVES 2

2 tablespoons butter
¼ cup diced onion
¼ cup diced green pepper
⅛ cup water
4 eggs
¼ teaspoon salt
¼ cup diced tomatoes
¼ cup cooked and diced bacon
¼ cup cooked and diced ham
¼ cup cooked and sliced sausage links
¼ cup diced deli roast beef
¾ cup shredded Cheddar cheese

1. In a skillet on medium heat, melt butter. Add onions and green peppers to the skillet.
2. In a mixing bowl, add water, eggs, and salt. Stir and beat well.
3. Pour egg mixture into the skillet and cook for 1–2 minutes to let the egg set. Add tomatoes and all the meats plus ½ cup of cheese.
4. Fold the omelette in half and top with remaining cheese.
5. Serve with salsa and sliced green onions.

IHOP Harvest Grain and Nut Pancakes

IHOP offers this healthier option to traditional pancakes. Instead of using regular pancake syrup, keep a supply of your favorite jams and jellies on hand. Pie fillings in the can are another nice alternative to put on top of your pancakes.

INGREDIENTS | SERVES 8

¾ cup rolled oats
¾ cup whole-wheat flour
1 teaspoon baking powder
2 teaspoons baking soda
½ teaspoon salt
1½ cups buttermilk
1 egg
¼ cup vegetable oil
¼ cup sugar
3 tablespoons chopped walnuts

1. Preheat a skillet or griddle on medium heat and spray with cooking oil. Grind oats in a food processor or blender until a fine consistency.

2. In a medium bowl, combine flour, oats, baking powder, baking soda, and salt. In another bowl, combine buttermilk, egg, oil, and sugar and mix with an electric mixer until smooth.

3. Combine the dry ingredients with the wet ingredients and mix. Add the nuts and mix.

4. Add ⅓ cup of batter onto a hot griddle or skillet and cook for 2–4 minutes per side, until brown.

IHOP Loaded Country Hash Brown Potatoes

This recipe is a skillet hash filled with meat and cheese. It is a great way to use leftover baked potatoes.

INGREDIENTS | SERVES 2

2 cold baked potatoes
½ cup cooking oil
2 teaspoons Lawry's Seasoned Salt
½ cup of cooked and diced breakfast meat
¼ cup cooked and diced onion and green peppers
½ cup of shredded American cheese

1. Dice the potatoes and leave the skin on.
2. Heat oil in a frying pan over medium heat.
3. Add the potatoes to the pan and season with salt.
4. Put in the cooked meat, onions, green peppers and top with cheese.
5. Cover with a lid and simmer for 6–8 minutes, until the potatoes are warm and the cheese is melted.

Potato Variations

These were a LTO (Limited Time Offering) on the menu at IHOP and came in 3 varieties. Ham, Swiss & Mushroom Browns were loaded with sautéed mushrooms, diced ham, and melted Swiss and Parmesan cheese and topped with green onions. Jack, Cheddar & Bacon Browns were stuffed with chopped hickory-smoked bacon and melted Cheddar and Monterey jack cheeses and topped with sour cream and green onions. Country Sausage Browns were overflowing with pork sausage links, cheddar cheese, and grilled onions and topped with creamy country gravy.

IHOP New York Cheesecake Pancakes

The New York Cheesecake Pancakes are a new item on the menu and have become one of their most popular signature pancakes. Top these pancakes with strawberry jam, whipped cream, or maple syrup.

INGREDIENTS | YIELDS 15 PANCAKES

1 (8-ounce) package cream cheese
2 cups Bisquick mix
½ cup graham cracker crumbs
¼ cup sugar
1 cup milk
2 eggs

1. Slice the cream cheese into 4 pieces and freeze overnight.
2. The next day, preheat a skillet or griddle on medium high.
3. In a large bowl, combine all the other ingredients.
4. Cut the frozen cream cheese into bite-size pieces and add to the batter.
5. Spray a skillet or griddle with cooking spray.
6. Add ⅓ cup of batter and cook about 2 minutes per side until done.

IHOP Stuffed French Toast

Using prepared cheesecake filling makes a quick and simple recipe that tastes amazingly similar to the stuffed French toast served at IHOP.

INGREDIENTS | SERVES 6

1 loaf of French bread
4 eggs
Splash of milk
2 tablespoons butter
1 (24.2-ounce) tub Philadelphia Ready to Eat Cheesecake Filling
Fresh strawberries or canned strawberry pie filling, for garnish
Whipped cream, for garnish

1. Slice bread into 1"-thick slices.
2. Beat eggs in a bowl with milk.
3. Dip the bread slices into the egg batter.
4. Add a few pats of butter to a skillet and allow it to melt.
5. Fry bread 2–3 minutes on each side until slightly brown.
6. Put a few tablespoons of the cheesecake filling on one piece of the toast.
7. Top with another slice.
8. Garnish with sliced strawberries or canned strawberry pie filling. Top with whipped cream.

McDonald's Yogurt Parfait

This is a healthy option for a quick breakfast on the run. Make these up ahead of time and store in the refrigerator. Place the granola is a separate bag and you can top it when ready to eat.

INGREDIENTS | SERVES 4

4 cups vanilla yogurt
2 (10-ounce) packages thawed sliced strawberries
⅓ cup thawed frozen blueberries
½ cup crunchy granola

1. Pour ½ cup of yogurt into a cup.
2. Top with ½ cup of strawberries.
3. Add 1 tablespoon of blueberries.
4. Pour ½ cup of yogurt over the fruit.
5. Top the yogurt with granola, and serve.

McDonald's Breakfast Burrito

Now you can get your fast food breakfast craving at home using this recipe, which can be modified according to your tastes.

INGREDIENTS | SERVES 4

4 ounces pork sausage
4 teaspoons minced onion
½ tablespoon minced mild green chilies
4 beaten eggs
Salt and pepper, to taste
4 (8") flour tortillas
4 slices American cheese

1. Preheat a skillet over medium heat.
2. Add sausage and onion to the skillet and sauté for 3–4 minutes, or until the sausage is browned.
3. Add the chilies and sauté for 1 minute more.
4. Pour eggs into the pan and scramble with the sausage, onion, and chilies. Season with salt and pepper.
5. Heat tortillas in the microwave on a moist paper towel for 1 minute.
6. Add the egg mixture and cheese to the tortilla and roll into a burrito.

The First Fast Food Breakfast
McDonald's pioneered the breakfast fast food concept with the introduction of the Egg McMuffin in 1972.

McDonald's Steak, Egg, and Cheese Bagel Sandwich

McDonald's currently serves only two types of bagel sandwiches. Since you are making them at home, you can put whatever you like on them such as ham, bacon, or sausage and switch the cheese to Monterey jack or Swiss.

INGREDIENTS | SERVES 2

1 beef cube steak, cut into 2 pieces
2 tablespoons Worcestershire sauce
1½ teaspoons garlic salt
1 teaspoon minced onion
2 tablespoons butter
2 split bagels
2 eggs
2 slices American cheese

1. Place the steaks in a plastic bag with the Worcestershire sauce, garlic salt, and onion.
2. Cook the steak on a George Foreman indoor grill for about 5 minutes, or until done. Remove.
3. Butter the insides of the bagel and toast on the grill.
4. Whisk the eggs in a small bowl.
5. Spray a skillet with nonstick spray and cook the eggs.
6. Once the egg has set, fold in half like an omelette and cut into 4 equal pieces.
7. Place the steak on the bottom of a bagel half, add egg and cheese, then top with the other half of the bagel.

Starbucks Bran Muffins

This recipe is a healthy muffin just like the ones served at your favorite coffee shop. Combine it with yogurt and fruit for a full breakfast meal.

INGREDIENTS | YIELDS 24 MUFFINS

2½ cups flour
2 teaspoons baking soda
1½ teaspoons salt
2 cups crushed bran cereal
½ cup chopped dried apple
½ cup dried cherries
1 cup boiling water
½ cup softened unsalted butter
1 cup sugar
½ cup honey
2 large eggs
2 cups buttermilk
½ cup walnut pieces

1. Preheat oven to 400°F. Line a muffin tin with baking cups.

2. In a small bowl, stir flour, baking soda, and salt.

3. In another bowl, combine bran cereal and dried fruit with the boiling water.

4. In a large bowl, beat butter until creamy. Gradually beat in sugar, honey, and eggs.

5. Add the buttermilk to the butter mixture and beat in. Then add the flour mixture, then bran mixture, and the walnuts.

6. Divide the batter into the lined muffin tins.

7. Bake muffins for 20 minutes.

Starbucks: More Than Just Coffee

Starbucks started business as a coffee bean roaster and retailer in the early 1970s and has become the largest coffeehouse company in the world. The expansion brought with it a line of food products that includes salads, sandwiches, pastries, and snacks.

CHAPTER 3

Appetizers

Applebee's Pico de Gallo
34

Applebee's Spinach and Artichoke Dip
34

Bennigan's Broccoli Bites
35

Carrabba's Bread Dipping Mix
36

Chi Chi's Seafood Nachos
36

Chili's Boneless Buffalo Wings
37

Chili's Chicken Fajita Nachos
38

Chili's Skillet Queso
39

Chili's Southwestern Eggrolls
40

Chili's Texas Cheese Fries
41

Dave and Buster's Philly Steak Rolls
42

Joe's Crab Shack Crab Dip
43

Joe's Crab Shack Crab Nachos
43

Johnny Carino's Italian Nachos
44

Olive Garden Bread Sticks
45

Olive Garden Fried Mozzarella
46

Olive Garden Smoked Mozzarella Fondue
47

Olive Garden Stuffed Mushrooms
48

Olive Garden Toasted Ravioli
49

Appetizers
(continued)

Olive Garden Tomato
Basil Crostini
50

Outback Steakhouse
Bloomin' Onion
51

Outback Steakhouse Bloomin'
Onion Dipping Sauce
52

Outback Steakhouse
Coconut Shrimp
52

Outback Steakhouse Creole
Marmalade Dipping Sauce
53

Red Lobster Cheddar
Bay Biscuits
53

T.G.I. Friday's Baked
Potato Skins
54

T.G.I. Friday's Nine Layer Dip
54

Applebee's Pico de Gallo

Pico de Gallo is a versatile accompaniment to Mexican dishes and eggs. You will use this recipe time and time again.

INGREDIENTS | SERVES 6

1 cup diced tomatoes
½ cup diced red onion
1 finely diced jalapeño pepper
⅛ cup roughly chopped cilantro leaves
½ teaspoon salt
¼ teaspoon black pepper
¼ teaspoon garlic powder
1 teaspoon salad oil
1 teaspoon white vinegar

1. In a medium bowl, add tomatoes, onion, and jalapeño.
2. Add the cilantro, salt, pepper, garlic powder, oil, and vinegar and mix gently.
3. Store the leftover pico de gallo in the refrigerator for up to 36 hours to add to your favorite dishes and salads.

Applebee's Spinach and Artichoke Dip

Anyone who has ever visited an Applebee's restaurant falls in love with their mouth-watering spinach-artichoke dip. Serve it with fresh bread or tortilla chips.

INGREDIENTS | SERVES 2

1 (14-ounce) can drained and chopped artichoke hearts
1 (10-ounce) box frozen chopped spinach
1 (10-ounce) jar Alfredo sauce
1 cup of shredded Parmesan and Romano cheese blend
2 diced Roma tomatoes
4 ounces softened cream cheese
½ cup shredded mozzarella cheese
1 teaspoon fresh minced garlic

1. Combine all the ingredients in a mixing bowl.
2. Spread the mixture into a small baking dish.
3. Bake in a 350°F oven for 30 minutes, or until the cheeses melt.

Bennigan's Broccoli Bites

These little fried nuggets are a great way to get the kids to eat their vegetables.

INGREDIENTS | SERVES 4

Broccoli Bites
2 cups frozen chopped broccoli
3 eggs
¾ cup shredded Colby cheese
¾ cup shredded Monterey jack cheese
5 tablespoons real bacon bits
1 tablespoon diced yellow onion
2 tablespoons flour
4 cups oil, for frying
Italian breadcrumbs, as needed

Honey-Mustard Dipping Sauce
¾ cup sour cream
⅓ cup mayonnaise
⅓ cup Dijon mustard
⅓ cup honey
4 teaspoons lemon juice

1. Thaw and drain broccoli thoroughly by pressing through a strainer. Beat the eggs in a mixing bowl with a whisk until well blended.

2. Place the broccoli, eggs, cheeses, bacon bits, onion, and flour into a plastic container. Stir together with a spatula until thoroughly combined. Refrigerate mixture for about 1 hour. This will help to bind the mix, making preparation much easier.

3. Heat about 4 cups oil in a fryer or deep pan at 350°F. Place the bread crumbs in a shallow pan. Scoop a 1 tablespoon portion of the broccoli mixture into the bread crumbs. Form each portion into a ball and coat it well in the bread crumbs.

4. Place the broccoli bites into the fry basket or frying pan. Make sure they do not stick together. Fry for 1 minute.

5. Remove and place onto a plate lined with paper towels to absorb excess oil.

6. For the dipping sauce, combine the sour cream, mayonnaise and mustard. Blend thoroughly using a whisk. Slowly pour in the honey and lemon juice and continue mixing until smooth and well combined. Serve with broccoli bites.

Carrabba's Bread Dipping Mix

...d-dipping spice sauce is a real favorite. Carrabba's serves the spices on a ...ll plate and the waiter adds olive oil. Serve with warm fresh bread.

INGREDIENTS | SERVES 3–4

...egano
1 tablespoon dried rosemary
1 tablespoon dried basil
1 tablespoon dried parsley
1 tablespoon garlic powder
1 tablespoon black pepper
1 tablespoon crushed red pepper
Salt, to taste

1. Combine the ingredients in a zip-top bag and crush.
2. Use 1 tablespoon of the mixture in the dipping bowl.
3. Drizzle the spices with olive oil and add a little fresh-squeezed lemon juice, if desired.

Chi Chi's Seafood Nachos

If you love seafood, this recipe is a must have. This modified nacho recipe is a healthier alternative to the traditionally greasy morsels. Serve them up as a tasty appetizer, a light snack, or even an exciting lunch.

INGREDIENTS | SERVES 2

16 large tortilla chips
1 (8-ounce) package Louis Kemp Crab Delights
1 (8-ounce) package Louis Kemp Lobster Delights
1 (8-ounce) thawed frozen package salad shrimp
1 cup shredded Monterey jack cheese

1. Spread tortilla chips on a 10" plate.
2. Layer the crab, lobster, and shrimp over the chips.
3. Sprinkle the cheese on top.
4. Microwave on medium until melted, 1½–2½ minutes.

Chili's Boneless Buffalo Wings

Chili's serves these spicy breaded chicken tenders with celery sticks and blue cheese, just like the famous wings, but without the bone.

INGREDIENTS | SERVES 2

2 teaspoons salt
½ teaspoon ground pepper
¼ teaspoon cayenne pepper
1 cup flour
¼ teaspoon paprika
1 egg
1 cup milk
2 boneless skinless chicken breasts
2–4 cups cooking oil
¼ cup hot sauce
1 tablespoon margarine

Recipe Variations

You can buy frozen chicken nuggets to make this recipe. Cook according to package directions and then toss in the hot sauce. For a lower-calorie option, use grilled chicken breast.

1. In a medium bowl, combine salt, peppers, flour, and paprika.

2. In another bowl, whisk together the egg and milk.

3. Slice each chicken breast into bite-size pieces.

4. Preheat oil in deep fryer or skillet.

5. Dip pieces of chicken into the egg mixture 1 or 2 at a time, then into the flour/spice mixture. Repeat so that each piece of chicken is double coated.

6. When all the chicken pieces have been breaded, arrange them on a plate and chill for 15 minutes.

7. Drop each piece of chicken into hot oil and fry for 5–6 minutes, or until the breading is golden brown.

8. In a small microwave-safe bowl, combine the hot sauce and margarine. Microwave for 20–30 seconds, or just until the margarine has melted.

9. When the chicken pieces are done frying, remove them to a plate lined with paper towels to absorb the excess oil.

10. Place the chicken pieces into a covered container. Pour the sauce over the chicken, put the lid on, and shake gently until each piece of chicken is coated with sauce.

Chili's Chicken Fajita Nachos

Yummy, crisp nachos get a special twist when topped with a fajita mixture. This recipe is sure to be a hit at your next party.

INGREDIENTS | SERVES 2

1 boneless skinless chicken breast, cut into strips
1 sliced Vidalia onion
1 bell pepper, cut into thin strips
1 envelope fajita seasoning mix
16 large tortilla chips
½ cup shredded Cheddar cheese
½ cup shredded Monterey jack cheese
16 jarred jalapeño pepper slices
1 cup shredded lettuce
½ cup thick and chunky salsa
2 tablespoons sour cream
2 tablespoons guacamole

1. Cook the chicken, onions, and bell peppers in a skillet according to fajita seasoning packet. Drain and set aside.

2. Place tortilla chips on a large microwave-safe plate.

3. Layer the cooked chicken fajita on top of the tortilla chips.

4. Add the cheeses on top of the chicken.

5. Place the jalapeño slices on top of the chicken.

6. Microwave the plate on medium 2–3 minutes, to melt the cheese.

7. Put lettuce, salsa, sour cream, and guacamole on top of the cheese.

Chili's Skillet Queso

Queso is turning up on many restaurant menus. Don't miss this easy appetizer. You can make it quickly and easily since it only contains two ingredients.

INGREDIENTS | SERVES 6–8

1 pound block Kraft Velveeta cheese
2 cans no-bean chili

Share an Appetizer

Chili's has joined a number of other restaurants in promoting the share an appetizer or dessert concept along with the entrée for a fixed price. The current promotion is the $20 dinner for 2, where you get 1 appetizer and 2 full-size entrées from a select list. Past promotions featured 3 courses for $20, where you share both the appetizer and dessert.

1. Cut the cheese into small chunks.
2. Place the cheese in a baking dish and add the chili.
3. Microwave on medium-high for 3–4 minutes, until the cheese melts. Stir frequently, every 30 seconds.

Chili's Southwestern Eggrolls

This recipe has an assortment of traditional Southwestern-style ingredients wrapped inside small tortillas and deep fried.

INGREDIENTS | SERVES 15

1 (16-ounce) can rinsed and drained black beans
1 (16-ounce) can drained corn
2 cups washed and drained fresh spinach
2 chopped jalapeños
2 pressed garlic cloves
¼ cup chopped fresh cilantro
¼ cup minced onion
½ teaspoon chili powder
½ teaspoon salt
¼ teaspoon fresh ground black pepper
2 cups grated Mexican cheese blend
15 small whole-wheat tortillas
Cooking oil
Prepared salsa
Sour cream

1. In a large mixing bowl, combine beans, corn, spinach, jalapeños, garlic, cilantro, onion, chili powder, salt, pepper, and cheese and mix well.

2. Put 2 tablespoons of mixture on each tortilla and roll into a thin eggroll.

3. Heat a frying pan to medium-high heat.

4. Using 1 tablespoon of cooking oil per 2–3 eggrolls, shallow fry in sauté pan.

5. Garnish with salsa and sour cream.

Chili's Texas Cheese Fries

Once you make these you will come back to this recipe time after time. Serve with ranch salad dressing on the side.

INGREDIENTS | SERVES 3–4

Half a (28-ounce) bag frozen steak fries
4 slices bacon
1 (8-ounce) bag shredded Cheddar cheese
Jalapeño pepper slices, to taste
Ranch salad dressing, for dipping

1. Spread the fries evenly over a cookie sheet and bake according to package directions.

2. Line strips of bacon on another cookie sheet and bake about 15–20 minutes, until crispy.

3. When the fries and bacon are done, remove from the oven.

4. Add a thick layer of cheese and jalapeños on top of the cooked fries, then crumble the bacon on top.

5. Return to the oven and bake for 8–10 minutes until the cheese melts.

Dave and Buster's Philly Steak Rolls

This appetizer is a Chinese twist on the traditional Philly cheese steak that we all love to eat.

INGREDIENTS | YIELDS 10

1 tablespoon vegetable oil
½ cup diced onions
1 box of Steakums (7 slices)
Salt and pepper, to taste
1 (15-ounce) jar of Cheez Wiz
10 egg roll wraps
2 cups vegetable oil, for frying

1. Heat 1 tablespoon of oil in a skillet over medium heat.

2. Add onion and cook, stirring frequently, for 2–3 minutes, until onion is translucent.

3. Break up Steakums pieces and add to skillet. Sprinkle salt and pepper to taste; cook and stir until steak is no longer pink (about 6 or 7 minutes). Remove from heat and set aside.

4. Place an egg roll wrap on a clean, dry surface with a corner facing you, like a baseball diamond.

5. Place 2 tablespoons of beef and onions onto the center of an egg roll wrap and top with 1–2 tablespoons of Cheese Wiz. Don't overfill your wrapper.

6. Fold the corner closest to you over mixture, then flap side corners over and roll. Use water or an egg wash to seal roll.

7. Heat and fill a high-sided pan with 1" of oil. Slowly add the rolls to oil and cook for 3 to 4 minutes, until golden brown on all sides.

8. Drain on paper towels, and serve warm with ketchup.

Joe's Crab Shack Crab Dip

Who doesn't love a good crab dip? Serve this restaurant copycat with tortilla chips, slices of bread, or crackers.

INGREDIENTS | SERVES 4

1 (5-ounce) can drained crab meat
1 (8-ounce) package softened cream cheese
3 tablespoons heavy whipping cream
2 teaspoons diced onion
2 teaspoons diced red pepper
2 teaspoons diced green pepper
2 teaspoons diced tomato
2 teaspoons diced green onion
2 teaspoons white wine
1 tablespoon Parmesan cheese
½ teaspoon Old Bay seasoning
Dash of Tabasco sauce, to taste

1. In a small microwave-safe dish, combine all the ingredients.

2. Microwave on medium power for 4 minutes.

3. Remove from microwave, stir, and serve with bread or chips.

Joe's Crab Shack Crab Nachos

What do you get when you combine crispy, salty chips with seafood? You get some amazingly delicious nachos.

INGREDIENTS | SERVES 3–4

16 baked tortilla chips
1 (8-ounce) package of chopped imitation crabmeat
¼ cup sour cream
¼ cup mayonnaise
2 tablespoons chopped onion
1 cup shredded Cheddar cheese
¼ cup sliced black olives
¼ teaspoon paprika

1. Arrange tortilla chips in a single layer on a baking sheet.

2. In a bowl, combine the crab, sour cream, mayonnaise, and onion. Spoon about 1 tablespoon onto each chip.

3. Sprinkle cheese, olives, and paprika on top of the chips.

4. Bake in a 350°F oven for 6–8 minutes, or until the cheese melts.

Johnny Carino's Italian Nachos

With this recipe, Carino's created a tasty change from the traditional Mexican nachos.

INGREDIENTS | SERVES 4

1 (12-ounce) package wontons
1 (1 pound) package ground pork
3–4 tablespoons olive oil
½ cup Alfredo sauce
1 (6-ounce) package grilled chicken pieces
2 diced Roma tomatoes
½ cup sliced olives
¼ cup pepperoncini peppers
Jalapeño peppers, to taste
1 cup shredded mozzarella cheese

About Carino's

Carino's Italian Grill is a United States-based chain of Italian food casual dining restaurants. It has more than 170 restaurants with branches in about thirty states. All the food is made from scratch and served family style on large serving platters meant to be shared.

1. Preheat oven to 400°F.
2. Cut the wontons on the diagonal to form triangles.
3. Cook pork in a sauté pan for 10–12 minutes until brown.
4. Toss wonton triangles in olive oil and place in a single layer on a baking sheet.
5. Bake for about 6 minutes, or until lightly brown. Remove from oven and place on paper towels to drain.
6. Pile the wontons on a large serving platter and drizzle them with Alfredo sauce.
7. Add pork, grilled chicken, tomatoes, olives, and peppers to the wontons. Top with mozzarella.
8. Microwave for 1–2 minutes, to melt the cheese.

Olive Garden Bread Sticks

Many people crave the bread sticks at Olive Garden and now you can make them at home in almost no time at all.

INGREDIENTS | SERVES 4–6

1 (10.5 ounce/6 count) package frozen bread sticks
2 tablespoons olive oil
¼ cup Parmesan cheese

Dipping Sauces

Olive Garden also serves dipping sauces for an extra charge. To get the restaurant feel, place some warm bowls of marinara and Alfredo sauce on the table to dip the bread sticks into.

1. Preheat oven to 350°F.
2. Brush each bread stick with olive oil.
3. Sprinkle the tops of the bread with Parmesan cheese.
4. Wrap in aluminum foil.
5. Bake for 12–15 minutes, according to package directions.

Olive Garden Fried Mozzarella

Everyone loves fried mozzarella sticks, and you can easily match the restaurant taste with this inexpensive recipe. Serve these with your favorite warm marinara sauce.

INGREDIENTS | SERVES 2–4

1 pound block mozzarella cheese
2 eggs
¼ cup water
1½ cups Italian bread crumbs
½ teaspoon granulated garlic
½ teaspoon dried oregano
½ teaspoon dried basil
⅔ cup flour
⅓ cup cornstarch

1. Preheat oil in a deep fryer to 350°F.
2. Slice the block of cheese lengthwise, into about ½" sections.
3. Cut each section in half.
4. In a small bowl, beat the eggs with water and set aside.
5. In another small bowl, mix the bread crumbs, garlic, oregano, and basil and set aside.
6. In another small bowl, blend the flour with the corn starch and set aside.
7. Dip the cheese in flour, then in egg wash, then coat with bread crumbs.
8. Place carefully in hot oil and fry until golden brown. This should only take a matter of seconds, so you need to watch them closely.
9. Drain on paper towels.

Olive Garden Smoked Mozzarella Fondue

This cheese dish is sure to be a hit at your next party. Serve with toasted bread sticks or fried mozzarella cheese.

INGREDIENTS | SERVES 8

6 cups of shredded Sargento 6 Cheese Italian Blend
3 tablespoons grated Parmesan cheese
3 tablespoons grated Romano cheese
1 cup sour cream
1 teaspoon Italian seasoning blend
½ teaspoon red pepper flakes
6 diced Roma tomatoes
Fresh minced parsley or basil
1 loaf of fresh Italian bread

1. Preheat the oven to 450°F.

2. In a large bowl, mix all the cheeses together. Add the sour cream and spices and stir until well combined.

3. Spray a medium casserole dish with nonstick spray. Add the cheese mixture and spread out evenly with a large spoon.

4. Bake the casserole on the center rack of the oven for 5 minutes, or until the cheese is melted and slightly bubbly on the edges.

5. Garnish with tomatoes and fresh herbs.

6. Slice the bread into ¼"–½" slices and place them on a lightly greased cooking sheet. Bake for about 5 minutes, until the bread is toasted.

Olive Garden Stuffed Mushrooms

These are the perfect appetizers for the mushroom lovers in your house.

INGREDIENTS | SERVES 4–6

1 (6-ounce) can clams
8–12 fresh mushrooms
1 finely minced green onion
⅛ teaspoon garlic salt
½ teaspoon minced garlic
1 tablespoon melted butter
1 teaspoon oregano leaves
½ cup Italian breadcrumbs
1 egg
2 tablespoons grated Parmesan cheese
1 tablespoon grated Romano cheese
2 tablespoons grated mozzarella cheese
¼ cup melted butter, for garnish
¼ cup grated mozzarella cheese, for garnish
Fresh minced parsley, for garnish

1. Preheat the oven to 350°F.
2. Drain and finely mince the clams, saving ¼ cup of clam juice for the stuffing.
3. Lightly oil a small baking dish.
4. Gently wash the mushrooms, pat dry, and remove the stems.
5. In a bowl, combine the clams, onions, garlic salt, minced garlic, butter, and oregano and mix well.
6. Add the bread crumbs, egg, and clam juice and mix well.
7. Add the cheeses and mix well.
8. Put about 1½ teaspoons of the stuffing mixture inside the mushroom cavity and slightly mound.
9. Place the stuffed mushrooms in the baking dish and pour ¼ cup melted butter over the top. Cover and bake in the oven for about 35–40 minutes.
10. Remove the cover and sprinkle ¼ cup of mozzarella on top and put back in the oven just long enough for the cheese to melt slightly (about 5–7 minutes).
11. Garnish with freshly diced parsley.

Olive Garden Toasted Ravioli

Serve these tasty appetizers with your favorite marinara sauce.

INGREDIENTS | SERVES 2–4

¼ cup water
2 eggs
1 teaspoon Italian seasoning
1 teaspoon garlic salt
1 cup plain bread crumbs
1 cup flour
1 (16-ounce) package meat-filled ravioli

1. In a bowl, mix the water and eggs and beat well. Set aside.
2. In another bowl, mix the Italian seasonings and garlic salt with the bread crumbs and set aside.
3. In a third bowl, measure the flour and set aside.
4. Heat vegetable oil in deep fryer or skillet to 350°F for deep frying.
5. Dip the ravioli in flour, then in the egg wash, then in bread crumbs and carefully place in hot oil.
6. Fry about 2–3 minutes until golden, remove from oil, and drain.

Olive Garden Tomato Basil Crostini

Most Italian restaurants serve some type of tomato bruschetta appetizer, which is served on grilled bread rubbed with garlic. This is a very inexpensive recipe to make at home.

INGREDIENTS | SERVES 4

4 chopped medium tomatoes
6–8 chopped fresh basil leaves
6 tablespoons extra-virgin olive oil
8 slices of crusty bread
2–3 cloves of garlic

1. In a medium bowl, mix the tomatoes, basil, and olive oil together.

2. Grill or toast the bread.

3. Rub the bread with garlic and top with the tomato mixture.

Outback Steakhouse Bloomin' Onion

The blooming onion from Outback may be one of the most popular appetizers in America; millions are sold every year. Now you can make these at home in no time at all.

INGREDIENTS | SERVES 4

Seasoned Flour
2 cups flour
4 teaspoons paprika
2 teaspoons garlic powder
½ teaspoon pepper
¼ teaspoon cayenne pepper

Batter
⅓ cup cornstarch
1½ cups flour
2 teaspoons minced garlic
2 teaspoons paprika
1 teaspoon salt
1 teaspoon pepper
24 ounces beer
1 Vidalia or Texas sweet onion

Blooming Onion History

Outback Steakhouse was the first national restaurant chain to serve the blooming onion when it opened back in 1988. Lonestar Steakhouse currently has it on the menu and Applebee's carried the appetizer in the past as the Awesome Blossom.

1. Preheat oil in a deep fryer to 375°F.
2. In a shallow bowl, combine all seasoned flour ingredients.
3. Prepare the batter: mix cornstarch, flour, and seasonings until well blended. Add the beer and mix well.
4. Cut about ¾" off top of onion and peel. Cut 12–16 vertical wedges, but do not cut through bottom root end. Remove about 1" of petals from center of onion.
5. Dip prepared onion in seasoned flour and remove the excess by shaking. Separate the petals and dip into the batter to coat thoroughly.
6. Gently place in the fryer basket and deep-fry 1½ minutes. Turn the onion over and fry an additional 1½ minutes. Drain on paper towels.
7. Place onion upright in shallow bowl and remove center core with a circular cutter or apple corer.

Outback Steakhouse Bloomin' Onion Dipping Sauce

This creamy and delicious sauce is the perfect companion for the blooming onion. One thing is for sure, everyone will wonder how you made this sauce.

INGREDIENTS | YIELDS ½ CUP

½ cup mayonnaise
2 teaspoons ketchup
2 tablespoons cream-style horseradish
¼ teaspoon paprika
¼ teaspoon salt
⅛ teaspoon dried oregano
Dash ground black pepper
Dash cayenne pepper

1. Mix all the ingredients in a small bowl with a lid.
2. Chill for at least 30 minutes in the refrigerator before serving.

Outback Steakhouse Coconut Shrimp

Coconut-crusted deep-fried shrimp is a popular appetizer on many restaurant menus. Red Lobster also has a version using coconut rum.

INGREDIENTS | SERVES 2

12 jumbo shrimp
1 (7-ounce) divided bag shredded coconut
2 tablespoons sugar
½ teaspoon salt
1 cup flour
1 cup beer

1. Peel and devein the shrimp. Leave the tails on.
2. In a medium bowl, combine ½ cup coconut, sugar, salt, flour, and beer. Mix well, cover, and refrigerate for at least 1 hour.
3. Preheat oil in a skillet or deep fryer to 350°F.
4. Pour the rest of the coconut flakes into a shallow bowl. Dip one shrimp at a time into the batter, then roll the battered shrimp in the coconut.
5. Fry the shrimp a few at a time for 2–3 minutes, or until the shrimp become golden brown. Drain on paper towels.

Outback Steakhouse Creole Marmalade Dipping Sauce

This sweet and tangy dipping sauce is the perfect accompaniment to the Coconut Shrimp recipe and is what makes this dish quite unique.

INGREDIENTS | YIELDS ½ CUP

½ cup orange marmalade
2 teaspoons Grey Poupon mustard
1 teaspoon white horseradish sauce
Dash Tabasco sauce
Salt, to taste

1. Combine all the ingredients in a small bowl.
2. Chill in the refrigerator for at least 30 minutes before serving.

Red Lobster Cheddar Bay Biscuits

Everyone's favorite cheese biscuit at Red Lobster is so easy to make that you will serve them all the time.

INGREDIENTS | SERVES 6–8

2 cups Bisquick baking mix
⅔ cup milk
½ cup shredded Cheddar cheese
½ cup melted butter
¼ teaspoon garlic powder

1. Preheat oven to 450°F.
2. In a large bowl, mix baking mix, milk, and cheese until a soft dough forms.
3. Drop by the spoonful onto an ungreased cooking sheet.
4. Bake for 8–10 minutes, or until golden brown.
5. Mix the butter and garlic powder.
6. Brush the butter mixture over warm biscuits before removing from cookie sheet.

T.G.I. Friday's Baked Potato Skins

This is another often-duplicated restaurant recipe and a great way to use leftover baked potatoes.

INGREDIENTS | SERVES 5

10 baked potato halves
1 tablespoon melted butter
Seasoned salt, to taste
¾ cup shredded Cheddar cheese
5 strips of cooked and crumbled bacon
1 green onion, diced

1. Preheat oven to 375°F.
2. Remove as much of the potato flesh as you can, leaving only the skins.
3. Brush potato shells with butter and season with salt.
4. Bake for 15–20 minutes, until crisp.
5. Remove and sprinkle with cheese, bacon, and onion.
6. Place back in the oven for 6–8 minutes, until the cheese has melted.
7. Serve with sour cream or ranch dressing.

Potato Skins History

T.G.I. Friday's has a long history of innovation in the restaurant industry. They have been credited with naming the happy hour, inventing Long Island Iced Tea, and creating loaded potato skins.

T.G.I. Friday's Nine Layer Dip

This is a Mexican dip loaded with flavor. It is not on the menu anymore, so the only way you can have it is to make it at home.

INGREDIENTS | SERVES 3–4

2 strips of diced bacon
1 (16-ounce) can of plain refried beans
1 (1.25-ounce) package of taco seasoning
½ cup sour cream
¾ cup shredded Cheddar cheese
¾ cup guacamole
⅓ cup diced tomatoes
2 tablespoons finely sliced green onions
2 tablespoons sliced black olives

1. Fry bacon in a skillet until done. Add refried beans and cook with the bacon and drippings.
2. Stir frequently and cook on low for 15 minutes.
3. Mix taco seasoning with sour cream and set aside.
4. Place the refried beans on a platter and spread 1" thick. Top the beans with ½ cup of cheese.
5. The next layer is ½ cup of the sour cream mixture. Top with ¾ cup guacamole.
6. Top with the diced tomatoes, onions, and black olives and garnish with ¼ cup of cheese.

CHAPTER 4

Soups, Stews, and Chilis

Applebee's Cheese Chicken
Tortilla Soup
56

California Pizza Kitchen Pea and
Barley Soup
57

Chili's Black Bean Soup
58

Chili's Chicken Enchilada Soup
59

Chili's Chicken Mushroom Soup
60

Chili's Southwest Chicken Chili
61

O' Charley's Loaded
Potato Soup
62

Olive Garden Angel Hair and
Three Onion Soup
63

Olive Garden Chicken and
Gnocchi Soup
64

Olive Garden Italian
Sausage Soup
65

Olive Garden Minestrone Soup
66

Olive Garden Pasta
e Fagioli Soup
67

Olive Garden Pasta Roma Soup
68

Olive Garden Seafood
Pasta Chowder
69

Olive Garden Zuppa
Toscana Soup
70

P.F. Chang's Wonton Soup
71

Red Lobster Clam Chowder
72

Ruby Tuesday White
Chicken Chili
72

Steak 'n Shake Chili
73

T.G.I. Friday's Broccoli
Cheese Soup
74

T.G.I. Friday's French
Onion Soup
74

Applebee's Cheese Chicken Tortilla Soup

This soup is quick to make, flavorful, and very filling. Serve with warm corn bread or tortillas.

INGREDIENTS | SERVES 6–8

2 tablespoons vegetable oil
2 teaspoons minced garlic
1 medium chopped onion
¼ cup chopped green pepper
1 (15 ounce) can tomato purée
4 cups chicken stock
1 teaspoon sugar
½ teaspoon salt
1 teaspoon chili powder
1 teaspoon Worcestershire sauce
10 (6") yellow corn tortillas
4 tablespoons flour
½ cup water
1 pound cooked chicken
1 cup cream
¼ cup nonfat sour cream
8 ounces Velveeta cheese, cut into 1" cubes

1. In a large stockpot over medium heat, add oil and sauté garlic, onions, and green peppers.
2. Add chicken stock, tomato purée, sugar, salt, chili powder, and Worcestershire sauce to the pot.
3. Bring to a boil, then reduce heat and simmer for 20 minutes.
4. Cut tortillas into ¼" strips and bake in the oven at 400°F for 6–8 minutes until crispy.
5. In a small bowl, mix flour and water, then whisk into the soup.
6. Add chicken and cream, bring to a boil, then simmer for 5 minutes.
7. Ladle into bowls and garnish with the sour cream, cheese, and tortilla strips.

California Pizza Kitchen Pea and Barley Soup

This unique soup is full of flavor and is a signature dish at CPK.

INGREDIENTS | SERVES 8

2 cups split peas
6 cups water
4 cups chicken broth
⅓ cup minced onion
1 large clove minced garlic
2 teaspoons lemon juice
1 teaspoon salt
1 teaspoon granulated sugar
¼ teaspoon dried parsley
¼ teaspoon white pepper
Dash dried thyme
½ cup barley
6 cups water
2 medium diced carrots
½ stalk diced celery

1. Rinse and drain the split peas and add them to a large pot with 6 cups of water, chicken broth, onion, garlic, lemon juice, salt, sugar, parsley, pepper, and thyme. Bring to a boil. Reduce heat and simmer for 75 minutes, or until the peas are soft.

2. While the peas are cooking, combine the barley with 6 cups of water in a saucepan. Bring to a boil, reduce heat, and simmer for 75 minutes, or until the barley is soft and most of the water has been absorbed.

3. Drain the barley in a colander and add it to the split peas. Add the carrots and celery and continue to simmer the soup for 15–30 minutes, or until the carrots are tender. Stir occasionally.

4. Turn off the heat, cover the soup, and let it sit for 10–15 minutes before serving.

Chili's Black Bean Soup

Serve this soup with some grilled quesadillas or a salad to make a complete meal.

INGREDIENTS | SERVES 8

¼ cup olive oil
¼ cup diced yellow onion
¼ cup diced carrot
¼ cup diced green bell pepper
1 cup boiling water
4 beef bouillon cubes
1½ quarts undrained canned black beans
2 tablespoons cooking sherry
1 tablespoon distilled white vinegar
2 tablespoons Worcestershire sauce
1 tablespoon granulated sugar
2 teaspoons garlic powder
2 teaspoons salt
½ teaspoon ground black pepper
2 teaspoons chili powder
8 ounces small-diced smoked sausage
1 tablespoon cornstarch
2 tablespoons water

1. In a medium stockpot, place the olive oil, onion, carrot, and bell pepper. Sauté the vegetables for 3–4 minutes, until they are tender.

2. In a saucepan, bring 1 cup of water to a boil, add the bouillon cubes, and allow them to dissolve.

3. Add the bouillon, beans, and remaining ingredients except the cornstarch and 2 tablespoons of water to the sautéed vegetables. Bring mixture to a simmer and cook approximately 15 minutes.

4. In a blender, purée 1 quart of the soup and put back into the pot.

5. In a separate bowl, combine the cornstarch and 2 tablespoons water. Add the cornstarch mix to the soup and bring to a boil for 1 minute.

Chili's Chicken Enchilada Soup

Serve this soup in cups or bowls, and garnish with shredded Cheddar cheese, crumbled corn tortilla chips, and pico de gallo.

INGREDIENTS | SERVES 12

1 tablespoon vegetable oil
1 pound chicken breast fillet
½ cup diced onion
1 pressed garlic clove
4 cups chicken broth
1 cup masa harina
3 cups water
1 cup enchilada sauce
16 ounces Velveeta cheese
1 teaspoon salt, or to taste
1 teaspoon chili powder
½ teaspoon cumin
Shredded Cheddar cheese, for garnish
Crumbled corn tortilla chips, for garnish

Rotisserie Chicken

Buy a cooked rotisserie chicken from the grocery store when you are in a hurry. They are great for sandwiches, soups, stews, and casseroles.

1. In a large pot over medium heat, add 1 tablespoon of oil. Add the chicken breasts and brown for 4–5 minutes per side. Set chicken aside.

2. Add onions and garlic to pot and sauté over medium heat for about 2 minutes, or until onions begin to become translucent. Add the chicken broth.

3. In a medium bowl, combine the masa harina with 2 cups of water and whisk until blended. Add the masa mixture to the pot with onions, garlic, and broth.

4. Add the remaining water, enchilada sauce, cheese, and spices to the pot and bring to a boil.

5. Shred the chicken into small, bite-size pieces and add to the pot. Reduce the heat and simmer for 30–40 minutes, or until thick.

Chili's Chicken Mushroom Soup

This is a hearty soup recipe full of root vegetables, sure to warm you on a cold day.

INGREDIENTS | SERVES 6–8

¼ cup (½ stick) butter
¼ cup diced celery
¼ cup diced carrots
¼ cup diced yellow onions
3 cups sliced mushrooms
½ cup flour
5½ cups chicken broth
Pinch of dried tarragon
¼ teaspoon thyme
1 teaspoon black pepper
½ teaspoon hot pepper sauce
1 teaspoon chopped fresh parsley
3 cups half-and-half
1½ teaspoons lemon juice
¾ pound cooked and diced chicken

1. In a large soup pot, melt the butter over medium heat.
2. Add the vegetables and sauté for 4–5 minutes, until tender.
3. Add the flour and stir constantly.
4. Slowly add the chicken broth.
5. Add herbs, pepper, pepper sauce, and parsley to the pot and stir well. Simmer for 10 minutes.
6. Stir in the half-and-half, lemon juice, and chicken. Bring to a simmer and cook 10 minutes.

Chili's Southwest Chicken Chili

Warm your taste buds with this flavorful chili recipe. If you are not a fan of chicken chili, this dish will change your mind.

INGREDIENTS | YIELDS 4 QUARTS

2 (15-ounce) cans navy beans
1 (15-ounce) can dark red kidney beans
¼ cup vegetable oil
½ cup onion, diced
1⅓ cups diced green bell peppers
2 tablespoons diced jalapeño peppers
3 tablespoons minced fresh garlic
4½ cups water
8 teaspoons chicken base
2 teaspoons lime juice
2 tablespoons sugar
3 tablespoons cornstarch
3 tablespoons ground cumin
2½ tablespoons chili powder
4 teaspoons ground paprika
4 teaspoons dried basil
2 teaspoons minced fresh cilantro
1½ teaspoons ground red pepper
½ teaspoon ground oregano
½ cup canned crushed tomatillos
1 (4-ounce) can diced green chilies, drained
3 pounds cooked diced chicken breasts
Shredded cheese of your choice
Sour cream, for garnish
Tortilla chips

1. Drain and rinse the beans.
2. In 5-quart or larger pot, heat oil over medium heat.
3. Add the onions, bell pepper, jalapeño, and garlic and sauté. Cook for 3–4 minutes, until the vegetables are tender.
4. In a large bowl, combine water, chicken base, lime juice, sugar, cornstarch, and seasonings. Add this to the vegetable mixture.
5. Add the tomatillos and green chilies to the pot and bring to boil.
6. Add the beans and chicken and simmer 10 minutes.
7. Garnish the soup with cheese, sour cream, and tortilla chips.

O' Charley's Loaded Potato Soup

A one-of-a-kind signature soup from O'Charley's sure to make you happy and full of all the flavors you love.

INGREDIENTS | SERVES 6–8

3 pounds red potatoes
¼ cup melted margarine
¼ cup flour
8 cups half-and-half
1 (16-ounce) block melted Velveeta cheese
Garlic powder, to taste
1 teaspoon hot pepper sauce
½ pound crispy fried bacon
½ cup shredded Cheddar cheese
½ cup chopped fresh parsley
½ cup chopped fresh chives

1. Peel and dice the potatoes into ½" cubes.
2. Place in a large stockpot, cover with water, and boil for 10 minutes.
3. In a separate soup pot, combine margarine and flour over low heat.
4. Stir constantly, gradually adding the half-and-half, until the liquid begins to thicken. Add the Velveeta and stir well.
5. Drain the potatoes and add to cream mixture.
6. Stir in garlic powder and hot pepper sauce. Cover and cook over low heat for 30 minutes, stirring occasionally.
7. Place into individual serving bowls and top with crumbled bacon, Cheddar, parsley, and chives.

About O'Charley's

O'Charley's has over 230 casual dining family restaurants in twenty different states. They serve freshly prepared steaks that are grilled to perfection, seafood, chicken, salads, desserts, and more. The loaded potato soup is one of the most popular soups of the day, and the restaurant copycat recipe is often requested.

Olive Garden Angel Hair and Three Onion Soup

Olive Garden has a vast selection of soups. This recipe combines the flavors of pasta with the traditional French onion soup.

INGREDIENTS | SERVES 6

½ pound pearl onions
1 medium thinly sliced red onion
1 medium thinly sliced Vidalia onion
4 tablespoons olive oil
6 cups chicken stock
Salt, to taste
¼ teaspoon red pepper flakes
½ pound angel hair pasta, broken in 2" pieces
¼ cup chopped Italian parsley
4 teaspoons grated Romano Cheese

1. Place the onions and oil in a large saucepan over low heat and sauté, stirring occasionally, for about 20 minutes, until the onions are soft.

2. Add the stock, salt, and pepper flakes and simmer for about 1 hour.

3. Add the pasta and parsley and cook until pasta is al dente. Sprinkle with grated Romano cheese.

Olive Garden Chicken and Gnocchi Soup

The chicken and gnocchi is one of the most popular soups on the menu at Olive Garden. Look for premade gnocchi in the frozen food section of your local supermarket.

INGREDIENTS | SERVES 6–8

⅓ cup butter
2 cloves minced garlic
1 pound cubed chicken
⅓ cup flour
Cracked pepper, to taste
2 cups whole milk
2 cups heavy cream
½ shredded carrot
1 stalk celery shredded
¼ cup shredded onion
½ cup torn fresh spinach
3 chicken bouillon cubes
1 (16-ounce) package frozen gnocchi

1. In a soup pot on medium heat, melt the butter and sauté the garlic for 2–3 minutes.

2. Add the chicken and cook 8–10 minutes until done.

3. Stir in the flour and pepper and mix well, cook for 2–3 minutes, until the flour is cooked into the chicken. Add the milk and heavy cream.

4. Add the carrots, celery, onion, and spinach. Drop 3 bouillon cubes into the pot.

5. Mix ingredients well, stirring occasionally. Cover and simmer for 10 minutes.

6. Add the frozen gnocchi to the pot. Cook 3–4 minutes more, until the gnocchi is done.

What Is Gnocchi?

Gnocchi is an Italian dumpling. Most gnocchi are potato based, but they can be made from all sorts of flours. Gnocchi are eaten as entrées or used as alternatives to pasta in soups. They are widely available dried, frozen, or fresh in vacuum-sealed packages in supermarkets and specialty stores.

Olive Garden Italian Sausage Soup

A wonderfully delicious soup created by the chefs at Olive Garden's Culinary Institute of Tuscany.

INGREDIENTS | SERVES 4

1 pound ground sweet Italian sausage
1 (10¾-ounce) can tomatoes
¼ teaspoon ground black pepper
1 cup white rice
6 cups beef broth
1 (10-ounce) box thawed and drained chopped spinach
Romano cheese, for garnish

1. Cook the sausage in a soup pot over medium heat for 10–12 minutes. Break the meat up with a fork as it cooks.
2. Add the tomatoes, rice, broth and black pepper. Bring the pot to a simmer.
3. Cook 12–15 minutes, or until the rice is tender.
4. Stir in the chopped spinach and let it simmer for a few minutes.
5. Ladle soup into bowls and garnish with cheese.

Garden Culinary Institute of Tuscany

Olive Garden's Culinary Institute of Tuscany is located in the heart of Italy's wine-growing region. Every year, hundreds of Olive Garden chefs travel to the institute to learn authentic Italian cooking skills, like how to choose the freshest ingredients and layering flavors to create the perfect meal.

Olive Garden Minestrone Soup

This classic Italian vegetable and pasta soup will become a family favorite. Serve with grilled cheese or a salad and bread sticks, just like a meal at Olive Garden.

INGREDIENTS | SERVES 8

3 tablespoons olive oil
¼ cup minced celery
4 cloves minced garlic
1 small minced onion
½ cup frozen Italian-style green beans
½ cup chopped zucchini
4 cups vegetable broth
2 (15-ounce) cans drained red kidney beans
2 (15-ounce) cans drained small white bean
½ cup shredded carrots
1 (14-ounce) can diced tomatoes, drained
3 cups hot water
2 tablespoons minced fresh parsley
1½ teaspoons dried oregano
1½ teaspoons salt
½ teaspoon pepper
½ teaspoon dried basil
¼ teaspoon dried thyme
4 cups fresh baby spinach
½ cup small shell pasta

1. Heat the olive oil over medium heat in a large soup pot.
2. Sauté celery, garlic, onion, green beans, and zucchini for 5 minutes.
3. Add the broth, beans, carrots, drained tomatoes, hot water, and spices.
4. Bring the soup to a boil. Reduce heat and simmer for 20 minutes.
5. Add spinach leaves and pasta. Cook for an additional 20 minutes.

Olive Garden Pasta e Fagioli Soup

Pasta e faioli means "pasta and beans" in Italian, and is a traditional meatless soup served by Italian peasants for centuries. The recipe contains ground beef, but it can be omitted to make a vegetarian dish.

INGREDIENTS | SERVES 6–8

2 pounds ground beef
1 chopped onion
3 chopped carrots
4 stalks chopped celery
2 (28-ounce) cans undrained diced tomatoes
1 (16-ounce) can drained red kidney beans
1 (16-ounce) can drained white kidney beans
3 (10-ounce) cans beef stock
3 teaspoons oregano
2 teaspoons pepper
5 teaspoons parsley
1 teaspoon Tabasco sauce (optional)
1 (20-ounce) jar spaghetti sauce
8 ounces pasta

1. Brown the beef in a skillet.
2. Drain the fat from beef and add to a slow cooker with everything except the pasta.
3. Cook on low for 7–8 hours, or on high for 4–5 hours.
4. During last 30 minutes, add the pasta and cook on high.

Olive Garden Pasta Roma Soup

*This simple Italian pasta soup is full of beans and vegetables.
Serve with garlic toast for dipping in the soup.*

INGREDIENTS | SERVES 6–8

2 (16-ounce) cans drained garbanzo beans
⅓ cup olive oil
1 cup julienned carrots
¾ cup diced onions
1 cup diced celery
¼ teaspoon minced garlic
6 slices cooked bacon
1½ cups canned drained chopped tomatoes
1 quart chicken broth
½ teaspoon black pepper
⅛ teaspoon ground rosemary
2 tablespoons chopped fresh parsley
½ cup cooked macaroni

1. Add the beans to a food processor and pulse on and off until the beans are mashed well.

2. Heat the oil in a large soup pot. Add the carrots, onions, celery, and garlic and sauté for 5 minutes on medium heat.

3. Add the remaining ingredients except pasta to the pot. Bring everything to a boil. Reduce heat to a simmer and cook for 20 minutes, stirring occasionally.

4. Add the pasta to the finished soup and serve immediately.

Olive Garden Seafood Pasta Chowder

A hearty and creamy seafood chowder is just the ticket for a cold mid-winter meal. Serve this soup with oyster crackers.

INGREDIENTS | **SERVES 6–8**

6 ounces small shells or bowtie pasta
3 ounces crab meat
6 tablespoons butter
½ pound sliced fresh mushrooms
2 (1-ounce) packages Newburg sauce
3 cups milk
1½ cups water
¼ cup dry white wine
¼ cup sliced green onions

1. Cook the pasta according to the package directions.
2. Sort the crab meat to remove any shell pieces.
3. Melt the butter in a 3-quart sauce pan. Add the mushrooms and sauté for 3 minutes.
4. Add the Newburg sauce and stir well.
5. Add the milk, water, and wine and stir well until the mixture comes to a boil. Reduce heat and simmer 5–8 minutes, stirring constantly.
6. Add the green onions, pasta, and crab. Stir to combine and heat another 5–10 minutes.

Olive Garden Zuppa Toscana Soup

This is a wonderful soup you can make at home, and one of the most requested restaurant copycat recipes from Olive Garden. Serve with some fresh crusty Italian bread.

INGREDIENTS | SERVES 6–8

1 pound Italian sausage, crumbled
½ pound smoked bacon, chopped
1 large chopped onion
2 large diced russet baking potatoes
2 (14.5-ounce) cans chicken broth
1 quart water
2 cloves minced garlic
Salt and pepper, to taste
2 cups chopped kale or Swiss chard
1 cup heavy whipping cream

1. Cook the sausage in a 300°F oven for approximately 30 minutes. Drain on paper towels.

2. Brown bacon in a small skillet over medium-high heat. Drain on paper towels.

3. Place the onions, potatoes, broth, water, and garlic in a soup pot. Cook on medium heat for 15 minutes, or until the potatoes are done.

4. Add the sausage and bacon. Sprinkle in salt and pepper to taste.

5. Simmer for another 10 minutes. Turn to low heat.

6. Add the kale and cream. Heat another 5–10 minutes.

P.F. Chang's Wonton Soup

This is a flavorful soup as good as any you can get at a Chinese restaurant.

INGREDIENTS | SERVES 10–12

For the Soup

4 cups chicken stock
2 cubed chicken breast halves without skin
1 pound peeled medium shrimp
1 cup torn fresh spinach
1 cup sliced mushrooms
1 (8-ounce) can drained water chestnuts
1 teaspoon light brown sugar
1 tablespoon Chinese rice wine or dry sherry
2 tablespoons soy sauce
1 teaspoon finely chopped green onion
1 teaspoon finely chopped fresh ginger

For the Homemade Wontons

½ pound pork, coarsely chopped
8 coarsely chopped medium shrimp
1 teaspoon light brown sugar
1 tablespoon Chinese rice wine or dry sherry
1 tablespoon soy sauce
1 teaspoon finely chopped green onion
1 teaspoon finely chopped fresh ginger
24 wonton wrappers

1. Bring the stock to a rolling boil. Add the remaining ingredients. Cook the chicken in the soup about 10 minutes.

2. For the homemade wontons, in a bowl, mix the pork and shrimp with brown sugar, rice wine, soy sauce, green onions, and ginger. Blend well and set aside for 25–30 minutes for the flavors to blend.

3. Place 1 teaspoon of the filling in the center of each wonton wrapper. Wet the edges of each wonton with a little water and press them together with your fingers to seal. Fold each wonton over.

4. To cook, add wontons to boiling chicken stock and cook for 4–5 minutes. Transfer to individual soup bowls and serve garnished with thinly sliced green onions.

Red Lobster Clam Chowder

This recipe makes a traditional New England clam chowder full of vegetables. You can serve it as a side dish, but this soup is hearty enough to have as a meal.

INGREDIENTS | SERVES 6–8

2 tablespoons butter
¼ teaspoon chopped garlic
1 cup diced onions
½ cup diced celery
½ cup diced leeks
2 tablespoons flour
4 cups milk
1 cup minced clams with juice
1 cup diced potatoes
1 tablespoon salt
1 teaspoon thyme
½ cup heavy cream

1. Melt the butter in a soup pot over medium heat. Sauté the garlic, onion, celery, and leeks for 3–4 minutes.
2. Remove from the heat, add flour, and mix well.
3. Return to the stove. Add the milk and stir.
4. Drain clams and add the juice to the soup. Bring to a boil, stirring often.
5. Reduce heat to a simmer. Add the potatoes and seasonings. Simmer for 10 minutes.
6. Add the clams and simmer for 5–8 minutes. Finish by adding the heavy cream.

Ruby Tuesday White Chicken Chili

White chili is a hearty stew, and delicious without the tomato base. Garnish this dish with sour cream, Monterey jack cheese, and fresh chopped cilantro as you would regular chili.

INGREDIENTS | SERVES 8

1 pound great northern beans
6 cups chicken stock
2 medium chopped onions
2 minced garlic cloves
6 cups diced cooked chicken
1 cup salsa
2 seeded and diced jalapeño peppers
2 diced chili peppers
1½ teaspoons oregano
2 teaspoons cumin
¼ teaspoon cayenne pepper
1 tablespoon vegetable oil
Salt, to taste

1. Soak beans in water overnight.
2. The next day, drain the beans. Add beans, chicken stock, and half the onions and garlic to a large stock pot.
3. Simmer for 2 hours, until the beans soften, stirring frequently. Add the chicken and salsa.
4. In a skillet, sauté peppers, spices, and the remaining onions and garlic in oil for 3–4 minutes. Add to the chili pot along with salt and pepper.
5. Simmer for 1 more hour.

Steak 'n Shake Chili

Steak 'n Shake's chili has an almost cult following. Serve it with oyster crackers, shredded cheese, sliced green onions, and sour cream.

INGREDIENTS | SERVES 4

2 tablespoons vegetable oil
½ small diced onion
1½ pounds ground beef
1 (10.5-ounce) can Campbell's French onion soup
½ teaspoon salt
1 tablespoon chili powder
2 teaspoons ground cumin
½ teaspoon black pepper
2 teaspoons cocoa
2 (15-ounce) cans chili beans
1 (6-ounce) can tomato paste
1 (8-ounce) can tomato sauce
1 cup cola

1. Place oil, onion, and hamburger in a large stockpot over medium heat.
2. Cook the hamburger for 7–9 minutes, until it has browned. Drain the excess oil.
3. Add the onion soup and simmer for a few minutes.
4. Add the rest of the ingredients to the pot.
5. Simmer on the stove for 1 hour.

T.G.I. Friday's Broccoli Cheese Soup

This soup is so good and so easy. Now you can create a restaurant copycat at home by tossing a few ingredients into a pot.

INGREDIENTS | SERVES 6

4 cups chicken broth
1 cup half-and-half
1 cup water
4 slices American cheese
½ cup flour
½ teaspoon dried onion flakes
¼ teaspoon black pepper
4½ cups bite-size broccoli florets

1. Combine all the ingredients except the broccoli into a large soup pot.
2. Bring to a boil, stirring constantly.
3. Reduce to a simmer.
4. Add the broccoli and simmer for 15 minutes, or until the broccoli is tender.
5. Garnish with shredded Cheddar cheese.

T.G.I. Friday's French Onion Soup

This is a classic French onion soup recipe that is served in many restaurants.

INGREDIENTS | SERVES 4

2 tablespoons butter
4 medium sliced onions
4 cups beef broth
1 tablespoon Worcestershire sauce
¼ teaspoon black pepper
Dash of dried thyme
1 cup French bread cubes
½ cup shredded mozzarella cheese

1. Melt the butter in a 2-quart saucepan over low heat.
2. Add the onions and cook 20 minutes, stirring occasionally. Add the broth, Worcestershire sauce, pepper, and thyme.
3. Increase the heat to medium-high and bring to a boil.
4. Reduce the heat to low, cover, and simmer for 5 minutes.
5. Divide soup into 4 individual serving crocks. Place the bread cubes on top of the soup and then add the cheese. Put the soup bowls under the broiler to melt the cheese until it turns slightly brown.

CHAPTER 5

Salads and Sandwiches

Applebee's Oriental
Chicken Salad
76

Arby's Roast Beef Sandwich
77

Arby's Barbecue Sauce
77

California Pizza Kitchen
Wedge Salad
78

California Pizza Kitchen Waldorf
Chicken Salad
79

Chili's Grilled Caribbean Chicken
Salad
80

Dave and Buster's
Muffaletta Salad
81

Golden Corral Seafood Salad
82

KFC Bean Salad
82

Olive Garden House Salad
83

Olive Garden Salad Dressing
83

Panera Bread Company Tomato
Mozzarella Salad
84

Quiznos Steakhouse
Dip Submarine
85

Starbucks Tarragon
Chicken Salad
86

Steak 'n Shake Frisco Melt
87

Subway Orchard Chicken Salad
88

Subway Veggie Delite Wrap
88

Subway Sweet Onion Chicken
Teriyaki Sandwich
89

T.G.I. Friday's Strawberry
Fields Salad
90

Wendy's Spicy Chicken Sandwich
91

Applebee's Oriental Chicken Salad

What makes this salad recipe so delicious is the tangy Asian salad dressing. This is sure to be one of your favorite dinner salads.

INGREDIENTS | SERVES 4

4 frozen breaded chicken tenderloins

Dressing
6 tablespoons honey
3 tablespoons rice wine vinegar
½ cup mayonnaise
2 teaspoons Dijon mustard
¼ teaspoon sesame oil

Salad
2 cups chopped green cabbage
2 cups chopped red cabbage
6 cups chopped romaine lettuce
1 shredded carrot
2 chopped green onions
¼ cup toasted sliced almonds
⅔ cup chow mein noodles

1. Preheat the oven and cook chicken tenders according to package directions.

2. Combine all the ingredients for the dressing in a small bowl. Stir well and chill in the refrigerator for 30 minutes.

3. Combine all the salad ingredients and toss with the dressing.

Arby's Roast Beef Sandwich

The barbecue sauce is what really makes this sandwich unique. This recipe will make you think that you are eating at Arby's restaurant.

INGREDIENTS | SERVES 4

1 pound thinly sliced deli roast beef
1 can beef broth
Butter, for brushing
4 plain hamburger buns
Arby's Barbecue Sauce (see below)

1. Place the roast beef and broth in a microwave-safe bowl. Heat for 1–2 minutes, until warm.

2. Add a light coating of butter to the inside of the bun and toast lightly in a skillet.

3. Place the warm roast beef on the bun. Pile as high as you like.

4. Add the barbecue sauce on top of the beef.

Arby's Barbecue Sauce

This is a simple barbecue sauce meant to top the roast beef sandwiches served at Arby's. You may store the sauce in the refrigerator for up to 2 months.

INGREDIENTS | YIELDS 1 CUP

1 cup ketchup
2 teaspoons water
2 teaspoons brown sugar
½ teaspoon Worcestershire sauce
½ teaspoon Tabasco sauce
¼ teaspoon onion powder
¼ teaspoon garlic powder
¼ teaspoon salt
¼ teaspoon pepper

1. Combine all the ingredients into a small sauce pan. Place over medium heat.

2. Stir constantly until the sauce boils.

3. Cook for 7–10 minutes.

4. Remove from heat and allow to cool.

California Pizza Kitchen Wedge Salad

The classic iceberg wedge salad has become very popular at many restaurants. Why only indulge in this dish at a nice steakhouse when it is so easy to serve at home?

INGREDIENTS | SERVES 2

1 head iceberg lettuce
Blue cheese dressing, to taste
2 peeled and chopped hardboiled eggs
6 slices chopped cooked bacon
Blue cheese crumbles, to taste
½ cup chopped tomatoes

1. Trim off any brown or dark green leaves on the head of lettuce.
2. Remove the inside core by tapping it on a counter top.
3. Cut the head of lettuce in half.
4. Trim the opposite ends so that the lettuce wedge will lay flat.
5. Top the lettuce with blue cheese dressing.
6. Add chopped eggs and bacon.
7. Finish the salad with blue cheese crumbles and tomatoes.

About California Pizza Kitchen

CPK is widely known for its innovative and nontraditional pizzas. The chain has over 230 locations in thirty-two states. The design of the restaurant revolves around an open kitchen centered around a wood-burning pizza oven. They also serve various kinds of pasta, salads, and desserts.

California Pizza Kitchen Waldorf Chicken Salad

This recipe includes some unique items not normally found in the traditional Waldorf salad.

INGREDIENTS | SERVES 2

Salad Dressing
1 cup olive oil
½ cup balsamic vinegar
2 tablespoons Dijon mustard
1 tablespoon minced garlic
½ teaspoon fresh ground black pepper
¼ teaspoon salt

Salad
6 cups mixed baby greens
½ cup diced celery
1 granny smith apple, chopped in bite-sized pieces
½ cup halved red seedless grapes
2 sliced grilled chicken breasts
½ cup candied walnuts
Crumbled gorgonzola cheese, to taste

1. Whisk all the ingredients for the dressing together in a bowl with a lid.

2. Chill the salad dressing and plates in the refrigerator for 30 minutes before serving.

3. Toss the greens, celery, and fruits together and place on the chilled plates.

4. Drizzle on the salad dressing.

5. Top the salad with chicken breast, candied walnuts, and gorgonzola.

Chili's Grilled Caribbean Chicken Salad

It's sweet, crunchy, and cool, and now it's yours. This salad features a honey-lime dressing for a taste of the islands.

INGREDIENTS | SERVES 4

4 boneless, skinless chicken breasts
½ cup teriyaki marinade

Honey-Lime Dressing

¼ cup Dijon mustard
¼ cup honey
1½ teaspoons sugar
1 tablespoon sesame oil
1½ cups apple cider vinegar
1½ teaspoons lime juice

Pico De Gallo

2 diced tomatoes
½ cup diced Spanish onions
2 teaspoons chopped jalapeño pepper
2 teaspoons minced cilantro
Pinch of salt

Salad

4 cups chopped leaf lettuce
4 cups chopped iceberg lettuce
1 cup chopped red cabbage
1 can drained pineapple chunks
4 handfuls of tortilla chips, broken into pieces

1. Marinate the chicken in teriyaki marinade for 2 hours in the refrigerator.

2. Mix all the ingredients for the dressing in a small bowl and chill for 30 minutes in the refrigerator.

3. Mix all the ingredients for the pico de gallo in a small bowl and chill for 30 minutes in the refrigerator.

4. Preheat the grill and grill the chicken breast for 5 minutes on each side, or until done. Cut into strips.

5. Toss the lettuce and cabbage in a large salad bowl.

6. Add the pico de gallo, pineapple, dressing, and tortilla chips.

7. Add the grilled chicken strips. Toss, and serve.

Dave and Buster's Muffaletta Salad

This cold pasta salad is a twist on the big round New Orleans muffaletta sandwiches, which contain Italian meats and cheeses.

INGREDIENTS | SERVES 4

24 slices pepperoni
2 ounces sliced salami
4 ounces sliced ham
4 ounces sliced turkey
1 cup sliced celery
4 tablespoons chopped green onion
1 cup roasted red peppers
¼ cup sliced black olives
½ cup chopped green salad olives
1¼ pounds spiral pasta
3 tablespoons Italian dressing
1½ cups assorted lettuce
¼ cup julienned spinach leaves
1 cup diced Roma tomatoes
1 cup Italian cheese blend
¼ cup shredded Asiago cheese

1. Cut the pepperoni, salami, ham, and turkey into thin julienne strips. Place the meats in a large salad bowl.
2. Add the celery, green onions, and roast peppers to the bowl.
3. Chop and add both types of olives to the bowl.
4. Add the cooked pasta.
5. Pour the Italian dressing on the pasta and toss everything together gently.
6. Place assorted lettuce and spinach on a cold serving platter, leaving a space in the middle for the pasta salad.
7. Pile the salad mixture high in the center of the platter.
8. Top the salad with tomatoes and cheeses.

Origins of the Muffaletta

The muffaletta's origins are from a grocery store in New Orleans that was near the farmer's market. The Italians would come in and order olive salad, lunch meats, cheese, and bread, so the owner of the store suggested that they make a sandwich out of it. Today, the muffaletta is served with the same ingredients and is large enough to serve several people.

Golden Corral Seafood Salad

This dish is perfect for a quick and light lunch. It may be served on top of salad greens, in a tortilla wrap, or on bread as a sandwich.

INGREDIENTS | SERVES 4–6

1 pound shredded imitation crab meat
1 cup diced celery
½ cup mayonnaise
¼ cup diced green onions
1 tablespoon lemon juice
3 peeled and chopped hardboiled eggs

1. Mix all the ingredients together in a medium-size bowl with a lid.
2. Refrigerate for at least 1 hour before serving to allow the flavors to blend.

KFC Bean Salad

A bean salad tastes better after it marinates 3–4 days, so make this dish ahead of time and you will be able to enjoy all of the rich flavors when you are ready to eat.

INGREDIENTS | SERVES 6

1 (16-ounce) can green beans
1 (16-ounce) can wax beans
1 (16-ounce) can kidney beans
1 medium small-diced green pepper
1 medium small-diced white onion
½ cup vegetable oil
½ cup cider vinegar
¾ cup sugar
1½ teaspoons salt
½ teaspoon black pepper

1. Drain and rinse all the beans.
2. Combine all the ingredients together in an airtight container
3. Marinate in the refrigerator, preferably 3–4 days.

Olive Garden House Salad

This classic Italian salad is sure to be a hit with friends and family. Serve it with some breadsticks and soup to create a true Olive Garden meal at home.

INGREDIENTS | SERVES 2

1 bag of American Blend salad mix
10 slices red onion
10 black olives
8 banana peppers
1 cup croutons
1 sliced tomato
Olive Garden Salad Dressing, to taste (see below)

1. Combine all the ingredients in a medium bowl with a lid.

2. Cool the salad and serving plates in the refrigerator for 1–2 hours.

3. Put the dressing on the bottom of the plates. Add the chilled salad ingredients on top of the dressing.

Soup, Salad, and Breadsticks

The all-you-can-eat soup, salad, and breadsticks promotion from Olive Garden is one of the most successful marketing campaigns of all time. It has been duplicated in many other restaurants chains, such as T.G.I. Friday's Endless Lunch and Chili's Bottomless Express Lunch.

Olive Garden Salad Dressing

Making the Olive Garden salad dressing at home is easy to do and tastes better than what you can buy off the grocery shelf. The dressing will keep for about 10 days if stored in an airtight container in the refrigerator.

INGREDIENTS | YIELDS 1 CUP

½ cup mayonnaise
⅓ cup white vinegar
1 teaspoon vegetable oil
2 tablespoons corn syrup
2 tablespoons Parmesan cheese
2 tablespoons Romano cheese
¼ teaspoon garlic salt
½ teaspoon Italian seasoning
½ teaspoon parsley flakes
1 tablespoon lemon juice
Sugar (optional)

1. Place all the ingredients in a blender. Blend until everything is mixed well.

2. If you find the dressing a bit tart for your tastes, add a little bit of sugar.

Panera Bread Company Tomato Mozzarella Salad

There is no shortage of sandwich places, but Panera Bread Company serves some of the best. The key to this recipe is buying a good loaf of crusty Italian bread from the bakery.

INGREDIENTS | SERVES 4

1 loaf focaccia bread
5 or 6 chopped ripe tomatoes
2 tablespoons fresh chopped basil
1 thin-sliced red onion
4 ounces cubed fresh mozzarella
Balsamic vinaigrette dressing

1. Cut bread into 4 wedges and place on plate.
2. In a small bowl, gently toss tomatoes, basil, and red onion together.
3. Place ¼ of the mixture on each wedge of bread and top with ¼ of cheese cubes.
4. Pour about 2 ounces of dressing over each serving.

About Panera Bread Company

The Panera Bread Company, also called the St. Louis Bread Company, is a chain of quick, casual restaurants with a bakery and café that sells bread, sandwiches, soups, salads, and bakery items. Their menu also includes seasonal cookies and a wide variety of coffee flavors.

Quiznos Steakhouse Dip Submarine

Quiznos has a variety of toasted deli sandwiches. This recipe features one of their signature submarines with an au jus dipping sauce.

INGREDIENTS | SERVES 2

Au Jus Dipping Sauce
1 tablespoon butter
1 tablespoon finely chopped onion
1 tablespoon flour
1 (1-ounce) packet au jus mix
1⅔ cups water

Sandwich Sauce
½ cup prepared Alfredo sauce
¼ cup mayonnaise
1 dash onion salt or garlic salt

Sandwich
1 loaf bakery French bread
¾ pound thin-sliced deli roast beef
½ cup shredded Swiss cheese
½ cup shredded Italian cheese blend

Toasted Submarine Sandwiches
Paninis are the latest trend in sandwich making. Americans define panini as a grilled or pressed sandwich served warm. You don't need to buy an expensive panini press, just use your George Forman grill. Put the sandwich inside the grill and place a heavy pot or skillet on top of it to press and toast the sandwich. This is a much quicker method than using the oven.

1. Preheat the oven broiler.

2. Melt the butter in a small saucepan over medium heat. Sauté the onions until tender (about 2–3 minutes).

3. Add the flour and the contents of the au jus mix packet. Gradually whisk in the water and allow it to simmer while you make the sandwich.

4. In a small bowl, mix together the Alfredo sauce, mayonnaise, and your choice of onion salt or garlic salt.

5. Slice the French bread with one horizontal slice to make a top and a bottom half. Spread the sauce evenly over both pieces of the sliced bread.

6. Place sandwich halves open faced onto a baking sheet. Put under the oven broiler for about 1 minute, until the sauce is bubbly and the edges of the bread barely start to brown.

7. Remove the tray from the oven. Arrange the roast beef over both sandwich halves, then sprinkle evenly with cheeses.

8. Broil for another minute, until the cheese melts and starts to brown. Remove from the oven.

9. Put the sandwich halves together and return to the broiler very briefly to lightly toast the top of the sandwich. Remove from the oven and slice sandwich into 4 even slices.

10. Serve with the au jus sauce in small bowls for dipping.

CHAPTER 5 SALADS AND SANDWICHES

Starbucks Tarragon Chicken Salad

This is a very good restaurant copycat recipe for their chicken salad with a unique dressing.

INGREDIENTS | SERVES 2

¼ cup mayonnaise
1 tablespoon fresh chopped tarragon
1 teaspoon lemon juice
2 cups ½" cubed cooked chicken
¼ cup finely chopped dried cranberries
1 stalk finely chopped celery
1 tablespoon finely chopped red onion

1. In a small bowl, create the dressing by combining the mayonnaise, tarragon, and lemon juice. Mix well.

2. In a medium bowl, add the chicken, cranberries, celery, and onion and lightly toss to mix.

3. Add the dressing and mix well.

Steak 'n Shake Frisco Melt

It seems that patty melts are popping up on the menu everywhere you go these days. This restaurant copycat recipe for Steak 'n Shake Frisco Melt is a winner, and one that you can make at home with just a few simple ingredients.

INGREDIENTS | SERVES 4

1 tablespoon ketchup
2 tablespoons Thousand Island dressing
1 pound ground beef
8 slices of bread
1 tablespoon butter or margarine
2 tablespoons diced onions
8 slices American cheese
4 slices Swiss cheese
4 lettuce leaves
4 slices of tomato

1. Combine the ketchup and salad dressing. Set aside.

2. Form ground beef into 8 thin patties. Fry or grill the burgers until cooked as desired. Set aside.

3. Lightly toast all 8 slices of bread.

4. To a skillet, add ½ tablespoon of margarine, and cook the onions for 2–3 minutes until softened. Remove the onions and set aside.

5. Layer as follows from bottom to top: bread, American cheese, burger, Swiss cheese, burger, American cheese, onions, salad dressing, and bread.

6. Place sandwich in skillet and toast 1–2 minutes on each side to melt the cheeses.

7. Serve with a lettuce leaf and a tomato slice

Subway Orchard Chicken Salad

Subway's new Orchard Chicken Sandwich is available for only a limited time. With this recipe, you can make it anytime you want and put it on fresh bread topped with your favorite veggies, just like Subway.

INGREDIENTS | SERVES 4

¼ cup plain nonfat yogurt
2 tablespoons light mayonnaise
2 teaspoons lemon juice
½ teaspoon sugar
1 cup cubed cooked chicken breast
½ cup diced celery
1 cup chopped red apples
¼ cup golden raisins or white grapes
¼ cup dried cranberries or cherries

1. Make the salad dressing in a small bowl by mixing together the yogurt, mayonnaise, lemon juice, and sugar.
2. Add the rest of the ingredients to a large bowl.
3. Pour the yogurt mixture over the chicken mixture. Toss well to mix.
4. Cover and chill for at least 2 hours.

Subway Veggie Delite Wrap

This light and low-calorie option on the menu at Subway is easy to create at home using simple ingredients. You may substitute your favorite vegetables or omit the ones that you don't like in this recipe.

INGREDIENTS | SERVES 1

¼ cup refried beans
1 slice of cheese of your choice
1 whole-wheat tortilla
½ cup shredded lettuce
½ cup diced tomato
¼ cup diced onion
4 pickle slices
3 diced olives
2 teaspoons fat-free Italian salad dressing
2 teaspoons honey mustard salad dressing

1. Spread the refried beans and cheese onto the tortilla.
2. Place on a plate and microwave for 30–60 seconds, until the cheese melts.
3. Add the vegetables, pickles, and olives on top of the melted cheese.
4. Drizzle the salad dressings on top of the vegetables.
5. Roll up like a burrito.

Subway Sweet Onion Chicken Teriyaki Sandwich

Subway's Sweet Onion Chicken Teriyaki Sandwich is one of the chains biggest selling subs. The sandwich is made with very common ingredients. What sets this sub apart from the others is the sweet onion sauce.

INGREDIENTS | SERVES 1

1 boneless, skinless chicken breast
¼ cup Lawry's teriyaki marinade
1 bakery-fresh sub roll
Sliced vegetables of your choice

Sweet Onion Sauce
½ cup light corn syrup
1 tablespoon red wine vinegar
1 tablespoon minced white onion
2 tablespoons white vinegar
1 teaspoon brown sugar
1 teaspoon balsamic vinegar
¼ teaspoon lemon juice
⅛ teaspoon salt
⅛ teaspoon poppy seeds
Pinch of cracked black pepper
Pinch of garlic powder

1. Place the chicken breast and marinade in a zip-top bag. Marinate the chicken in the refrigerator for at least 30 minutes.

2. Combine all the sauce ingredients into a small microwave-safe bowl. Heat for 1–2 minutes, until the mixture boils.

3. Stir well, cover, and let cool.

4. Cook the chicken on a George Foreman grill or stovetop grill pan. Slice into ¼" strips.

5. Place the chicken on a sub roll. Add whatever vegetables you like.

6. Pour the sweet onion sauce over the chicken and vegetables.

T.G.I. Friday's Strawberry Fields Salad

The restaurant doesn't serve this salad anymore. That's the great thing about copycat recipes—if it is something you like that goes off the menu, you can still make it at home. Frozen strawberries may be used if fresh ones are not available.

INGREDIENTS | SERVES 2

Glazed Pecans
1 cup chopped pecans
¼ cup dark brown sugar
1 tablespoon water

Strawberry Glaze
12 strawberries
¼ cup balsamic vinegar
¼ cup granulated sugar
2 tablespoons water

Salad
1 head red leaf lettuce
1 head romaine lettuce
2 ounces shredded Parmesan cheese
6 ounces balsamic vinaigrette dressing
Cracked pepper, to taste

1. In a small sauté pan on medium heat, mix the chopped pecans with brown sugar and water. Cook for 4–5 minutes. Set aside.

2. Slice the strawberries into ¼" slices.

3. In a small bowl, mix the vinegar, sugar, and water with the sliced strawberries. Set aside.

4. Chop the lettuces into 2" pieces.

5. In a large bowl, toss the lettuces, Parmesan, vinaigrette, and pecans.

6. Strain the strawberries from the glaze and place on top of the salad. Add the cracked black pepper to the top of the salad.

New Salads at T.G.I. Friday's

T.G.I. Friday's innovative menu is constantly changing. Currently there are 6 salads, and 3 of them are new. The salads they are serving now are a Santa Fe Chopped Salad, Chicken Caesar Salad, Cobb Salad, Italian Wedge Salad, Southwest Wedge Salad, and the Classic Wedge Salad.

Wendy's Spicy Chicken Sandwich

This super-crispy chicken sandwich with a hint of spiciness will feed your fast food craving. If you like it really hot, add more hot pepper sauce to your taste.

INGREDIENTS | SERVES 4

Vegetable oil for frying
⅓ cup hot pepper sauce
⅔ cup water
1 cup all-purpose flour
2½ teaspoons salt
4 teaspoons cayenne pepper
1 teaspoon coarse-ground black pepper
1 teaspoon onion powder
½ teaspoon paprika
⅛ teaspoon garlic powder
4 boneless, skinless chicken breasts
4 plain hamburger buns
8 teaspoons mayonnaise
4 tomato slices
4 lettuce leaves

1. Preheat oil in a deep fryer to 350°F.
2. Mix the pepper sauce and water in a small bowl.
3. In a different bowl, combine the flour, salt, cayenne pepper, black pepper, onion powder, paprika, and garlic powder.
4. Pound each of the chicken pieces until about ⅜" thick. Trim them if necessary to help them fit on the bun.
5. Coat each piece of chicken with the flour and roll it in the watered-down pepper sauce. Coat it in the flour mixture again and set it aside. Repeat for other fillets.
6. Fry the chicken for 10 minutes, or until they are brown and crispy. Remove to paper towels to drain.
7. Prepare sandwiches by grilling the hamburger buns in a hot fry pan. Spread 2 teaspoons of mayonnaise on each bun.
8. Build the sandwiches by adding tomato, lettuce, and chicken.

CHAPTER 6

Fast Food and Treats

Auntie Anne's Soft Pretzels
94

A&W Coney Island Sauce
95

Burger King Chicken Fries
96

Carl's Jr. Six Dollar Burger
97

Carl's Jr. Western
Bacon Cheeseburger
98

Domino's Cinna Stix
99

Hardee's Mushroom Swiss
Burger
100

In-n-Out Double-Double Burger
100

Jack in the Box Mini Buffalo
Chicken Sandwiches
101

KFC Crispy Strips
102

KFC Twister
103

KFC Pepper Mayonnaise Sauce
103

Long John Silver's Beer-
Battered Fish
104

Long John Silver's Fish Tacos
105

Long John Silver's Baja Sauce
105

McDonald's Fillet of Fish
106

Mrs. Fields Chocolate
Chip Cookies
107

Sonic Fritos Chili Cheese Wraps
108

Sonic Hickory Burger
108

Taco Bell Crispitos
109

White Castle Sliders
110

Auntie Anne's Soft Pretzels

You can create this popular mall food at home. Auntie Anne's has more than 1,500 locations nationwide.

INGREDIENTS | YIELDS 12

1½ cups warm water
1⅛ teaspoons active dry yeast
2 tablespoons brown sugar
1⅛ teaspoons salt
1 cup bread flour
3 cups regular flour
2 cups warm water
2 tablespoons baking soda
Coarse salt, to taste
4 tablespoons melted butter

1. Preheat oven to 400°F.
2. Add water to a mixing bowl and sprinkle yeast into it. Stir to dissolve.
3. Add the brown sugar and salt. Stir to dissolve.
4. Add the flour and knead the dough until it is smooth and elastic.
5. Let the dough rise at least ½ hour.
6. While dough is rising, prepare a baking soda water bath with 2 cups water and 2 tablespoons of baking soda. Be certain to stir often.
7. After the dough has risen, pinch off bits of dough and roll into a long rope (about ½" or less thick) and shape.
8. Dip each pretzel in the soda solution and place on greased baking sheet. Allow the pretzels to rise again. Sprinkle with coarse salt.
9. Bake them in the oven for about 10 minutes, or until golden. Brush with melted butter and serve.

A&W Coney Island Sauce

For a taste of summer on the boardwalk any time of year, this A&W copycat sauce recipe can't be beat. Serve it on your favorite hotdogs.

INGREDIENTS | YIELDS 25 CUPS

5 pounds hamburger
2 small onions, finely chopped
64 ounces Hunt's Tomato Paste
64 ounces Hunt's Tomato Purée
1½ cups granulated sugar
⅓ cup cider vinegar
2 tablespoons chili powder
1 tablespoon pepper
1 tablespoon celery seed
3 tablespoons plus 1 teaspoon salt

1. Brown the hamburger and onions in a large skillet. Drain the excess oil.

2. Add the remaining ingredients and simmer for 3½ hours.

3. Stir frequently so that the sauce will not stick to the pan.

Burger King Chicken Fries

These are a fairly new item on the Burger King menu. This restaurant copycat recipe is easy to make since it uses a prepared seasoning mix.

INGREDIENTS | SERVES 2

1 package boneless skinless chicken breasts
½ cup flour
½ cup Zatarain's Fish-Fri
1 egg
1 tablespoon water
Vegetable oil for frying

1. Butterfly the chicken breasts. Cut them down the middle to separate the breast halves. Cut into the shape of French fries with meat scissors or a knife.

2. Put the flour and Fish-Fri into 2 separate zip-top plastic bags.

3. In a small bowl, lightly beat the egg with the water.

4. Place 4 chicken fries at a time into the flour bag. Shake off the excess flour.

5. Dip them into the egg wash, shake off the excess, then shake in the Fish-Fri.

6. Place each chicken fry on a plate to reserve for frying.

7. Heat the oil in a skillet on medium-high. Fry the chicken fries in batches so they do not touch, turning, until they are golden brown (about 4–5 minutes or until they float).

8. Drain on paper towels.

Carl's Jr. Six Dollar Burger

Hardees and Carl's Jr. serve these giant hamburgers and compare them to the burgers you get at popular casual restaurants. This meaty recipe will give you the restaurant feeling at home.

INGREDIENTS | SERVES 1

½ pound ground beef
Salt and pepper, to taste
1 large hamburger bun
3 teaspoons mayonnaise
2 teaspoons ketchup
1 teaspoon mustard
3–4 dill pickle slices
1 leaf of iceberg lettuce
2 slices of tomatoes
4–5 red onion rings

1. Preheat barbecue or indoor grill to medium heat.
2. Form the ground beef into a patty that is slightly larger than the bun. Generously salt and pepper each side of the patty.
3. Grill the burger on the grill 3–4 minutes per side, or until done.
4. Brown the faces of the bun in a hot skillet over medium heat.
5. Spread 1½ teaspoons of mayonnaise on the top and bottom buns.
6. Spread the ketchup and mustard on the top bun.
7. Arrange pickle slices on the bottom bun. Add lettuce, tomato, and onion on top of the pickles.
8. Place the cooked burger on the bun and top with cheese.

Carl's Jr. Western Bacon Cheeseburger

This recipe provides all the classic ingredients in a typical western hamburger served at many restaurants, without the big price tag. Add some French fries and you have a fast food meal at home.

INGREDIENTS | SERVES 1

2 frozen onion rings
¼ pound ground beef
2 slices of bacon
1 sesame seed hamburger bun
2 tablespoons barbecue sauce
1 slice of American cheese

1. Bake onion rings according to package directions.
2. Form hamburger into a patty and cook for 4–5 minutes per side, until done.
3. In a small skillet, fry bacon until crispy.
4. Toast the faces of the bun.
5. Spread BBQ sauce on the top and bottom of the bun.
6. Place both onion rings on the bottom of the bun.
7. Add cooked hamburger, cheese, and bacon.

Domino's Cinna Stix

Pizza dough isn't just for pizza. This sweet recipe was created by Dominos employees looking for a quick snack using the ingredients they had on hand. This recipe will be especially appreciated by the kids in the family.

INGREDIENTS | YIELDS 12–16

1 package of refrigerated pizza dough
¼ cup melted margarine
½ cup sugar
2 teaspoons cinnamon

Icing

1 pound powdered sugar
1 tablespoon milk
1 tablespoon melted butter
¼ teaspoon vanilla extract

1. Preheat the oven to 350°F.

2. Roll out the pizza dough to a large rectangle.

3. Brush the melted margarine over the dough.

4. In a small bowl, mix the sugar and cinnamon.

5. Sprinkle the mixture liberally over the pizza dough. Cut the dough in half and then slice into smaller sticks.

6. Place the dough on a lightly greased cookie sheet and bake for 15 minutes.

7. In a small bowl, mix together all the icing ingredients.

8. Serve icing alongside the sticks for dipping.

Hardee's Mushroom Swiss Burger

This recipe uses simple canned ingredients to make a burger as good or even better than the original.

INGREDIENTS | SERVES 4

1 (10.75-ounce) can Campbell's Golden Mushroom soup
1 small can sliced mushrooms
1 teaspoon Worcestershire sauce
½ teaspoon Accent seasoning
½ teaspoon Lawry's Seasoned Salt
¼ teaspoon ground pepper
1 pound hamburger
4 slices Swiss cheese

1. Mix the mushroom soup, mushrooms, and Worcestershire sauce together.
2. Place mixture in a small sauce pan over low heat and let simmer.
3. Mix the Accent, Seasoned Salt, and pepper into the hamburger.
4. Form the hamburger into 4 patties and fry in a skillet or grill for 4–5 minutes per side until done.
5. Put each patty onto a bun and add the Swiss cheese and mushroom sauce.

In-n-Out Double-Double Burger

Give this recipe a try—it will become one of your favorite ways to prepare a hamburger.

INGREDIENTS | SERVES 1

1 plain hamburger bun
⅓ pound ground beef
2 slices American cheese
1 tablespoon Thousand Island salad dressing
1 slice fresh tomato
1 lettuce leaf
1 thin slice of onion

1. Preheat a frying pan or the grill. Lightly toast both halves of the hamburger bun and set aside.
2. Divide the beef into 2 even portions and form into patties. Season the patties with salt and pepper. Cook for 4–5 minutes per side.
3. Place a slice of cheese on each hamburger patty and melt the cheese.
4. Assemble from bottom to top: bun, salad dressing, tomato, lettuce, burger, onion, burger, and then bun top.

In-n-Out

The In-n-Out restaurant chain has developed an almost cult following for its hamburgers in the Western states.

Jack in the Box Mini Buffalo Chicken Sandwiches

These little slider sandwiches are fun and easy to make. They would be perfect to nibble on during a football game or cocktail party.

INGREDIENTS | YIELDS 24

1 (2-pound) package frozen chicken nuggets

2 (12-ounce/12-count) packages ready-made Kings Hawaiian dinner rolls

24 teaspoons ranch salad dressing

24 teaspoons Frank's RedHot sauce

24 small pieces iceberg lettuce

1. Prepare the chicken nuggets according to package directions. You will need 1 chicken nugget for each roll.

2. Split the rolls open with a serrated knife. Coat the bottom of each roll with ranch dressing.

3. Place a chicken nugget on top of the dressing.

4. Add 1 teaspoon of hot sauce to each nugget.

5. Cover the chicken with lettuce, then the top of the roll.

KFC Crispy Strips

KFC is the leader in chicken quick-serve chains. These chicken strips will match the flavor of the restaurant and satisfy your fast food craving.

INGREDIENTS | SERVES 6

6 chicken breasts
Vegetable oil for frying
1 egg
1 cup milk
2 cups flour
2½ teaspoons salt
¾ teaspoon pepper
⅛ teaspoon garlic powder
⅛ teaspoon paprika
⅛ teaspoon baking powder

1. Cut the chicken breasts into strips.
2. Preheat the oil in a skillet or deep fryer to 350°F.
3. In a small bowl, beat the egg and milk.
4. In another bowl, combine the flour and spices.
5. Dip the chicken strips 1 at a time into the egg mixture.
6. Then dip in the flour coating.
7. Fry a few strips at a time until they are golden brown. Cook for about 5 minutes or until the strips float.
8. Drain on a paper towel to absorb excess oil.

KFC Twister

You may use the recipe for KFC crispy strips in this book or buy chicken strips from your local supermarket deli to prepare this dish.

INGREDIENTS | SERVES 1

1 large flour tortilla
KFC Pepper Mayonnaise Sauce (see below)
2 cooked breaded chicken breast strips
A small amount of thinly sliced lettuce
2 slices of tomato, diced

1. Microwave the tortilla for 30–45 minutes to soften and make it easier to fold.
2. Cover the tortilla with the mayonnaise sauce.
3. Lay the chicken tenders end-to-end lengthwise on top of the tortilla.
4. Add lettuce, tomato, and more of the mayonnaise sauce on top of the chicken.
5. Fold like a burrito and enjoy.

The Twister

The Twister was KFC's answer to the current craze for sandwich wraps in the restaurant industry. They simply used their chicken strips and created a special sauce to top them with.

KFC Pepper Mayonnaise Sauce

This is a recipe for a simple sauce to put on top of your Twister to make it taste like what is served at KFC.

INGREDIENTS | YIELDS ½ CUP

½ cup mayonnaise
1 teaspoon black pepper
1 teaspoon lemon juice

1. Combine all the ingredients in a small bowl with a lid.
2. Store in the refrigerator for up to 2 weeks.

Long John Silver's Beer-Battered Fish

The secret to the Long John Silver's taste is the batter they use to dip their fish, chicken, and shrimp into. This recipe is very easy since it uses a prepared mix. The best type of fish to use is cod, tilapia, or trout.

INGREDIENTS | SERVES 2–4

Vegetable oil, for frying
1 cup McCormick Golden Dipt Beer Batter for Seafood mix
⅔ cup beer
1½ pounds fish fillets

1. Pour oil into a deep fryer or large heavy skillet, filling no more than ⅓ full. Heat oil to 375°F.

2. In a medium bowl, stir batter mix and beer until smooth.

3. Cut fish into serving-size pieces.

4. Dip fish into batter and shake off any excess.

5. Carefully add the fish a few pieces at a time into the hot oil. Cook 3–5 minutes, turning once to brown evenly. The fish is done when it is golden brown and flakes easily with a fork.

6. Drain the fried fish on paper towels.

Long John Silver's Fish Tacos

Long John Silver's just recently added fish tacos to their menu. You can substitute grilled fish for a light alternative.

INGREDIENTS | SERVES 1

1 soft flour tortilla
1 Long John Silver's Beer-Battered Fish Filet (Chapter 6)
½ cup shredded lettuce
Long John Silver's Baha Sauce (see below), to taste

1. Heat the flour tortilla in the microwave for 30–45 seconds to soften.
2. Place the fish fillet in the center of the tortilla.
3. Add the lettuce and Baja Sauce on top of the fish.
4. Fold like a burrito and serve.

Long John Silver's Baja Sauce

The Baja sauce originated in southern California and inspired the recipe for Long John Silver's fish tacos. Use this sauce liberally on your tacos.

INGREDIENTS | YIELDS 1½ CUPS

½ cup sour cream
½ cup mayonnaise
2 teaspoons taco seasoning
1 small diced jalapeño pepper
¼ cup fresh lime juice
½ cup chopped fresh cilantro

1. Combine all the ingredients into a small bowl with a lid. Mix well.
2. Store in the refrigerator for up to 2 weeks.

McDonald's Fillet of Fish

This recipe tastes better than the original and contains less fat since the fish is baked instead of fried.

INGREDIENTS | SERVES 1

1 Gorton's breaded fish fillet
1 plain hamburger bun
1 tablespoon mayonnaise
1 teaspoon minced onion
1 teaspoon sweet relish
Pinch of salt
1 slice American cheese

1. Cook the fish according to the package instructions. You may bake or fry.
2. Lightly grill the bun.
3. In a small bowl, mix together the mayonnaise, minced onion, relish, and salt to make the tartar sauce.
4. Place the fish on the bottom of the bun.
5. Add the cheese and tartar sauce on top of the fish.

Fillet of Fish

The Fillet of Fish was created by McDonald's in 1963. It is a very easy sandwich to create using frozen fish from Gorton's of Gloucester, which supplied the fish to all the restaurants when the concept was developed.

Mrs. Fields Chocolate Chip Cookies

This popular mall cookie started from scratch in a home kitchen and spread across the nation. You can create it at home with simple ingredients.

INGREDIENTS | YIELDS 30 COOKIES

1 cup softened butter
½ cup granulated sugar
1½ cups firmly packed brown sugar
2 large eggs
2½ teaspoons vanilla
2½ cups all-purpose flour
¾ teaspoon salt
1 teaspoon baking powder
1 teaspoon baking soda
½ (18-ounce) bag semisweet chocolate chips

1. Preheat the oven to 350°F.
2. In a large mixing bowl, cream together the butter, sugars, eggs, and vanilla.
3. In another bowl, mix together the flour, salt, baking powder, and baking soda.
4. Combine the wet and dry ingredients.
5. Stir in chocolate chips.
6. Make golf ball-sized dough portions and place 2" apart on an ungreased cookie sheet.
7. Bake 9–10 minutes, or until edges are light brown.

Mrs. Fields
Mrs. Fields was founded in the late 1970s by a woman named Debbie Fields. She and her husband opened a store in California selling homemade cookies, which grew into over 1,200 franchises throughout the United States.

Sonic Fritos Chili Cheese Wraps

This restaurant copycat recipe provides a crunch in your sandwich. Feel free to add or substitute items in the ingredients to match your tastes.

INGREDIENTS | SERVES 4

1 (19-ounce) can mild chili
3 cups Fritos corn chips
4 flour tortillas
1 cup shredded mild Cheddar cheese
¼ cup diced green onions

1. In a small saucepan, cook the chili on medium-high heat until bubbling. Remove from the stove.

2. Mix the Fritos in with the chili.

3. Place ¼ of the chili mixture down the middle of each tortilla.

4. Sprinkle ¼ cup of cheese on top of the chili. Add the diced onions to taste.

5. Fold into a burrito.

6. Microwave for 15–20 seconds to melt the cheese.

Sonic Hickory Burger

Burgers come in all shapes and sizes. If this is one that you crave and there is no Sonic near you, pull out this recipe and a frying pan.

INGREDIENTS | SERVES 1

¼ pound ground beef
Salt and pepper, to taste
1 tablespoon butter
1 large plain white hamburger bun
1 tablespoon Kraft Hickory Barbecue Sauce
1 tablespoon chopped white onion
⅓ cup chopped lettuce

1. Preheat a skillet to medium heat.

2. Shape the ground beef into a patty. Season with salt and pepper.

3. Melt the butter in the skillet. Lightly brown the bun. Remove and set aside.

4. In the same skillet, grill beef 3–4 minutes per side, until done.

5. Build the burger from the bottom by adding the barbecue sauce, onion, lettuce, burger, and then top bun.

Taco Bell Crispitos

Taco Bell came up with this snack by using what they had on hand, which is mainly lots of tortillas. This recipe is an easy-to-create sweet when you're in a hurry.

INGREDIENTS | YIELDS 20

Vegetable oil for frying
½ cup sugar
⅛ cup cinnamon
5 flour tortillas

1. Preheat oil in a skillet or deep fryer to 350°F.
2, In a small bowl, mix the sugar and cinnamon.
3. Quarter the tortillas with a knife or pizza cutter.
4. Deep fry the triangles in small batches for about 30 seconds on each side, until they turn brown.
5. Place on paper towels to drain.
6. Coat with the sugar and cinnamon mixture.

White Castle Sliders

The mini sandwich trend has surfaced in bars and pubs as well as major restaurant chains across the country. This recipe uses a few short cuts to make a big batch in a hurry.

| INGREDIENTS | YIELDS 24 SLIDER SANDWICHES |

2 pounds ground beef
1 (.75-ounce) package dry onion soup mix
¼ cup Worcestershire sauce
2 (12-ounce/12-count) packages ready-made Kings Hawaiian dinner rolls
Condiments of your choice

1. Preheat oven to 350°F.
2. In a large mixing bowl, combine the ground beef, soup mix, and Worcestershire sauce.
3. Divide the mixture into 2 large rectangular sheet cake pans. Spread the meat out flat with your hands.
4. Bake for 20 minutes. Drain the excess oil.
5. Cut the meat into small squares with a pizza cutter.
6. Slice each dinner roll in half to use as a bun.
7. Add your favorite toppings to each mini burger.

Origins of the Slider

The slider was invented by White Castle, the oldest fast food chain in the country. They coined the phrase "slyder" to describe their little square hamburger patties in 1932. White Castle burgers sold for a nickel a piece in the 1940s and still have a cult-like following to this day.

CHAPTER 7

Steakhouse Favorites

Applebee's Bourbon
Street Steak
112

Applebee's Southwest Steak
113

Houston's Hawaiian
Steak Marinade
114

LongHorn Steakhouse
Steak Marinade
114

Lone Star Steakhouse
Steak Sauce
115

Morton's Garlic Green Beans
115

O'Charley's Black and Blue
Steak Salad
116

Olive Garden Steak Tuscano
117

Outback Steakhouse
Aussie Fries
118

Outback Steakhouse
Sautéed Mushrooms
118

Outback Steakhouse Shrimp on
the Barbie
119

Outback Steakhouse
Steak Seasoning
120

Outback Steakhouse
Sweet Potato
120

Ponderosa Steak Sauce
121

Sizzler Cheese Toast
121

Steak & Ale
Burgundy Mushrooms
122

Texas Roadhouse Honey
Cinnamon Butter
123

Texas Roadhouse Steak Rub
123

Applebee's Bourbon Street Steak

This Cajun-style dish is named after the famous street in the French Quarter in New Orleans.

INGREDIENTS | SERVES 4

½ cup bottled steak sauce
¼ cup bourbon whiskey
1 tablespoon honey
2 teaspoons prepared mustard
4 beef steaks

1. In a zip-top plastic bag, combine the steak sauce, whiskey, honey, and mustard.

2. Add the steaks and refrigerate for 2 hours, or overnight.

3. Preheat the grill to medium-high heat.

4. Grill the steaks for 12–15 minutes, to the desired degree of doneness.

Applebee's Southwest Steak

Applebee's serves the Southwest steak with skin-on garlic mashed potatoes and garlic bread.

INGREDIENTS | SERVES 2

4 shakes blackened-steak seasoning
2 beef steaks
Butter, as needed
1 cup julienne-cut yellow onions
½ cup julienne-cut red peppers
½ cup julienne-cut green peppers
Salt, to taste
Pepper, to taste
Garlic powder, to taste
2 slices Cheddar cheese
2 slices Monterey jack cheese

1. Preheat the grill.
2. Add the steak seasoning to both sides of the steaks.
3. Grill steaks to desired doneness.
4. Melt butter in a skillet over medium heat and sauté the onion and peppers for 2–3 minutes. Season with salt, pepper, and garlic.
5. Reduce the heat and simmer until the steak is cooked.
6. For final minute of steak cooking, top each steak with 1 slice of Cheddar and 1 slice of Monterey jack.
7. Plate the steak with the onions and peppers.

Houston's Hawaiian Steak Marinade

Here's a popular version of Houston's marinade used on their Hawaiian rib eye steaks. It is also good on chicken.

INGREDIENTS | YIELDS 3 CUPS

½ cup apple cider
½ cup pineapple juice
1 cup soy sauce
1 cup brown sugar
1½ teaspoons garlic powder
1½ teaspoons ginger

1. Put all the ingredients in a saucepan.
2. Cook over medium heat for 10–15 minutes, until the sauce thickens.
3. Store the sauce in the refrigerator for up to 2 weeks.

Houston's
Houston's Restaurants serve seafood and traditional American fare. Houston's are casual dining restaurants, with a full bar and a soothing décor of copper and wood. The average dinner is about $20.

LongHorn Steakhouse Steak Marinade

LongHorn Steakhouse restaurant serves beef, ribs, and chops in an inviting western atmosphere. Use this marinade to get a restaurant-quality steak.

INGREDIENTS | YIELDS 2 CUPS

1 cup bourbon
1 cup light teriyaki sauce
1 tablespoon brown sugar
1 tablespoon garlic juice

1. Combine all the ingredients in a small bowl.
2. Stir to mix all the flavors.
3. Brush on steaks while grilling.

LongHorn Steakhouse
LongHorn Steakhouse is a restaurant chain with about 330 restaurants with a western Texas theme. They are best known for serving various kinds of grilled steaks, but they also grill fresh fish and chicken.

Lone Star Steakhouse Steak Sauce

The sauce you use is just as important to a good restaurant steak as the way you cook it.

INGREDIENTS | YIELDS 1 CUP

½ cup butter
2 tablespoons Worcestershire sauce
¾ teaspoon black pepper
2 drops hot pepper sauce
½ cup lemon juice
1 minced small clove garlic
½ teaspoon dry mustard
Salt, to taste

1. Melt butter in a small saucepan over medium heat.
2. Combine the rest of the ingredients in the pan.
3. Cook for 10–15 minutes, until the sauce thickens.

Morton's Garlic Green Beans

This dish is quick, easy, and a great accompaniment to almost any meal.

INGREDIENTS | SERVES 4–6

½ stick unsalted butter
1 chopped shallot
3 cloves minced garlic
1 pound thawed frozen French-cut green beans
Salt, to taste
Freshly ground white pepper, to taste

1. In a large sauté pan over medium heat, melt the butter until bubbling but not browned.
2. Add the shallot and garlic and sauté until softened, about 30 seconds.
3. Add the beans and toss a couple of times.
4. Add the salt and pepper and continue to sauté until all is hot throughout, approximately 2 minutes.

O'Charley's Black and Blue Steak Salad

If you want a hearty and filling entrée salad, O'Charley's makes one of the best using fan-sliced steak and blue cheese.

INGREDIENTS | SERVES 1

1 (6-ounce) sirloin steak
2 tablespoons melted margarine
1–2 tablespoons Cajun seasoning
1¼ cups shredded Parmesan cheese
1¼ cups large croutons
3½ cups chopped romaine lettuce
¼ cup Caesar dressing
3 slices Roma tomato
¼ cup crumbled blue cheese
¼ cup cooked diced bacon

O'Charley's

O'Charley's serves moderately priced menu items such as steak, chicken, pasta, and seafood. The current marketing promotion offers 2 entrées for $15 from a select menu.

1. Preheat the grill.

2. Brush one side of the sirloin with margarine and sprinkle to taste with the Cajun seasoning.

3. Place seasoned-side down on the grill.

4. While first side is cooking, brush second side with margarine and sprinkle with additional seasoning.

5. Cook about 2 minutes; turn and cook 2–3 minutes more, or to desired degree of doneness. Cut the steak into ½" slices.

6. In a large bowl, sprinkle about half the Parmesan and half the croutons over the romaine. Add the dressing and toss well.

7. Place in a chilled pasta bowl or large soup plate and sprinkle with remaining Parmesan cheese.

8. Add the tomato slices and top with sliced steak, blue cheese, bacon, and remaining croutons.

Olive Garden Steak Tuscano

This is a recipe for grilled steak brushed with Italian herbs. Olive Garden serves this dish with Tuscan potatoes.

INGREDIENTS | SERVES 4

4 beef steaks
8 sprigs fresh rosemary
½ cup extra-virgin olive oil
Coarse salt, to taste
Freshly ground pepper, to taste

1. Bring the steaks to room temperature 1 hour before cooking.
2. Preheat the grill.
3. Remove the fresh rosemary from the sprigs, wash, and pat dry.
4. Put it in a pan with the olive oil and heat without letting it boil.
5. Remove the rosemary sauce from the heat and let it infuse for 30 minutes or more.
6. Generously salt and pepper both sides of the steaks.
7. Grill steaks for 10–15 minutes, to the desired degree of doneness, brushing the steaks with the olive oil mixture while grilling.

Outback Steakhouse Aussie Fries

French fries are always offered on the menu at steakhouses and these are loaded with flavor.

INGREDIENTS | SERVES 6

1 pound frozen French fries
1 cup Mexican cheese blend
6 pieces cooked crumbled bacon

1. Preheat deep fryer to 350°F.
2. Preheat oven to 350°F.
3. Fry the French fries in small batches according to the package directions.
4. Drain the fries on paper towels.
5. Place them on a baking sheet and top with the cheese and bacon.
6. Bake for 10 minutes, or until the cheese melts.

Outback Steakhouse Sautéed Mushrooms

Most steakhouses offer toppings for their steaks, and sautéed mushrooms are one of the most popular.

INGREDIENTS | SERVES 4–6

1 (10½-ounce) can beef broth
½ cup diced onion
2 (8-ounce) cans or jars of small whole mushrooms, plus the juice of one
⅓ cup burgundy wine

1. Place the beef broth in a saucepan and simmer the onions for 15 minutes.
2. Add the mushrooms and wine and simmer for another 15 minutes.

Outback Steakhouse Shrimp on the Barbie

This recipe is meant to be served as an appetizer, but you can double it to serve as an entrée.

INGREDIENTS | SERVES 4

Marinade and Shrimp

½ cup melted butter
½ cup olive oil
½ cup mixed minced fresh parsley, thyme, and cilantro
3 tablespoons fresh lemon juice
3 large crushed garlic cloves
1 tablespoon minced shallot
Salt, to taste
Ground black pepper, to taste
1½ pounds unpeeled medium to large shrimp

Dipping Sauce

2 cups mayonnaise
2 cups sour cream
½ cup tomato chili sauce
½ teaspoon cayenne pepper

1. In a large bowl, combine the first 8 ingredients.
2. Mix in the shrimp and marinate in the refrigerator for 5 hours.
3. Combine all the dipping sauce ingredients into a bowl and mix well. Chill until needed.
4. Preheat the grill.
5. Thread the shrimp onto skewers.
6. Grill the shrimp for about 2 minutes per side.

Outback Steakhouse Steak Seasoning

Use this recipe to make mouthwatering steaks just like the ones at Outback.

INGREDIENTS | YIELDS 4 TEASPOONS

2 teaspoons salt
1 teaspoon paprika
½ teaspoon black pepper
¼ teaspoon onion powder
¼ teaspoon garlic powder
¼ teaspoon cayenne pepper
Dash coriander
Dash turmeric

1. Mix all ingredients together in a small bowl.
2. Rub the spices on each side of the steak before grilling.

Outback Steakhouse Sweet Potato

A sweet potato is a delicious alternative to the ordinary spuds served at most steakhouses.

INGREDIENTS | SERVES 1

1 large sweet potato
2 tablespoons shortening
2–3 tablespoons salt
3 tablespoons softened butter
3 tablespoons honey
1 teaspoon cinnamon

1. Preheat the oven to 350°F.
2. Rub the outside of the potato with shortening and sprinkle with salt.
3. Bake the potato for 45–60 minutes, or until soft.
4. Split the potato in half lengthwise.
5. Whip together the butter and honey, and put on each half of the potato.
6. Sprinkle cinnamon on top of the butter and honey.

Ponderosa Steak Sauce

This sweet and tangy sauce is the perfect accompaniment to a well-prepared steak.

INGREDIENTS | YIELDS 1 CUP

⅓ cup Heinz 57 Sauce
⅓ cup Worcestershire Sauce
⅓ cup A-1 Steak Sauce
2 tablespoons light corn syrup

1. Combine all the ingredients into a bottle with tight-fitting cap.
2. Shake well before using.
3. Keep refrigerated. Will keep up to 2 months.

Sizzler Cheese Toast

Texas toast is another popular item on the menu at many steakhouses, and the addition of cheese makes it even better.

INGREDIENTS | SERVES 6–8

1 pound slightly softened butter
1 cup grated Parmesan cheese
Sliced Italian bread

Sizzler

Sizzler is a budget restaurant chain with more than 270 locations throughout the U.S. Their ultimate value meal offers a 6 ounce signature steak and salad bar for around $10. The endless salad bar features hot appetizers and a custom dessert bar.

1. In a small bowl, cream together the butter and cheese with a fork.
2. Preheat a griddle or large frying pan over medium-high heat.
3. Spread the cheese mixture on bread slices about ¼" thick.
4. Place the bread cheese-side down on a griddle.
5. Cook until the cheese has browned.

Steak & Ale Burgundy Mushrooms

Here is another mushroom recipe to use on top of your steaks.

INGREDIENTS | SERVES 6–8

1¼ pounds mushrooms
8 cups water
¼ cup lemon juice
4 tablespoons margarine
¾ cup diced yellow onions
¼ teaspoon garlic powder
⅓ teaspoon ground white pepper
1 tablespoon beef bouillon granules
½ cup burgundy wine

1. Clean and thoroughly dry the mushrooms.

2. Combine the water and lemon juice in a covered saucepan and bring to a boil.

3. In another saucepan, melt the margarine and sauté the onions for 5 minutes.

4. In a bowl, add the spices and bouillon to the wine. Whisk until the bouillon has dissolved. Add the wine mixture to the onions.

5. Simmer over medium heat for about 10 minutes. Remove from heat.

6. Add the mushrooms to the boiling lemon water, then return to a boil.

7. Remove the blanched mushrooms from the heat and thoroughly drain. Add the mushrooms to the wine sauce and stir until blended.

Texas Roadhouse Honey Cinnamon Butter

Dinner rolls go well with steaks, and this flavored butter makes them taste even better.

INGREDIENTS | YIELD 1 CUP

1 cup softened butter
⅓ cup sweetened condensed milk
½ teaspoon corn syrup
1 teaspoon cinnamon, to taste

1. Place all the ingredients in a food processor. Blend until the mixture is smooth.

2. Store the butter in the refrigerator for up to 2 weeks.

Texas Roadhouse Steak Rub

Spice rubs are another way to add flavor to your steaks, and this one has a spicy kick.

INGREDIENTS | SERVES 4

1 tablespoon black pepper
½ tablespoon ancho chile powder
1 tablespoon Worcestershire sauce
½ tablespoon Dijon mustard
½ teaspoon ground cumin
½ teaspoon ground cayenne pepper
½ tablespoon minced garlic
½ teaspoon salt

1. Mix all the ingredients in a bowl. It should be the consistency of a thick paste.

2. Baste the tops and sides of the steaks on both sides as you grill.

Marinades and Rubs

Too many cooks overlook marinades and rubs. To highlight the flavor of your steaks and create a restaurant-quality meal, you should consider one or the other. Marinades contain acidic ingredients in liquid form, which can tenderize the beef, and rubs are made with spices and meant to be rubbed into the meat before cooking.

CHAPTER 8

Bar Food

Applebee's Baby Back Ribs
126

Applebee's Garlic and Peppercorn Fried Shrimp
127

Applebee's Garlic Mashed Potatoes
128

Applebee's Tequila Lime Chicken
129

Applebee's Veggie Patch Pizza
130

Bahama Breeze Calypso Shrimp Pasta
131

Bahama Breeze Jamaican Marinade
132

Bahama Breeze Vegetable Sauté
133

Chili's Cajun Chicken Pasta
134

Chili's Margarita Grilled Chicken
134

Chili's Monterey Chicken
135

Hooters Hot Wings
136

Hooters Hot Wing Sauce
137

Ruby Tuesday Chicken Quesadillas
138

Ruby Tuesday Sonora Chicken Pasta
139

T.G.I. Friday's Dragonfire Chicken
140

T.G.I. Friday's Jack Daniels Grilling Sauce
141

T.G.I. Friday's Sizzling Chicken and Cheese
142

T.G.I. Friday's Spicy Cajun Chicken Pasta
143

Tommy Bahama Crab Cakes
144

Applebee's Baby Back Ribs

Now you can enjoy those spicy, sweet, delicious Applebee's Baby Back Ribs any time you like at home with this simple recipe.

INGREDIENTS | SERVES 6

3 racks pork baby back ribs
1 cup ketchup
¼ cup apple cider vinegar
3 tablespoons dark brown sugar
3 tablespoons Worcestershire sauce
1 teaspoon liquid smoke
½ teaspoon salt

1. Put the ribs in a large pot with enough water to cover them. Bring the water to a boil, reduce heat, and cover. Simmer for 1 hour, or until ribs are fork tender.

2. Mix all the remaining ingredients together in a medium pan. Bring to a boil, reduce heat, and simmer uncovered. Cook for 30 minutes, stirring often, or until the sauce is slightly thickened.

3. Heat the broiler. Place the ribs meat-side down on the broiler pan, Brush the ribs with half the sauce.

4. Broil 4"–5" from heat source for 6–7 minutes. Turn the ribs over and brush with remaining sauce.

5. Broil 6–7 minutes longer, or until the edges are slightly charred.

Applebee's Garlic and Peppercorn Fried Shrimp

Make the best garlic pepper shrimp with this easy recipe.

INGREDIENTS | SERVES 4

1 pound (61–90) thawed shrimp
Vegetable oil, as needed
½ cup flour
¼ teaspoon salt
2 teaspoons divided fresh cracked black pepper
1 teaspoon garlic powder
½ teaspoon paprika
1 teaspoon sugar
2 eggs
1 cup bread crumbs

Applebee's

Applebee's Neighborhood Grill & Bar serves mainstream American dishes such as salads, shrimp, chicken, and pasta. There is also a section of choices under 550 calories.

1. Clean and peel the shrimp. Leave the tails on.
2. Fill a fryer 2"–3" deep with oil and heat to 350°F.
3. In a bowl, combine the flour, salt, 1 teaspoon pepper, garlic powder, paprika, and sugar.
4. In another bowl, beat eggs slightly.
5. In a third bowl, mix the bread crumbs and 1 teaspoon pepper.
6. Coat the shrimp with flour mixture, then eggs, then bread crumb mixture, being careful to shake off excess between steps and not overcoat.
7. Fry for 2–3 minutes, or until golden brown.

Applebee's Garlic Mashed Potatoes

Roasted garlic mashed potatoes is an extremely popular dish, both at home and in restaurants.

INGREDIENTS | SERVES 8

4 whole cloves of garlic
2 pounds red potatoes
½ cup milk
¼ cup heavy cream
3 tablespoons butter
Salt and black pepper, to taste

1. Preheat the oven to 400°F.

2. Place garlic cloves on a sheet of heavy-duty aluminum foil. Wrap the garlic tightly and roast for approximately 45 minutes, or until soft. Unwrap the garlic and let it cool until touchable.

3. Wash and rinse the potatoes. It is not necessary to peel the potatoes, unless you desire.

4. Place the potatoes in a large pot and boil for 20 minutes. Remove them from the heat and drain them in a colander.

5. Peel the garlic cloves. Combine them with the potatoes and all other ingredients and mash with a potato masher.

Applebee's Tequila Lime Chicken

Many restaurants are using alcohol to flavor their dishes, including this recipe, which you're sure to enjoy.

INGREDIENTS | SERVES 1

½ cup lime juice
¼ cup tequila
1 boneless skinless chicken breast
1 tablespoon salsa
3 tablespoons ranch dressing
½ cup tortilla chips
¼ cup shredded Cheddar jack cheese

1. Pour the lime juice and tequila into a sealable plastic bag. Add the chicken and allow it to marinate for 2–3 hours.
2. Preheat the grill to medium-high heat and also preheat the broiler.
3. Remove the chicken from the marinade. Grill it for 10 minutes, or until thoroughly cooked.
4. Combine salsa and ranch dressing in a small bowl.
5. Scatter the tortilla chips on an oven-safe plate.
6. Place the chicken on top of the tortilla chips.
7. Pour the dressing mixture over the chicken.
8. Cover the chicken with the cheese.
9. Place the chicken under the broiler until cheese is melted.

Applebee's Veggie Patch Pizza

Use the Applebee's Spinach and Artichoke Dip to make this pizza. Serve as a meal with a salad for a meatless dinner.

INGREDIENTS | SERVES 1

1 (10") flour tortilla
½ cup Applebee's Spinach and Artichoke Dip (Chapter 3)
½ teaspoon Italian seasoning
Black pepper, to taste
Garlic powder, to taste
Salt, to taste
½ cup sliced mushrooms
¼ cup diced tomatoes
½ cup shredded mozzarella cheese
1 tablespoon shredded Parmesan/Romano cheese

1. Preheat oven to 350°F.
2. Spray a pizza pan with cooking spray. Place tortilla on pan.
3. In a small bowl, mix the dip and spices together.
4. Spread the mixture evenly over the tortilla.
5. Top the pizza with tomatoes, mushrooms, and cheeses.
6. Bake for 10 minutes, until the cheese melts.

Bahama Breeze Calypso Shrimp Pasta

Cook up a bit of the islands at home with this Caribbean-inspired dish.

INGREDIENTS | SERVES 4

½ cup chicken broth
½ cup clam juice
1 clove chopped garlic
2 tablespoons blackening seasoning
Cayenne pepper, to taste
1 teaspoon dried thyme
1 pound of medium-size peeled shrimp
½ teaspoon each salt and pepper
8 tablespoons butter
½ cup thin-sliced green onion
½ cup heavy cream
3 cups cooked linguine or spaghetti
4 tablespoons diced tomatoes

1. Place broth, clam juice, garlic, blackening seasoning, cayenne, and thyme in a bowl and mix well.

2. Cover the bowl with a lid and refrigerate until needed.

3. Season the shrimp with salt and pepper.

4. In a skillet over medium heat, melt the butter. Add the shrimp and onions and cook for 2–3 minutes until they begin to turn opaque.

5. Add the broth mixture and cream to the skillet. Bring the sauce to a boil and reduce heat.

6. Add the pasta to the sauce. Cook for an additional 2 minutes to heat the pasta.

7. Garnish with diced tomatoes.

Bahama Breeze Jamaican Marinade

Try this recipe on chicken or steak for a taste of the Caribbean island flavors, just like the dishes served at Bahama Breeze restaurant.

INGREDIENTS | YIELDS 1½ CUPS

¼ cup olive oil
2 tablespoons Jamaican Jerk seasoning
¼ cup orange juice
2 tablespoons soy sauce
¼ cup rice wine vinegar
1 tablespoon dark Jamaican rum
Juice of 1 lime
1 seeded and minced habanero pepper
2 cloves minced garlic
½ cup chopped red onion
2 chopped green onions
½ teaspoon Creole seasoning

1. Combine all the ingredients in a small bowl with a lid. Stir with a whisk.
2. Cover and refrigerate. Can be stored for up to 2 weeks.

Bahama Breeze

Bahama Breeze is a restaurant chain specializing in Caribbean-flavored fresh seafood, chicken, and steaks. The menu features such dishes as Jerk chicken pasta, seafood, paella, tropical entrée salads, and cocktails.

Bahama Breeze Vegetable Sauté

This restaurant sauté recipe will have your family and friends wanting more vegetables.

INGREDIENTS | SERVES 4

2 teaspoons extra-virgin olive oil
½ red bell pepper julienned
½ yellow bell pepper julienned
½ green bell pepper julienned
½ seeded and sliced chayote squash
1 stick sliced celery
1 large clove garlic minced
¼ cup chicken broth
8 sliced mushrooms
1 teaspoon chopped fresh thyme
¼ teaspoon white pepper
2 tablespoons dry white wine
½ teaspoon salt

1. Heat olive oil over high heat and sauté the vegetables for 3–4 minutes, stirring often.

2. Reduce heat to low and add the remaining ingredients.

3. Cook the vegetables, stirring often, for 2 more minutes.

Chili's Cajun Chicken Pasta

Serve up a spicy dinner with this hot and creamy linguini tossed with chicken strips sautéed with Cajun seasoning.

INGREDIENTS | SERVES 2

2 boneless skinless chicken breast halves, cut into strips
2 teaspoons Cajun seasoning
2 tablespoons butter or margarine
1–2 cups heavy cream
¼ teaspoon dried basil
¼ teaspoon lemon pepper seasoning
¼ teaspoon salt
⅛ teaspoon pepper
⅛ teaspoon garlic powder
4 ounces cooked linguine or fettuccine
Grated Parmesan cheese, to taste

1. Place chicken and Cajun seasoning in a resealable plastic bag. Rub and shake to coat the chicken well.

2. In a large skillet over medium heat, melt the butter and sauté the chicken. Cook about 5–7 minutes, then reduce the heat.

3. Add the cream and seasonings. Stir for 5 minutes, until the sauce thickens.

4. Add the pasta and toss. Heat for another 5 minutes. Garnish with Parmesan cheese.

Chili's Margarita Grilled Chicken

The popular and unique Margarita Grilled Chicken on the menu at Chili's Bar and Grill is quite easy to make at home.

INGREDIENTS | SERVES 4

1 cup liquid margarita mix
4 boneless, skinless chicken breasts
Fresh ground black pepper, to taste

Chili's

Chili's Bar and Grill is a large casual dining chain with more than 1,400 restaurants. They serve American food with a Tex-Mex influence. The menu offers tacos, fajitas, and quesadillas as well as traditional American steaks, ribs, and hamburgers.

1. Pour the margarita mix into a zip-top bag.

2. Add the chicken breasts and marinate for 2 hours in the refrigerator.

3. Drain, and dust chicken with black pepper.

4. Heat a skillet to medium-high heat. Spray the skillet with nonstick cooking oil.

5. Cook the chicken for 3–4 minutes per side, or until done.

Chili's Monterey Chicken

If your family likes barbecue chicken, then this is a recipe that they will enjoy.

INGREDIENTS | SERVES 1

1 boneless, skinless chicken breast
Salt and pepper, to taste
2 teaspoons barbecue sauce
2 slices of well cooked bacon
¼ cup mixture Monterey jack and sharp Cheddar cheeses
2 slices diced tomatoes
1 teaspoon chopped chives

1. Pound the chicken breast until it is flattened. Season with salt and pepper.

2. Heat a skillet to medium-high heat and spray with nonstick cooking oil.

3. Cook the chicken for 4–5 minutes per side, or until done. Transfer the chicken to a microwave-safe serving plate.

4. Top the chicken breast with barbecue sauce, bacon, and cheeses.

5. Microwave for 1–2 minutes, until the cheese melts.

6. Sprinkle with tomatoes and chives.

Hooters Hot Wings

Buffalo chicken wings are a staple on most restaurant menus. This recipe makes a big batch for a crowd, which would be a great addition to any party.

INGREDIENTS | SERVES 12

3 cups flour
2½ teaspoons salt
1 teaspoon paprika
¼ teaspoon cayenne pepper
5 pound bag of chicken wings
Hooter's Hot Wing Sauce (Chapter 8)

History of Hot Wings
The first spicy chicken wings were served at the Anchor Bar Restaurant in Buffalo, New York, in 1964. It is probably one of the most duplicated restaurant recipes in the world.

1. In a large mixing bowl, combine flour and spices.
2. Cut chicken into wings and drumettes. Wash and allow to drain.
3. Coat the wings with flour mixture and refrigerate for 90 minutes.
4. Preheat a deep fryer to 350°F.
5. Fry wings in hot oil for 8–10 minutes until golden brown. Do not crowd the wings, and fry in batches.
6. Place the wings on paper towels to remove excess oil.
7. When all the wings are fried, place in a large bowl.
8. Add the hot wing sauce and mix completely.

Hooters Hot Wing Sauce

The must-have recipe for your wings.

INGREDIENTS | YIELDS 2 CUPS

3 sticks of softened butter
½ cup Tabasco sauce
3 tablespoons brown sugar
2 tablespoons chili sauce
1 tablespoon balsamic vinegar
¾ teaspoon salt
¾ teaspoon paprika
⅜ teaspoon cayenne pepper

1. Mix all the ingredients together.
2. Store in the refrigerator for up to 2 weeks.

Hooters in the Supermarket

If you are pressed for time, just pick up a bottle or two of the hot wing sauce, which is available at your local grocery store nationwide.

Ruby Tuesday Chicken Quesadillas

This is a great recipe for a party appetizer, but can be a meal when combined with rice and a salad, as well.

INGREDIENTS | SERVES 1

1 (5-ounce) chicken breast half, boned and skinned
¼ cup Italian salad dressing
1 (12") flour tortilla
2 tablespoons margarine
1 cup shredded Cheddar or Monterey jack cheese
1 tablespoon plus ¼ cup diced tomato
1 tablespoon diced jalapeño pepper
Cajun seasoning, to taste
½ cup shredded lettuce
¼ cup sour cream
¼ cup salsa, for dipping

Ruby Tuesday

The Ruby Tuesday franchise has over 680 restaurants. The menu features premium seafood, handcrafted hamburgers, steaks, ribs, chicken, and combo platters. The fit and trim menu offers dishes under 700 calories.

1. Place the chicken breast in a bowl with the Italian dressing. Allow to marinate for 30 minutes in the refrigerator.

2. Grill chicken for 5 minutes, until done, and cut into ¼" pieces. Set aside.

3. Brush one side of the tortilla with margarine and place in frying pan over medium heat.

4. On one half of tortilla, add the cheese, 1 tablespoon tomatoes, peppers, and Cajun seasoning. Make sure to spread to the edge of the half and top with diced chicken.

5. Fold the empty tortilla side on top, and flip over in the pan so that cheese is on top of chicken.

6. Cook for 1–2 minutes per side, until very warm throughout. Remove the quesadilla from the pan to a serving plate and cut into wedges on one side of plate.

7. On the other side of the plate, put the lettuce, topped with ¼ cup tomatoes then sour cream. Serve your favorite salsa in a small bowl on the side.

Ruby Tuesday Sonora Chicken Pasta

This is a great recipe with a Mexican flavor that makes a spicy and festive meal.

INGREDIENTS | SERVES 2

6 tablespoons butter or margarine
½ cup finely chopped onion
1 small minced clove garlic
⅓ cup all-purpose flour
1 cup hot water
1 tablespoon chicken stock
1 cup half-and-half
Pinch of salt
½ teaspoon sugar
¼ teaspoon hot sauce
1 teaspoon lemon juice
¼ teaspoon cayenne pepper
¾ cup shredded Parmesan cheese
¾ cup cubed Velveeta cheese
¾ cup prepared salsa
½ cup sour cream
10 ounces cooked penne pasta
1 (6-ounce) boneless, skinless chicken breast
⅓ cup spicy black beans
¼ cup diced tomatoes, for garnish
1 teaspoon sliced green onion, for garnish

1. Preheat the grill.
2. Melt butter in a saucepan and add the onion and garlic. Sauté for 2–3 minutes until the onions are transparent.
3. Stir in the flour to make a roux and cook for 5 minutes, stirring often.
4. Mix the hot water, chicken stock, and half-and-half. Add the mixture slowly to roux, stirring constantly. Allow to cook for 5 minutes. The sauce should have the consistency of honey.
5. Add the salt, sugar, hot sauce, lemon juice, cayenne, and Parmesan to the sauce and stir to blend. Do not allow to boil.
6. Add the Velveeta and stir until melted. Add the salsa and sour cream and blend.
7. Place the pasta into a mixing bowl. Add the cheese sauce and toss to coat evenly.
8. Grill the chicken for 5 minutes per side until done. Slice into ¼" thick strips.
9. Place the chicken on top of pasta and ladle black beans on top. Sprinkle with tomatoes and green onions.

T.G.I. Friday's Dragonfire Chicken

The restaurant uses a hot and spicy Chinese kung pao sauce to give this dish its flavor.

INGREDIENTS | SERVES 4

4 boneless, skinless chicken breasts

Marinade
½ cup olive oil
½ cup honey
3 tablespoons rice vinegar
2 tablespoons lime juice
1 finely chopped jalapeño
2 teaspoons minced garlic
1 tablespoon diced onion
¾ tablespoon salt

Kung Pao Sauce
¼ cup water
2 tablespoons rice vinegar
½ cup dark brown sugar
4 tablespoons soy sauce
1 tablespoon Asian-style chili sauce
1 tablespoon finely minced garlic
1 tablespoon finely minced ginger

1. In a blender on high speed, combine the marinade ingredients for 1 minute.

2. In a small bowl, combine all ingredients for Kung Pao sauce and whisk together.

3. Pound the chicken breasts flat. Marinate in zip-top bag for 2–3 hours.

4. Grill chicken breasts about 5 minutes per side until done.

5. Drizzle the chicken with Kung Pao Sauce before serving.

T.G.I. Friday's Jack Daniels Grilling Sauce

Whiskey gives this sauce a restaurant-quality taste and is good on any type of meat you would like to grill.

INGREDIENTS | YIELDS 3 CUPS

1 tablespoon onion powder
1 tablespoon garlic powder
1 tablespoon Tabasco sauce
1 cup pineapple juice
½ cup whiskey
2 cups brown sugar
2 beef bouillon cubes
4 tablespoons Worcestershire sauce

1. Combine all ingredients in a small saucepan over high heat.
2. Bring the sauce to a boil.
3. Reduce heat and simmer for 15 minutes.
4. Allow the sauce to cool, and use as a sauce on a grilled meat.

T.G.I. Friday's Sizzling Chicken and Cheese

This dish is a modified Mexican dish served in a hot pan, fajita style.

INGREDIENTS | SERVES 2

2 (4-ounce) chicken breasts
2 tablespoons chopped garlic
2 tablespoons chopped parsley
1 teaspoon crushed red chilies
¼ teaspoon black pepper
¼ teaspoon salt
4 divided tablespoons olive oil
1 julienned green pepper
1 julienned red pepper
1 julienned yellow onion
4 cups cooked mashed potatoes
½ cup shredded Chihuahua white cheese
2 slices American cheese

1. Pound the chicken breasts to an even thickness.
2. In a zip-top bag, combine garlic, parsley, chilies, pepper, salt, and 2 tablespoons olive oil.
3. Place the chicken breasts in the marinade and refrigerate for 2–4 hours.
4. In a cast iron skillet over medium heat, heat remaining olive oil and sauté the chicken breasts for 5 minutes per side until they reach a golden brown color. Remove from the pan.
5. Sauté the peppers and onion for 2–3 minutes, until al dente. Remove from the skillet.
6. Heat a cast iron skillet on the burner until very hot. Place the mashed potatoes in the skillet, then add the cheeses, peppers, and onions.
7. Put the chicken on top of the potatoes. Cook until heated through. Serve from the hot skillet.

T.G.I. Friday's Spicy Cajun Chicken Pasta

The flavors of New Orleans and Italy come together in this spicy Alfredo pasta recipe.

INGREDIENTS | SERVES 2

½ divided stick butter
1 chopped green bell pepper
1 chopped red bell pepper
½ sliced and quartered white onion
1 clove pressed garlic
2 boneless, skinless chicken breast halves
2 teaspoons olive oil
1 medium chopped tomato
4–6 sliced mushrooms
1 cup chicken stock
¼ teaspoon salt
¼ teaspoon cayenne pepper
¼ teaspoon paprika
¼ teaspoon white pepper
¼ teaspoon dried thyme
12 ounces hot, cooked fettuccine
2 teaspoons chopped fresh parsley

1. In a large skillet over medium-high heat, melt 2 tablespoons butter and sauté the bell peppers, onion, and garlic for 8–10 minutes.

2. Cut the chicken breasts into bite-size pieces.

3. In a medium-size pan heat olive oil over high heat and cook the chicken, stirring, for 5–7 minutes, or until the chicken shows no pink.

4. Add the chicken to the pan with the vegetables, along with the tomatoes, mushrooms, chicken stock, cayenne, paprika, salt, pepper, and thyme. Continue to simmer for 10–12 minutes, until it thickens.

5. Toss the fettuccine with the remaining 2 tablespoons of butter.

6. Serve the dish by dividing the noodles onto 2 plates. Divide the chicken and vegetable sauce evenly and spread it over the top of the noodles. Divide the parsley and sprinkle it over the top.

Tommy Bahama Crab Cakes

These delicious crab cakes are easy to prepare and will be a hit with family and guests.

INGREDIENTS | SERVES 6–8

1¾ pounds lump crabmeat
1½ tablespoons finely chopped green onion
4 tablespoons minced red onion
3 tablespoons minced yellow onion
1 egg
½ tablespoon Old Bay Seasoning
1 tablespoon salt
2 tablespoons Panko bread crumbs
3 tablespoons flour
1 teaspoon black pepper
1 teaspoon celery salt
3 tablespoons butter

1. Mix all the ingredients in a medium bowl. Be careful not to break up the crabmeat.

2. Portion the crab cakes into 6 large or 8 small patties.

3. Place a nonstick sauté pan on medium heat and melt the butter.

4. Brown crab cakes on both sides.

CHAPTER 9

Mexican

Chevys Fresh Mex Fuego Spice Mix
146

Chevys Fresh Mex San Antonio Veggies
146

Chevys Fresh Mex Habanero Steak Fajitas
147

Chi-Chi's Baked Chicken Chimichangas
148

Chi-Chi's Margarita Marinade
149

Chi-Chi's Seafood Enchiladas
150

Chipotle Cilantro Lime Rice
151

Chipotle Marinated Chicken
152

Chipotle Pork Carnitas
153

Chipotle Steak Barbacoa
154

El Pollo Loco Chicken
155

El Torito Guacamole
156

El Torito Veggie Mix
156

Qdoba Mango Salsa
157

Taco Bell Enchiritos
158

Taco Bell Fiesta Bowls
159

Taco Bell Fire Border Sauce
159

Taco Bell Mexican Pizza
160

Taco Bell Santa Fe Gorditas
161

Chevys Fresh Mex Fuego Spice Mix

Use this seasoning mix on tortilla chips, vegetables, popcorn, and as a rub for steaks, chops, chicken, or fish.

INGREDIENTS | YIELDS 1 CUP

¼ cup paprika
2 teaspoons cayenne
2 tablespoons salt
2 teaspoons ground white pepper
2 tablespoons black pepper
2 tablespoons garlic powder
2 tablespoons chili powder
2 tablespoons oregano

1. Combine all ingredients. Mix well.
2. Store the mixture in an airtight container out of direct sunlight. It will keep for up to 6 months.

Chevys Fresh Mex San Antonio Veggies

These fajita vegetables can be served with almost any Mexican dish.

INGREDIENTS | YIELDS 4 CUPS

2 tablespoons olive oil
2 cups thinly sliced yellow onions
1 tablespoon Chevys Fresh Mex Fuego Spice Mix (see above)
1 cup thinly sliced red bell peppers
1 cup thinly sliced green bell peppers

1. In a sauté pan over high heat, heat olive oil until it smokes.
2. Add the onions and spice mix and sauté 4 minutes.
3. Add the peppers and sauté 2 more minutes.

Chevys Fresh Mex

Chevys Fresh Mex is a chain of Mexican restaurants that started in California. They now have about 100 locations in the U.S. Chevys promises that everything on the menu is made daily.

Chevys Fresh Mex Habanero Steak Fajitas

Serve San Antonio Veggies, flour tortillas, shredded cheese, sour cream, guacamole, and homemade salsa with these smoking-hot steak fajitas.

INGREDIENTS | SERVES 4

2 ounces achiote paste
½ cup red wine vinegar
¼ cup olive oil
¾ cup pineapple juice
½ cup chopped yellow onion
3 cloves peeled garlic
2 tablespoons salt
½ teaspoon white pepper
3 stemmed jalapeños
½ cup stemmed habanera peppers
2 pounds skirt steak

1. In a blender, combine all the ingredients except the skirt steak to form a marinade.

2. Pour marinade into a zip-top bag. Add the meat to the marinade and refrigerate 24 hours.

3. Grill meat on a charcoal or gas grill, turning every 2–3 minutes, until meat reaches desired doneness.

4. Slice steak across the grain at an angle to create wide, thin strips for serving.

Chi-Chi's Baked Chicken Chimichangas

Chi-Chi's restaurants were known for their fun atmosphere and great Mexican food. This recipe is easy to make using leftover chicken.

INGREDIENTS | SERVES 6

½ cup chopped onion
2 minced garlic cloves
2 tablespoons olive oil
½ tablespoon chili powder
1 (16-ounce) jar salsa
½ teaspoon cumin
½ teaspoon cinnamon
Pinch of salt
2½ cups cooked and shredded chicken
6 (10") flour tortillas
1 cup refried beans
Olive oil, for basting
Sour cream
Guacamole

Chi-Chi's

All the Chi-Chi's restaurants in the United States have closed. They still have a line of grocery products in supermarkets inspired by the restaurant that features salsas and tortillas in various varieties and flavors.

1. Preheat the oven to 450°F.
2. In a large saucepan, sauté onion and garlic in oil for 2–3 minutes until tender.
3. Stir in the chili powder, salsa, cumin, cinnamon, and salt.
4. Add the chicken and cook for 5 minutes to incorporate flavors. Remove pan from heat. Allow to cool.
5. Grease a large baking dish.
6. Working with 1 tortilla at a time, spoon a heaping tablespoon of beans down the center of each tortilla.
7. Top with ½ cup of the chicken mixture.
8. Fold up the bottom, top, and sides of tortilla and secure with wooden toothpicks, if necessary.
9. Place in the baking pan, seam-side down. Brush all sides with the oil.
10. Bake 20–25 minutes, or until golden brown and crisp, turning every 5 minutes.
11. Serve with sour cream and guacamole on the side.

Chi-Chi's Margarita Marinade

Who knew that classic drinks like mojitos and margaritas could make such great flavorings for meat and seafood?

INGREDIENTS | YIELDS 1 CUP

1 (10-ounce) can drained diced tomatoes and green chilies
¼ cup orange juice
¼ cup tequila
¼ cup vegetable oil
2 tablespoons fresh lime juice
1 tablespoon honey
1 teaspoon minced garlic
1 teaspoon grated lime peel
2 pounds boneless steak, chicken, or pork

1. In a large zip-top plastic food bag, combine all the ingredients except the meat. Mix well.
2. Add meat, seal the bag, and turn over several times to coat thoroughly.
3. Place bag in refrigerator, turning bag occasionally, 8 hours, or overnight.
4. Heat the broiler. Remove meat from marinade, reserving marinade. Place meat on the broiler pan.
5. Broil 7"–8" from heat source until desired doneness.
6. In a small saucepan, bring marinade to a boil and boil for 1 minute.
7. Serve the marinade on top of the meat.

Chi-Chi's Seafood Enchiladas

Crab- or shrimp-stuffed enchiladas are a popular item on the menu at many Mexican restaurants.

INGREDIENTS | YIELDS 8

1 (10-ounce) can cream of chicken soup
½ cup chopped onions
Dash nutmeg
Dash ground black pepper
8 ounces real or imitation chopped crab
1¾ divided cups shredded Monterey jack cheese
8 (6") flour tortillas
1 cup milk

1. In a mixing bowl, stir together soup, onion, nutmeg, and pepper.

2. In another bowl, combine half of the soup mixture, crab, and 1 cup of the Monterey jack. Set aside.

3. Wrap the tortillas in a paper towel. Microwave on high for 30–60 seconds.

4. Place ⅓ cup of the crab mixture on each tortilla.

5. Roll up and place seam-side down in a greased 12" × 7½" dish.

6. Stir milk into the reserved soup mixture, and pour over enchiladas. Microwave the dish, covered, on high for 12–14 minutes.

7. Sprinkle with the remaining cheese. Let stand for 10 minutes.

8. Add a dash of hot pepper sauce, if desired.

Chipotle Cilantro Lime Rice

Cilantro is a key herb in Mexican cooking, and this rice dish is great as a side dish or inside a burrito.

INGREDIENTS | SERVES 2–4
1 teaspoon olive oil
⅔ cup white rice
1 lime
1 cup water
½ teaspoon salt
2 teaspoons fresh cilantro

1. In a 2-quart heavy saucepan, heat oil over low heat.
2. Add rice and the juice from half of lime. Stir for 1 minute.
3. Add water and salt. Bring to a full boil.
4. Cover and turn down to a simmer over low heat.
5. Cook until the rice is tender and the water is absorbed, about 25 minutes.
6. Add the cilantro and the juice from the other half of the lime.
7. Fluff rice with a fork.

Chipotle Marinated Chicken

Here is the recipe straight from Chipotle for their marinade. It is also good to use with steak.

INGREDIENTS | SERVES 4

1 (2-ounce) package dried ancho chilies
6 cloves of garlic
½ quartered red onion
¼ cup vegetable oil
2 tablespoons chopped fresh oregano
2 teaspoons cumin powder
1 teaspoon black pepper
4 (6-ounce) chicken breasts

1. Soak dry chilies overnight in water, until soft. Remove seeds.

2. Place chilies, garlic, onion, oil, oregano, cumin, and pepper in a food processor and purée until smooth.

3. In a medium baking dish, spread the mixture over the chicken.

4. Refrigerate at least 1 hour, or up to 24 hours.

5. Remove the chicken from the marinade and grill for 5 minutes per side until done.

Chipotle

Chipotle Mexican Grill currently has over 1,000 locations, and has been a leader in promoting organic ingredients. The restaurants have served more naturally raised meat than any other chain in the United States.

Chipotle Pork Carnitas

Mexican pork carnitas are slow-cooked, spicy, shredded pork shoulder served with tortillas and salsa.

INGREDIENTS | SERVES 10–12

Salt and pepper, to taste
1 (3-pound) pork shoulder roast
2–3 tablespoons olive oil
1 thinly sliced onion
4 medium tomatoes
½ teaspoon dried oregano
1 teaspoon cumin powder
2 bay leaves
2 whole cloves
2 dried chipotle chilies
¾ cup water or meat stock

1. Preheat the oven to 325°F.
2. Salt and pepper the pork and allow the meat to come to room temperature.
3. Add olive oil to a large oven-proof pan.
4. Sear the pork in the pan over medium-high heat for 5 minutes per side.
5. Remove the pork from the pan and let it rest for 10–15 minutes.
6. Add onions and cook over low heat for 2–3 minutes until translucent.
7. Return the pork to the pan and add the remaining ingredients.
8. Cover and place in the oven. Cook for 2–3 hours, until the internal temperature reaches 140°F–150°F.
9. Let the roast rest for 10–15 minutes before slicing.

Chipotle Steak Barbacoa

Chipotle is known for its large burritos using all-natural ingredients with the choice of chicken, pork carnitas, or barbacoa steak.

INGREDIENTS | SERVES 12

2 diced onions
3 tablespoons olive oil
8 minced garlic cloves
1 tablespoon taco seasoning
1½ tablespoons oregano
1 (.36-ounce) can of chipotle in adobo sauce
1 cup chicken broth
1 cup water
1 bay leaf
2 tablespoons white vinegar
3 pounds beef roast

1. Take everything but the roast and put it in a blender. Blend for 1–2 minutes until it is all ground up.
2. Add some of the sauce to the bottom of a slow cooker.
3. Place roast in the slow cooker pot and pour the rest of the sauce over the meat.
4. Slow cook for 8–10 hours.

El Pollo Loco Chicken

Try this El Pollo Loco marinade recipe for chicken that tastes like it came from the restaurant.

INGREDIENTS | SERVES 4

¾ cup Heinz Chili Sauce
Juice of 1 lemon
Juice of 1 large orange
2 tablespoons vegetable oil
2 tablespoons vinegar
2 teaspoons sugar
2 teaspoons garlic powder
1 teaspoon Worcestershire sauce
Tabasco sauce, to taste
4 boneless chicken breasts

1. For the marinade, mix all ingredients in a baking dish.
2. Add chicken and marinate for at least 4 hours, or up to 24 hours.
3. Remove the chicken from the marinade and discard marinade.
4. Cook chicken on a hot grill for about 10 minutes on each side.

El Pollo Loco

El Pollo Loco means "the crazy chicken" in Spanish. The chain specializes in marinated grilled chicken that is flame broiled over an open grill right before your eyes. The restaurants are mostly in the southwest and California. The menu offers healthy options with steamed fresh vegetables and salads in addition to the chicken.

El Torito Guacamole

Guacamole is an avocado dip and side dish that has become very popular throughout the restaurant world. Serve it in salads, burritos, and on burgers.

INGREDIENTS | SERVES 2–4

2 halved avocados
1 small crushed diced chili pepper
Juice of ½ lime
½ cup pico de gallo
1 tablespoon garlic powder

1. Cut open the avocado, remove the pit, and scoop the avocado flesh into a mixing bowl.
2. Add the chili peppers to the avocado, along with the lime juice, and mash with a fork.
3. Add the remaining ingredients and mix well.

El Torito

El Torito means "the little bull" in Spanish. The chain specializes in authentic Mexican dishes, and they prepare fresh guacamole tableside.

El Torito Veggie Mix

Mexican home cooking features more fruit and vegetables than you might imagine. Give this recipe a try for something different on the menu at home.

INGREDIENTS | YIELDS 3½ CUPS

1 cup corn kernels
1 cup diced zucchini
½ cup diced yellow onions
½ cup diced tomatoes
½ cup diced roasted Anaheim chiles
2 teaspoons salt
½ teaspoon black pepper
2 cloves finely chopped fresh garlic
½ teaspoon fresh chopped oregano

1. Place all ingredients in a mixing bowl and mix well.
2. Saute in a skillet for 6–8 minutes until all the vegetables are cooked.

Qdoba Mango Salsa

This spicy, fruity blend of fresh ingredients will turn any dish into an exciting new favorite.

INGREDIENTS | YIELDS 4½ CUPS

2 cups diced mangoes
1 medium peeled, seeded, and diced cucumber
1 finely minced jalapeño
1 diced medium red pepper
¼ diced red onion
¼ cup fresh chopped cilantro
Juice of 1 lime
1 tablespoon sugar
1 pinch salt

Place all ingredients in a medium bowl and mix well.

Qdoba

Qudoba Mexican Grill is a fast casual Mexican chain with over 450 restaurants throughout the United States. Customers order a handcrafted meal right in front of them using fresh ingredients and innovative flavors.

Taco Bell Enchiritos

This burrito enchilada hybrid vanished from the menu at Taco Bell, so the only way you can enjoy this dish is to make it at home.

INGREDIENTS | SERVES 10

1 pound ground beef
¼ cup flour
1 tablespoon chili powder
1 teaspoon salt
½ teaspoon dried minced onion
½ teaspoon paprika
¼ teaspoon onion powder
Dash garlic powder
½ cup water
1 (16-ounce) can refried beans
10 large flour tortillas
½ cup diced onion
1 (10-ounce) can red chili sauce
2 cups shredded Cheddar cheese

1. In a medium bowl, combine the ground beef with the flour, chili powder, salt, minced onion, paprika, onion powder, and garlic powder.
2. In a skillet over medium heat, add the seasoned beef mixture to the water.
3. Mix well and break up the meat as it cooks. Sauté for 8–10 minutes, or until browned.
4. Heat the refried beans in the microwave for 2 minutes on high.
5. Wrap the tortillas in a moist towel and microwave for 1 minute on high.
6. Spoon about 3 tablespoons of refried beans down the center of each tortilla.
7. Spoon 3 tablespoons of beef on top of the beans, followed by a couple teaspoons of diced onion.
8. Fold the two sides of the tortilla over the beans and meat and flip the tortilla over onto a plate.
9. Spoon a couple tablespoons of red sauce over the top of the tortilla and sprinkle a couple tablespoons of the shredded Cheddar cheese.
10. Heat for 30–45 seconds in the microwave, or until the cheese on top begins to melt.

Taco Bell Fiesta Bowls

These popular side dishes at Taco Bell feature spicy rice, potatoes, or beans.

INGREDIENTS | SERVES 4

1 (6.8-ounce) package of Spanish Rice-A-Roni
1 (15-ounce) can chili with beans
1 (16-ounce) can beef tamales
1 cup shredded Cheddar cheese
1 (14½-ounce) can diced tomatoes

1. Prepare the rice according to package directions.
2. Spoon the chili and tomatoes into an 8" square baking dish.
3. Cut the tamales into 1" pieces. Top the chili with the tamales.
4. Heat in the microwave for 4 minutes on high.
5. Add the rice and cheese on top and microwave for 3 minutes on high, until the cheese melts.

Taco Bell Fire Border Sauce

For years, Taco Bell customers had only a mild or hot taco sauce. This recipe is for true hot sauce freaks.

INGREDIENTS | YIELDS 3 CUPS

1 (6-ounce) can tomato paste
3 cups water
3 tablespoons vinegar
3 tablespoons minced canned jalapeño slices
1 tablespoon chili powder
1 tablespoon minced onion
2 teaspoons salt
2 teaspoons cornstarch
1 teaspoon cayenne pepper
1 teaspoon sugar
¼ teaspoon onion powder
Dash garlic powder

1. In a medium saucepan, combine the tomato paste and water and whisk until smooth.
2. Add the remaining ingredients and stir until combined.
3. Heat over medium-high heat until it begins to boil. Continue to cook for about 3 minutes, stirring often. Remove from heat.
4. When sauce has cooled, pour it into a sealed container and refrigerate. Can be stored for up to 2 weeks.

Taco Bell Mexican Pizza

Pizza is found all over the world in many forms. Try this Mexican-style pizza for a unique version of an old favorite.

INGREDIENTS | SERVES 4

½ pound ground beef
½ teaspoon salt
¼ teaspoon dried minced onion
¼ teaspoon paprika
1½ teaspoons chili powder
2 tablespoons water
1 cup cooking oil
8 (6") flour tortillas
1 (16-ounce) can refried beans
⅔ cup mild salsa
⅓ cup diced tomato
1 cup shredded Cheddar cheese
1 cup shredded Monterey jack cheese
¼ cup chopped green onion
¼ cup sliced black olives

1. Preheat the oven to 400°F.
2. Cook the ground beef over medium heat for 7–10 minutes until brown, then drain.
3. Return meat to pan and add the salt, onion, paprika, chili powder, and water. Let mixture simmer over medium heat for 10 minutes, stirring often.
4. Heat the oil in a frying pan over medium-high heat.
5. When oil is hot, fry each tortilla for about 30–45 seconds per side and drain on paper towels. Tortillas should become golden brown.
6. Heat refried beans in the microwave for 1–2 minutes.
7. Place 4 tortillas on a baking sheet. For each pizza, spread ⅓ cup beans on a tortilla. Next add ⅓ cup meat, then another tortilla.
8. Top each of the second tortillas with 2 tablespoons of salsa.
9. Divide the tomato, cheeses, green onion, and olives evenly on top of the salsa.
10. Bake for 8–12 minutes.

Taco Bell Santa Fe Gorditas

What makes this dish unique is the sauce. It is no longer on the menu at Taco Bell, so make it at home using this recipe.

INGREDIENTS | SERVES 4

- 2 tablespoons mayonnaise
- 2 tablespoons chili sauce
- 1 teaspoon lemon juice
- 2 teaspoons vinegar
- 1 (10-ounce) can drained black beans
- 1 (10-ounce) can drained whole kernel corn
- 1 large finely diced bell pepper
- 1 small onion, diced
- 2 tablespoons finely chopped fresh cilantro
- 4 cooked boneless chicken breasts
- 4 pita bread rounds
- ½ cup shredded Cheddar cheese

1. In a small bowl, mix mayonnaise, chili sauce, lemon juice, and vinegar. Let chill for a minimum of 30 minutes.

2. In a medium bowl, mix the black beans, corn, bell pepper, onion, and cilantro. Let chill for at least 30 minutes

3. Slice the chicken breasts into thin strips.

4. Grill the pita bread in a pan 1–2 minutes per side until the bread is hot and flexible.

5. Spread the mayonnaise mixture between each pita round and top with the strips of chicken.

6. Top with the bean mixture and cheese.

CHAPTER 10

Asian

Benihana Fried Rice
164

Benihana Hibachi
Meat Marinade
164

Benihana Sesame Chicken
165

Bennigan's Bamboo Chicken
and Shrimp Skewers
166

Panda Express Beijing Beef
167

Panda Express Chow Mein
168

Panda Express Kung Pao
Chicken, Shrimp, or Beef
169

Panda Express
Mandarin Chicken
170

Panda Express Orange Chicken
171

Panda Express Spicy Chicken
172

P.F. Chang's
Chicken Lettuce Wraps
173

P.F. Chang's
Coconut Curry Vegetables
174

P.F. Chang's
Dan Dan Noodles
175

P.F. Chang's Firecracker Shrimp
176

P.F. Chang's
Lemon Pepper Shrimp
177

P.F. Chang's Mongolian Beef
178

P.F. Chang's
Singapore Street Noodles
179

P.F. Chang's Spare Ribs
180

P.F. Chang's Spicy Eggplant
181

P.F. Chang's
Szechuan Chicken Chow Fun
182

P.F. Chang's Zodiac Noodles
183

Benihana Fried Rice

Make delicious fried rice just like the cooks at Benihana with this terrific copycat. You can have a professional-quality meal made right in your own kitchen.

INGREDIENTS | SERVES 4

5 tablespoons butter
1 cup chopped onion
1 cup chopped carrots
⅔ cup chopped green onions
3 teaspoons sesame seeds
5 eggs
1 cup cooked rice
5 tablespoons soy sauce
Salt, to taste
Pepper, to taste

1. Melt butter in a large skillet. Add onions, carrots, and green onions. Sauté for 2–3 minutes until carrots are translucent. Set aside.

2. Heat the oven to 350°F. Place sesame seeds in a shallow pan. Bake 10–15 minutes, shaking pan occasionally, until golden brown.

3. Lightly grease another skillet and scramble the eggs.

4. Combine rice, vegetables, sesame seeds, and eggs. Add soy sauce, stir, and salt and pepper to taste.

Benihana Hibachi Meat Marinade

This is a copycat of the Benihana Hibachi Steak, Shrimp, Chicken, or Scallops served at the restaurant.

INGREDIENTS | SERVES 4

Marinade
1 tablespoon grated apple
2 tablespoons soy sauce
1 tablespoon grated garlic
1 tablespoon sesame oil
1 tablespoon sesame seeds

Choose Meat
¾ pound thin-sliced boneless beef top loin steaks
¾ pound boneless chicken, cut into bite-size pieces
¾ pound deveined shrimp
¾ pound scallops

1. Mix all the marinade ingredients in a small bowl.

2. Marinate meat in the sauce for 30 minutes, or longer.

3. Heat a frying pan or flat grill on high heat.

4. Stir-fry the meat a few minutes until desired doneness.

Benihana Sesame Chicken

Sesame chicken is a dish commonly found in Chinese restaurants. This is the recipe you've been looking for; it makes a perfect sesame chicken.

INGREDIENTS	SERVES 1

1 teaspoon soybean oil
1 (5-ounce) skinned, boneless chicken breast
Salt and pepper, to taste
½ teaspoon lemon juice
½ teaspoon sesame seeds
2 mushrooms, sliced into 8 pieces
1 teaspoon soy sauce

1. Add the oil to a heated nonstick skillet.
2. Sprinkle chicken with salt and pepper, if desired.
3. Cook for about 8 minutes, or until chicken is white in appearance and firm to the touch.
4. Sprinkle with lemon juice and sesame seeds.
5. Add the mushroom slices and soy sauce and cook 2–3 minutes more. Serve hot.

Benihana
Benihana started out as a small restaurant in New York City before becoming a national chain. Diners sit around large tables where chefs chop, slice, stir-fry, and grill as part of the teppanyaki style of cooking.

Bennigan's Bamboo Chicken and Shrimp Skewers

Fix these delicious teriyaki skewers as appetizers for your next party or serve them with rice for a full Chinese meal.

INGREDIENTS | SERVES 4

3 chicken skewers
3 shrimp skewers

Marinade
½ cup fresh jalapeños
½ cup garlic
½ cup fresh minced ginger
½ cup fresh lemon juice
2½ cups soy sauce
1¼ cups sesame oil
1½ cups brown sugar

Peanut Sauce
⅔ cup crunchy peanut butter
1½ cups unsweetened coconut milk
¼ cup lemon juice
2 tablespoons soy sauce
2 tablespoons brown sugar
1 teaspoon grated fresh ginger
4 cloves minced garlic
½ teaspoon cayenne pepper
¼ cup chicken stock
¼ cup heavy cream
1 cup lo mein noodles

1. Combine all the ingredients for the marinade in a bowl. Place the skewers in a long shallow dish. Pour the marinade over the skewers and refrigerate 2–4 hours.

2. Remove the skewers from the marinade and place onto a well-oiled section of the grill or large sauté pan. Cook the chicken and shrimp for 3–4 minutes, until done.

3. To make the peanut sauce, in a saucepan over medium heat, combine peanut butter, coconut milk, lemon juice, soy sauce, brown sugar, ginger, garlic, and cayenne. Cook for about 5 minutes until consistency of heavy cream, stirring frequently.

4. Transfer to a blender and pulse briefly 3–4 times. Add the chicken stock and heavy cream. Blend for 1 minute, or until it is smooth and creamy.

5. Toss the cooked lo mein noodles with ½ cup peanut sauce.

6. Place the skewers on top of noodles.

Panda Express Beijing Beef

This recipe from the fast food restaurant will be a crowd pleaser for people who like Chinese dishes.

INGREDIENTS | SERVES 4

Marinade
1 egg
¼ teaspoon salt
2 tablespoons water
1 tablespoon cornstarch
1 pound flank steak, sliced into thin strips

Sauce
4 tablespoons water
4 tablespoons sugar
3 tablespoons ketchup
2 tablespoons vinegar
¼ teaspoon crushed chili pepper
2 teaspoons cornstarch

Other
6 tablespoons cornstarch, for dusting
Oil, for frying

Vegetables
1 teaspoon garlic, minced
1 medium diced red bell pepper
1 medium diced green bell pepper
1 medium sliced white onion

1. In a bowl or sealable bag, combine all marinade ingredients and mix well. Add beef slices and marinate for 15 minutes.

2. While beef is marinating, mix all of the sauce ingredients together in a bowl and refrigerate.

3. When the beef is done marinating, coat the slices with 6 tablespoons of cornstarch.

4. Remove any excess cornstarch and deep fry (either in a deep fryer or wok) in batches until floating or golden brown. Drain on paper towels.

5. Add a couple tablespoons of oil to the wok, add garlic, and stir-fry for 10 seconds. Add the peppers and onions and stir-fry for 2 minutes. Remove vegetables and set aside.

6. Pour sauce into the wok and heat until boiling.

7. In a serving dish, add beef and vegetables and coat with the sauce.

Slicing Beef
Most Chinese recipes call for thin strips of meat. It is much easier to make thin cuts if the meat is partially frozen. Cut meat across the grain; it will be easier to eat and have a better appearance.

Panda Express Chow Mein

Chow mein is a Chinese American dish of bits of meat and vegetables served over noodles.

INGREDIENTS | SERVES 1

1 tablespoon vegetable oil
2 diced green onions
1½ cups sliced Napa cabbage
¼ cup sliced celery
¼ cup bean sprouts
¼ teaspoon granulated sugar
½ cup chicken broth
½ tablespoon soy sauce
1 teaspoon sesame oil
½ tablespoon cornstarch dissolved in 1 tablespoon cold water
Red pepper flakes, to taste
¼ pound cooked vermicelli noodles

1. In a large heavy skillet, heat the vegetable oil until it is hot but not smoking. Stir-fry the onions, cabbage, celery, and sprouts for 3 minutes, or until the cabbage is wilted.

2. Add the sugar, broth, soy sauce, and sesame oil and simmer for 3 minutes.

3. Stir the cornstarch mixture, stir it into the vegetable mixture, and bring the liquid to a boil.

4. Season the dish with red pepper flakes. Reduce heat and simmer for 5 minutes until heated through and serve over noodles.

Panda Express Kung Pao Chicken, Shrimp, or Beef

Put some spice in your life with this Chinese restaurant favorite. You may substitute thinly sliced shrimp or beef for the chicken.

INGREDIENTS | SERVES 4

1 pound ½" cubed chicken breast
1 small egg
¼ cup water
¼ cup cornstarch
½ teaspoon salt
2 green onions
⅓ cup water
2½ tablespoons soy sauce
1 tablespoon cornstarch dissolved in 1 tablespoon cold water
1 teaspoon rice wine vinegar
2 divided tablespoons vegetable oil
1 chunked red pepper
1 chunked green pepper
1 chunked small zucchini
1 teaspoon minced garlic
¼ teaspoon red pepper flakes
¼ teaspoon ground ginger
Sugar, to taste
⅓ cup dry-roasted peanuts
4 cups cooked white rice

1. In a zip-top bag, combine meat with egg, water, cornstarch, and salt; marinate, chilled, for at least 30 minutes.

2. Slice the green onions, both the white part and greens, into ½" pieces.

3. Combine water and soy sauce, stir in dissolved cornstarch and rice wine vinegar, and chill.

4. About 20 minutes before serving time, heat about 1 tablespoon of oil in a hot wok. Stir meat, drain, and discard marinade.

5. Quickly stir-fry the meat 60–90 seconds. Transfer to a large container.

6. Stir-fry the peppers until almost tender. Add the onions and zucchini, remove, and reserve with meat.

7. Heat the remaining oil and stir-fry garlic and season with pepper flakes and ginger.

8. Stir the reserved sauce mixture before pouring into seasoned garlic. Heat through to thicken. Sweeten to taste with sugar, adding a bit more ginger and/or red pepper flakes, as needed.

9. Add cooked food to sauce and stir in peanuts. Serve over hot rice.

Panda Express Mandarin Chicken

This dish is very similar to a sauce loved by millions from Panda Express.

INGREDIENTS | SERVES 6

⅔ cup sugar
¼ cup soy sauce
1 tablespoon lemon juice
1 teaspoon vegetable oil
1 teaspoon minced fresh garlic
½ teaspoon minced fresh ginger
4 teaspoons arrowroot
¼ cup water
6 skinless chicken thighs

1. Preheat grill on high.

2. In a small saucepan, combine sugar, soy sauce, lemon juice, oil, garlic, and ginger.

3. In another small bowl, combine water with arrowroot and stir until arrowroot is dissolved.

4. Add arrowroot mixture to saucepan and turn heat to high. Stir often while bringing mixture to a boil, then reduce heat and simmer for 4–6 minutes, or until sauce is thick.

5. When the grill is hot, rub each chicken piece with oil and cook for 4–6 minutes per side, or until completely cooked. Chicken should have browned in spots.

6. When the chicken is done, chop it into bite-size pieces. Pour the pieces into a large frying pan over medium heat.

7. Heat until chicken sizzles, reduce heat, and cover chicken until ready to serve. Spoon chicken into a medium bowl, then pour all the sauce over the chicken and stir until well coated.

Panda Express Orange Chicken

Panda Express has lots of great dishes, but none is as legendary as the orange chicken. This restaurant copycat recipe lets you make your own version of their delicious favorite.

INGREDIENTS | SERVES 6

2 pounds boneless chicken breast
1 egg
Dash of salt
Dash of pepper
Vegetable oil
½ cup plus 1 tablespoon cornstarch
¼ cup flour
1 teaspoon sesame oil
1 teaspoon minced ginger
1 teaspoon minced garlic
¼ teaspoon red pepper flakes
¼ cup chopped green onions
Zest from 1 orange
1½ tablespoons soy sauce
5 tablespoons sugar
5 tablespoons white vinegar
1 tablespoon rice wine
¼ cup water
1½ tablespoons water

1. Preheat oil in a wok or deep skillet to 375°F.
2. Cut chicken into small squares and place in a bowl.
3. In a separate bowl, add egg, salt, pepper and 1 tablespoon of oil and mix well. Add cornstarch and flour and mix well. Add chicken to the mixture and coat well.
4. Cook chicken until the pieces are cooked through, about 5 minutes. Remove from the pan and drain.
5. In a clean skillet or wok lightly greased with 1 tablespoon of oil, add ginger and garlic and heat for a few seconds, until you can smell the mixture.
6. Add pepper flakes and onions to the ginger and garlic mixture and sauté for 15 seconds. Add orange zest. Add the soy sauce, sugar, vinegar and rice wine and bring the mixture to a boil. Combine the chicken with the orange sauce, mix well.
7. Combine the chicken with the orange sauce and mix well.
8. Add water to the remaining 1 tablespoon cornstarch and mix well. Combine cornstarch mixture with chicken and orange sauce and heat for about 5 minutes until sauce has thickened up. Stir in sesame oil. Remove from the heat and serve immediately.

Panda Express

Panda Express, with over 1,200 restaurants, is the largest chain of Chinese fast food restaurants in the United States. No MSG is added to any of the items on the menu. They offer a "create your own combo" meal whereby you choose a 2- or 3-entrée plate, and they offer quite a few low calorie options.

Panda Express Spicy Chicken

Panda Express is a quick stop when you are in the mood for Chinese. Why not make your own takeout tonight with this restaurant copycat recipe for spicy stir-fry chicken bursting with Asian flavors.

INGREDIENTS | SERVES 4

1 tablespoon cornstarch
2 tablespoons water
½ cup vegetable oil
¾ pound diced seasoned chicken
⅓ cup diced onion
¼ cup diced red bell pepper
½ cup diced chayote squash
8 pieces whole dry chili pepper
½ teaspoon crushed garlic
½ teaspoon crushed ginger
¼ cup roasted peanuts
¾ teaspoon crushed red chili pepper
½ teaspoon cooking wine
1 teaspoon soy sauce
2 tablespoons chicken broth
1 teaspoon granulated sugar
1 dash sesame oil

1. In a small bowl, mix the cornstarch and water and set aside.
2. Heat a pot of boiling water to cook the squash.
3. At the same time, heat ¼ cup of oil in wok until hot. Add chicken and stir-fry for 5 minutes until done.
4. Add onions and bell peppers and stir quickly (about 2–3 minutes) until crisp. Remove, drain, and set aside.
5. Add the squash to the boiling water for 60 seconds, or until crisp and done. Remove, drain, and set aside.
6. Heat 2 tablespoons of oil in wok until hot. Add the chili peppers, garlic, and ginger. Stir-fry for 2–3 minutes until fragrant.
7. Add all the remaining ingredients except cornstarch mixture.
8. Bring to a boil. Slowly stir in the cornstarch mixture. Add chicken and vegetables.
9. Coat the dish evenly with the sauce.

P.F. Chang's Chicken Lettuce Wraps

Lettuce wraps were the restaurant world's way of serving low-carb meals during that crazy diet fad. This dish of quickly cooked spiced chicken and vegetables tastes great if you are watching your calories.

INGREDIENTS | SERVES 6

8 dried shiitake mushrooms

Cooking Sauce
1 tablespoon Hoisin sauce
1 tablespoon soy sauce
1 tablespoon dry sherry
2 tablespoons oyster sauce
2 tablespoons water
1 teaspoon sesame oil
1 teaspoon sugar
2 teaspoons cornstarch

Marinade and Chicken
1 teaspoon cornstarch
2 teaspoon dry sherry
2 teaspoon soy sauce
2 teaspoon water
Salt and pepper, to taste
1½ pounds boneless skinless chicken breasts

Other
5 tablespoons vegetable oil
1 teaspoon minced fresh ginger
2 cloves minced garlic
2 small dried chilies (optional)
2 minced green onions
1 (8-ounce) can minced bamboo shoots
1 (8-ounce) can minced water chestnuts
1 (1-pound) package prepared Chinese rice noodles
6 large iceberg lettuce leaves

1. Cover mushrooms with boiling water, let stand 30 minutes, then drain. Cut and discard stems and mince mushrooms. Set aside.

2. In a bowl, mix all the ingredients for the cooking sauce and set aside.

3. In a medium bowl, combine cornstarch, sherry, soy sauce, water, salt, pepper, and chicken. Stir to coat chicken thoroughly. Stir in 1 teaspoon oil and let sit 15 minutes to marinate.

4. Heat a wok or large skillet to medium-high. Add 3 tablespoons oil, then add chicken and stir-fry for 3–4 minutes. Set aside.

5. Add 2 tablespoons of oil to the pan. Add ginger, garlic, chilies (if desired), and onion and stir-fry about 1 minute or so.

6. Add mushrooms, bamboo shoots, and water chestnuts and stir-fry an additional 2 minutes.

7. Return chicken to pan. Add cooking sauce and cook for 5 minutes until thickened and hot.

8. Break the noodles into small pieces and cover the bottom of a serving dish with them. Pour the chicken mixture over the top of the noodles. Spoon some of the mixture onto a lettuce leaf and roll.

P.F. Chang's Coconut Curry Vegetables

Borrowing the flavors of South East Asia, this is a delicious stir-fry of vegetables. For a really saucy dish to serve over rice or noodles, double the sauce ingredients and the cornstarch mixture.

INGREDIENTS | SERVES 2–4

- 3 cups broccoli
- 1 cup thinly sliced carrots or whole sugar snap peas
- ½ cup canned coconut milk
- 2 tablespoons soy sauce
- ½ teaspoon curry powder
- 1½–2 tablespoons packed brown sugar
- 2 teaspoons unseasoned rice vinegar or cider vinegar
- 2 teaspoons canola oil
- 2 teaspoons cornstarch dissolved in 1½ tablespoons cold water
- 1 small onion, cut into ¾" cubes
- 1 small cubed red bell pepper
- 1 cup halved mushrooms
- 2 tablespoons sesame oil

P.F. Chang's

P.F. Chang's China Bistro operates over 200 restaurants, specializing in gluten-free American Chinese food. The menu features a wide variety of rice and noodle dishes along with lunch bowls and small plates. They just introduced a new line of premium frozen foods based on their recipes that can be found in supermarkets nationwide.

1. In plain boiling water, separately blanch the broccoli and carrots for 3–4 minutes until tender crisp. Drain and rinse under cold water to stop the cooking. Drain again.

2. Combine coconut milk, soy sauce, curry powder, brown sugar, and vinegar. Taste and adjust the sugar to your liking.

3. Heat a wok or wide skillet over high heat until. Add the canola oil and swirl to glaze the pan.

4. Add the onions and bell pepper and stir-fry until tender-crisp, about 3–4 minutes.

5. Add the mushrooms and stir until hot, 2–3 minutes more.

6. Add the blanched vegetables and toss to mix.

7. Stir the sauce and add it to the pan. Bring it to a simmer, tossing to combine.

8. Stir the cornstarch mixture to recombine and add it to the pan.

9. Stir until the sauce turns glossy, about 10 seconds.

10. Add the sesame oil and toss to mix.

P.F. Chang's Dan Dan Noodles

Dan Dan noodles are a classic dish of Chinese cuisine. It consists of a spicy sauce containing preserved vegetables.

INGREDIENTS | SERVES 4

1 teaspoon oil
½ teaspoon chili paste
½ teaspoon minced garlic
1½ teaspoons minced green onion
4 ounces cooked ground chicken
2 ounces soy sauce
1 ounce cooking wine
1 teaspoon oyster sauce
1 teaspoon granulated sugar
7 ounces chicken stock
2 teaspoons cornstarch
2 teaspoons water
¼ ounce cooked egg noodles
Bean sprouts
Julienned cucumbers

1. Heat a wok or large skillet, add oil, and sear the chili paste, garlic, and green onion for 5 seconds.

2. Add chicken, tossing and stirring for 10 seconds. Add all soy sauce, wine, oyster sauce, sugar, and chicken stock. Simmer for 20 seconds.

3. In a small bowl, mix cornstarch and water and add to thicken the sauce.

4. Pour the sauce over a serving plate of hot noodles.

5. Garnish with bean sprouts and cucumbers.

P.F. Chang's Firecracker Shrimp

Do you love that firecracker shrimp that you get in a Chinese restaurant? This recipe will be one that you want to try.

INGREDIENTS | SERVES 2

1 ounce water
1 teaspoon cornstarch
2 tablespoons canola oil
7 baby carrots, halved lengthwise
8 ounces shrimp
½ cup water chestnut slices
24 snow peas
1 large chopped garlic clove
1 large chopped green onion
1 tablespoon chili paste
¼ teaspoon ground white pepper
2 teaspoons ground bean sauce
2 tablespoon sherry
Fresh chopped cilantro, for garnish

Sauce

2 tablespoons soy sauce
2 teaspoons sugar
⅛ cup water
2 teaspoons white vinegar

1. In a small bowl, combine the water and cornstarch and set aside.

2. In another bowl, combine the sauce ingredients and set aside.

3. Heat a large sauté pan or wok until smoking. Add oil and carrots and sauté for 2 minutes until the color of carrots brightens.

4. Add the shrimp and stir-fry about 3 minutes until about halfway cooked.

5. Add water chestnuts, snow peas, and garlic. Sauté for about 1 minute.

6. Add the onions. Add the chili paste, pepper, bean sauce, and when you smell the "nuttiness" of the bean sauce (about 2 minutes), reduce heat and add sherry.

7. Add the sauce mixture and let it boil briefly (about 2 minutes). Add cornstarch mixture and stir until thickened.

8. Garnish with chopped cilantro.

P.F. Chang's Lemon Pepper Shrimp

This dish might look hard, but all you need to do is read through the recipe once and follow the directions to make a great restaurant-quality meal.

INGREDIENTS | SERVES 4

1 tablespoon vegetable oil
2 tablespoons chopped garlic
½ teaspoon minced ginger
⅓ cup soy sauce
2 teaspoons cornstarch
¾ cup water
¼ cup dark brown sugar
2 teaspoons lemon juice
2 teaspoons coarse ground pepper
1 pound peeled medium shrimp
½ cup cornstarch
1 cup vegetable oil
4 thin quartered lemon slices
1 teaspoon vegetable oil
2 large green onions
1 cup bean sprouts
Dash of salt and pepper

1. To make the sauce, heat 1 tablespoon of oil in a wok or large saucepan over medium heat. Sauté the garlic and ginger for about 15 seconds.

2. Add the soy sauce, then dissolve the cornstarch in the water and add to the pan.

3. Add brown sugar, lemon juice and black pepper and bring mixture to a boil. Simmer for 2 minutes, then remove from the heat.

4. Coat all the shrimp generously with cornstarch. Let the shrimp sit for about 5 minutes so the cornstarch will adhere better.

5. Heat a cup of oil in a wok or large skillet over medium heat. Add the shrimp to the pan and sauté for 3–4 minutes, or until the shrimp starts to turn light brown. Strain the shrimp out of the oil with a slotted spoon or spider and dump the oil.

6. Place the shrimp back in the wok along with the lemon slices and sauté for 1 minute, then add the sauce. Toss to coat the shrimp thoroughly. Cook for another minute or so, until the sauce thickens.

7. As the shrimp cooks, in a separate medium saucepan, heat up 1 teaspoon of oil. Cut the green part of the onions into 3" lengths. Add them with the bean sprouts to the hot oil, along with a dash of salt and pepper. Sauté for 2 minutes, until onions begin to soften.

8. Build the dish by pouring the onions and sprouts onto a serving plate. Pour the shrimp over the veggies, and serve.

P.F. Chang's Mongolian Beef

Mongolian beef is a dish served in Chinese restaurants consisting of sliced beef stir-fried with vegetables.

INGREDIENTS | SERVES 4

2 teaspoons vegetable oil
½ teaspoon minced ginger
1 tablespoon chopped garlic
½ cup soy sauce
½ cup water
¾ cup dark brown sugar
1 pound flank steak
¼ cup cornstarch
1 cup vegetable oil
2 large green onions

1. To make the sauce, in a medium saucepan over medium heat, heat 2 teaspoons of vegetable oil. Add the ginger and garlic, then quickly add the soy sauce and water.

2. Dissolve the brown sugar, then raise the heat to about medium and boil for 2–3 minutes, or until the sauce thickens. Remove it from the heat.

3. Slice the steak against the grain into ¼" thick bite-size slices. Dip the pieces into the cornstarch to apply a very thin dusting to both sides of each piece of beef. Let sit for about 10 minutes so the cornstarch sticks.

4. As the beef sits, heat up 1 cup of oil in a wok or large skillet over medium heat until it's nice and hot, but not smoking (about 2 minutes).

5. Add the beef to the oil and sauté for 2 minutes, or until the beef just begins to darken on the edges. Stir the meat around a little so that it cooks evenly. After a couple minutes, use a large slotted spoon or a spider to take the meat out and put onto paper towels. Pour the oil out of the wok or skillet.

6. Put the pan back over the heat, place the meat back into it and simmer for 1 minute.

7. Add the sauce and, stirring, cook for 1 minute.

8. Add the onions and cook for 1 minute. Remove the beef and onions with tongs or a slotted spoon to a serving plate.

P.F. Chang's Singapore Street Noodles

This is a delicious noodle dish with chicken and shrimp and the trademark curry flavor.

INGREDIENTS | SERVES 4

Singapore Sauce
2 tablespoons white vinegar
¼ cup curry powder
¼ cup soy sauce
1 cup vegetarian oyster sauce
¼ cup Sriricha chili sauce
¼ cup ketchup

Remaining Ingredients
2 gallons water
1 pound rice stick noodles
4 tablespoons canola oil
½ pound medium-size shrimp
8 ounces julienned chicken
1 tablespoon chopped garlic
1 cup julienned cabbage
½ cup julienned carrots
2 medium diced tomatoes
1 bunch sliced green onions
⅓ cup shallots
¼ bunch roughly chopped cilantro
1 quartered lime
1 teaspoon sesame oil

1. In a bowl, combine all the ingredients for the sauce, mix well, and set aside.

2. Bring water to a rolling boil. Place rice sticks in boiling water for 2 minutes. Drain, then rinse under rapid running hot water for 1 minute, and drain well again. Toss noodles with 2 tablespoons of canola oil and set aside.

3. In a hot wok, stir-fry shrimp and chicken in 2 tablespoons canola oil until just done, about 2 minutes.

4. Add garlic, cabbage, carrots, and tomatoes and stir-fry for 1 minute.

5. Add noodles and stir-fry 1 minute more.

6. Add 1 cup vinegar mixture and stir-fry until ingredients are well incorporated, about 2 minutes. Add onions, shallots, cilantro, lime juice and sesame oil and toss briefly.

P.F. Chang's Spare Ribs

One of the most popular dishes on P. F. Chang's appetizer menu is the spare ribs that come slathered with an Asian barbecue sauce.

INGREDIENTS | SERVES 2

1 cup ketchup
1 cup light corn syrup
½ cup hoisin sauce
½ cup water
⅓ cup packed light brown sugar
2 tablespoons minced onions
1 tablespoon rice vinegar
12–16 cups water
1 rack pork spareribs
4 cups vegetable oil
1 teaspoon sesame seeds
1 tablespoon diced green onion

1. To make the sauce, in a medium saucepan over medium heat, combine the ketchup, corn syrup, hoisin sauce, water, brown sugar, onions and vinegar. Bring mixture to a boil, then reduce heat and simmer for 5 minutes, until thick. Cool.

2. Heat 12–16 cups of water in a large saucepan or Dutch oven. Add a couple teaspoons of salt.

3. As water boils, trim the excess fat and meat off and slice between the bones of each rib to separate. When the water is boiling, toss the ribs in and boil for 12–14 minutes. Remove ribs to a plate to cool.

4. In a large saucepan over medium, heat vegetable oil to 375°F.

5. When the oil is hot, drop 4–6 ribs in at a time. Fry for 2–4 minutes, or until meat browns.

6. Drain on a rack or paper towels. Fry all the ribs before moving on to the next step.

7. Heat a wok or large skillet over medium heat. When the pan is hot, add the ribs and sauce, toss the ribs to coat. Simmer the ribs in the sauce, stirring, for about 1 minute. Remove to a serving plate when they are all coated with sauce.

8. Sprinkle the ribs with sesame seeds and green onions.

P.F. Chang's Spicy Eggplant

This stir-fry recipe gives the eggplant a unique flavor with the addition of a fiery sauce added to the mix.

INGREDIENTS | SERVES 4

1 pound peeled eggplant
1 tablespoon cornstarch
4 tablespoons water, divided
2 tablespoons oyster sauce
2 tablespoons soy sauce
1 tablespoon white vinegar
1 tablespoon sugar
1 teaspoon chili paste
½ teaspoon ground bean sauce
½ teaspoon sesame oil
Vegetable oil, for frying
1 teaspoon minced garlic

1. Cut the eggplant into 1" cubes.
2. In a small bowl, combine the cornstarch and 2 tablespoons water to make a paste. Set aside.
3. In another bowl, combine oyster sauce, soy sauce, vinegar, sugar, chili paste, bean sauce, sesame oil, and 2 tablespoons water. Mix well.
4. In a wok, add 1 tablespoon of vegetable oil and fry eggplant for 1 minute. Remove and drain on paper towels.
5. On high heat, stir-fry garlic for 5 seconds, then add the spicy sauce. Reduce the heat and let sauce simmer 20 seconds. Add the eggplant and simmer for another 10 seconds.
6. Stir in the cornstarch paste a little at a time until you get the consistency of peanut butter.

P.F. Chang's Szechuan Chicken Chow Fun

This is a nice dinner for two. Stay in and cook instead of going out to eat and still have a great meal.

INGREDIENTS | SERVES 2

Sauce
- 2 tablespoons soy sauce
- 2 tablespoons vinegar
- 2 tablespoons granulated sugar
- 1 teaspoon oyster sauce
- 1 teaspoon mushroom soy sauce
- 2 tablespoons water

Remaining Ingredients
- 1 (14-ounce) package chow fun noodles (wide rice noodles sold at most Asian markets)
- 2 teaspoons vegetable oil
- 1 teaspoon minced garlic
- 1 teaspoon chili paste
- 4 ounces cooked ground chicken
- 2 tablespoons shredded black fungus mushrooms
- 2 tablespoons sesame oil
- 1 teaspoon Szechuan preserved vegetables, for garnish
- 2 tablespoons minced green onion, for garnish

1. In a small bowl, combine the sauce ingredients and set aside.
2. Separate the noodles and cover with plastic wrap until ready to use.
3. Heat a wok and add vegetable oil. Stir-fry garlic and chili paste for 5–7 seconds.
4. Add ground chicken and sear with garlic and chili paste. Add mushrooms and sauce and stir-fry for 3–4 minutes.
5. Drop the noodles into the wok, stirring, a handful at a time.
6. Continue cooking until the noodles have absorbed all the flavors and are hot. Add sesame oil.
7. Serve into bowls or plates. Garnish with Szechwan preserved vegetables and onions.

P.F. Chang's Zodiac Noodles

Thin strands of rice noodles are combined with vegetables and a spicy Kung Pao sauce in this dish.

INGREDIENTS | SERVES 4

5 ounces rice vermicelli
3 teaspoons vegetable oil
8 chili pods
3 ounces pork loin, cut into thin strips
1 teaspoon garlic
1½ ounces ham
2 diced green onions
¼ cup sliced cabbage, cut into thin strips
¼ cup sliced shiitake mushroom
⅛ teaspoon salt
2 tablespoons soy sauce
1 teaspoon oyster sauce
1 teaspoon sugar
½ teaspoon sesame oil

1. Soak vermicelli in very hot water for 1 hour.

2. Bring a pot of water to a boil, add vermicelli, and boil for 1 minute.

3. Rinse under warm water for 1 minute, drain well, then mix with 1 teaspoon of vegetable oil.

4. Heat a wok over high heat for 1–2 minutes, until it begins to smoke.

5. Add vegetable oil, then chili pods and pork. Stir-fry for 2–3 minutes until pork is almost done.

6. Add garlic, ham, onion, cabbage, and mushrooms and stir for 10–15 seconds.

7. Add vermicelli, salt, soy sauce, oyster sauce, sugar, and sesame oil. Stir-fry for 2–3 minutes until all the ingredients are mixed well.

CHAPTER 11

Italian

Buca di Beppo Chicken Limone
186

Buca di Beppo Chicken Marsala
187

Buca di Beppo Penne Cardinale
188

Buca di Beppo Chicken Saltimbocca
189

Carino's Angel Hair with Artichokes
190

Carino's Five Meat Tuscan Pasta
191

Carino's Grilled Chicken Bowtie Festival
192

Carino's Spicy Shrimp and Chicken
193

Carrabba's Linguine Pescatore
193

Carrabba's Meatballs
194

Carrabba's Pasta Weesie
195

Carrabba's Mussels in Wine Sauce
196

Little Caesars Crazy Sauce
197

Olive Garden Capellini Pomodoro
198

Olive Garden Chicken Milanese
199

Olive Garden Chicken Scampi
200

Olive Garden Penne Romana
201

Olive Garden Tuscan Garlic Chicken
202

Italian
(continued)

Olive Garden Venetian
Apricot Chicken
203

Papa John's Garlic Sauce
204

Pizza Hut Cavatini
204

Pizza Hut Stuffed Crust Pizza
205

Romano's Macaroni Grill
Carmela's Chicken
206

Romano's Macaroni Grill
Penne Rustica
207

Romano's Macaroni Grill
Shrimp Portofino
208

Buca di Beppo Chicken Limone

This is a fantastic, easy lemon chicken recipe. Serve it with green beans and roasted potatoes or a nice salad.

INGREDIENTS | SERVES 4

1 large egg
3 tablespoons lemon juice
⅓ cup flour
⅛ teaspoon garlic powder
⅛ teaspoon paprika
4 boneless skinless chicken breast halves
¼ cup melted butter or margarine
1½–2 teaspoons chicken bouillon cubes
½ cup hot water
1 tablespoon capers, for garnish
Lemon wedges, for garnish

1. In a small bowl, combine the egg and 1 tablespoon of lemon juice and beat well.

2. In another bowl, combine flour, garlic powder, and paprika and stir well.

3. Put the chicken breast between 2 sheets of waxed paper and pound until the chicken is flattened and even in thickness.

4. Dip the chicken in the egg mixture then dredge in flour mixture.

5. In a large skillet over medium-high heat, cook the chicken in butter 2–3 minutes on each side, until brown.

6. Dissolve bouillon in hot water and add to chicken along with 2 tablespoons of lemon juice. Bring to a boil, cover, and reduce heat.

7. Simmer 10–15 minutes, or until the chicken is done. Garnish with capers and lemon slices.

Buca di Beppo Chicken Marsala

Chicken Marsala is an elegant and delicious Italian dish that is also really easy to make.

INGREDIENTS | SERVES 4

4 boneless skinless chicken breasts
1 cup flour
Salt and pepper, to taste
1 tablespoon oregano
2 tablespoons olive oil
1 tablespoon butter
2 cups Marsala wine
3 cups chicken stock
1¼ cups sliced fresh mushrooms
4 minced garlic cloves
1 (16-ounce) package cooked linguini or spaghetti

Buca di Beppo

There are over eighty of these restaurants operating nationwide. The chain specializes in immigrant southern Italian food, which is served family style and meant to be shared among the dining party.

1. Place chicken breasts one at a time between 2 sheets of waxed paper. Pound until they are about ¼" thick.
2. In a small bowl, combine flour, salt, pepper, and oregano.
3. Dredge chicken in flour until coated thoroughly.
4. Heat the olive oil and butter in a large skillet.
5. Fry chicken breasts until they are almost fully cooked, about 3 minutes each side. Remove from pan.
6. Deglaze the pan with the wine. Make sure to scrape all the brown bits on the bottom of the pan and mix with the wine.
7. Add chicken stock, mushrooms, and garlic. Cook the broth on medium-high for 10 minutes, or until the sauce has been reduced by half.
8. Add chicken breasts back into the pan and cook for another 10 minutes. The sauce should become thick.
9. Serve over pasta.

Buca di Beppo Penne Cardinale

This recipe is a chicken pasta dish with a creamy, slightly spicy sauce.

INGREDIENTS | SERVES 4–6

1 pound chicken tenders
¾ cup olive oil
½ cup green onions
¼ cup chopped garlic
1 teaspoon salt
2 teaspoon crushed red pepper flakes
½ cup white wine
1¼ cups quartered artichokes
1½ cups cream
2 pats butter
1¾ pounds cooked penne pasta
¾ cup grated Romano cheese

1. Cut the chicken in half lengthwise.
2. In a large sauté pan, heat olive oil and sauté onions and garlic 3–4 minutes, until slightly browned.
3. Add the chicken, salt, and red pepper. Cook for an additional 3–4 minutes, until the chicken is done.
4. Deglaze the pan with white wine. Add artichokes and cream. Reduce the sauce until it starts to thicken. Cook for 4–5 minutes.
5. Remove the pan from the heat and incorporate the butter. Toss with the cooked penne and then the Romano cheese.

Buca di Beppo Chicken Saltimbocca

The name "saltimbocca" means "jump into the mouth" because a dish is that delicious.

INGREDIENTS | SERVES 4

1 tablespoon salt
4 (5-ounce) chicken breasts
1 tablespoon chopped fresh sage
4 thin slices prosciutto ham
3 ounces olive oil
1 ounce all-purpose flour
4 ounces white wine
5 ounces artichoke hearts, quartered
2 ounces fresh lemon juice
2 ounces heavy cream
1 tablespoon butter
½ ounce capers

1. Lightly salt the chicken breasts and sprinkle evenly with sage.

2. Place the prosciutto on top of the chicken and pound it into the breast until the thickness of the chicken measures ⅜".

3. In a sauté pan, heat the olive oil over medium heat.

4. Lightly flour the flattened chicken.

5. Place chicken into the pan, Prosciutto side down. Brown one side, turn and brown the other side.

6. Drain off excess oil, and deglaze with white wine. Add the artichokes, lemon juice, cream, and butter and cook until sauce is thickened.

7. On a large platter, place the chicken breasts topped with reduced sauce and garnish with capers.

Carino's Angel Hair with Artichokes

You can put together a hearty and healthy meal quickly with this recipe.

INGREDIENTS | SERVES 4

3 tablespoons extra-virgin olive oil
1 teaspoon fresh chopped garlic
14 large shrimp
1 cup quartered artichoke hearts
1 cup diced Roma tomatoes
1 cup chopped black olives
4 tablespoons capers
Salt and pepper, to taste
¼ cup chopped fresh basil
1 pound angel hair pasta, cooked
2 tablespoons shredded Parmesan
Fresh chopped parsley, for garnish

1. In a sauté pan on medium, add olive oil, garlic, shrimp, and artichokes. Let shrimp cook and let garlic turn a golden color to develop flavor (about 3–4 minutes).

2. Add tomatoes, black olives, capers, salt, and pepper. Let ingredients thoroughly heat while mixing. Cook 5–6 minutes.

3. Remove from the heat and toss in fresh basil.

4. Place cooked pasta in a mound on service plate and top with ingredients from sauté pan, then garnish with Parmesan and parsley.

Carino's Five Meat Tuscan Pasta

Grill up some extra Italian sausage to make this pasta dish in a hurry.

INGREDIENTS | SERVES 4

2 tablespoons olive oil
2 teaspoons chopped garlic
½ cup sliced cooked Italian sausage
½ cup diced ham
½ cup chopped bacon
¼ cup chopped pepperoni
¼ cup diced green bell peppers
¼ cup diced yellow onions
Salt and pepper, to taste
2½ cups meat sauce
1 (16-ounce) box cooked bowtie pasta
¼ cup shredded Asiago cheese
¼ cup shredded Parmesan cheese

1. In a large sauté pan over medium heat, add the olive oil, garlic, sausage, ham, bacon, pepperoni, bell peppers, onions, salt, and pepper. Sauté 8–10 minutes until bacon is cooked and peppers and onions are soft.

2. Add meat sauce and pasta and toss together.

3. Place the pasta on a serving plate and garnish with Asiago and Parmesan cheeses.

Chef Boyardee

Did you know that Chef Boyardee was a real person and that Betty Crocker was not? Chef Boyardee was an Italian American immigrant named Ettore Boiardi who opened a restaurant in the early 1920s. The demand for his recipes grew into the canned products we know today. Betty Crocker is a fictional character created in the 1920s by General Mills to give a personalized response to consumer product questions.

Carino's Grilled Chicken Bowtie Festival

The Bowtie Festival is a favorite on the menu at Carino's. It features fresh vegetables and chicken tossed in a creamy tomato sauce.

INGREDIENTS | SERVES 4

2 tablespoons melted butter
⅛ cup diced red onion
1 teaspoon chopped fresh garlic
¼ cup diced Roma tomatoes
¼ cup diced cooked bacon
1 cup sliced cooked chicken
Salt, pepper, and garlic salt, to taste
1 ounce heavy cream
⅛ cup Asiago cheese
1 (16-ounce) jar of Ragu Alfredo sauce
1 (16-ounce) box cooked bowtie pasta

1. In a heated sauté pan combine butter, onions, garlic, tomatoes, bacon, chicken, salt, pepper, and garlic salt.

2. After 3–4 minutes, when the onions turn translucent, add the cream and Asiago.

3. Once the cheese and cream have reduced (about 6–8 minutes), add the Alfredo sauce and pasta.

4. Toss and combine well.

5. Allow to cool a few minutes for the sauce and cheese to thicken.

Carino's Spicy Shrimp and Chicken

This signature dish from Carino's is bound to become a family favorite.

INGREDIENTS | SERVES 4

2 chicken breasts
2 tablespoons melted butter
20 peeled medium shrimp
3 cups sliced mushrooms
1 cup hydrated sundried tomatoes
1 cup sliced green onions
Salt and pepper, to taste
2 cups heavy cream
⅓ cup grated Pecorino Romano cheese
Cayenne pepper, to taste
1 (16-ounce) box cooked penne pasta

1. Grill chicken breasts 5 minutes per side until done. Cool and slice into ¼" thick strips.
2. Add butter to a large sauté pan over medium heat. Add shrimp, chicken, mushrooms, sundried tomatoes, onions, salt, and pepper. Sauté for 3–4 minutes until shrimp and mushrooms are cooked.
3. Add cream, cheese, and cayenne pepper. Let cream reduce by half (about 6–8 minutes) while thoroughly combining all ingredients.
4. Toss pasta with contents of sauté pan.

Carrabba's Linguine Pescatore

The linguine pescatore features a variety of seafood in a spicy red sauce.

INGREDIENTS | SERVES 2

3 shrimp
3 scallops
6–8 mussels
1¼ cups marinara sauce
Salt and white pepper, to taste
12 ounces cooked linguine

1. Cook all the ingredients except the linguine over medium heat in a covered sauté pan for about 5 minutes until the shrimp turns pink and the mussels pop open.
2. Toss with linguine.
3. Garnish and serve.

Carrabba's Meatballs

This simple restaurant copycat recipe for meatballs tastes just like the ones served at Carrabba's. It uses a combination of meats and will make you happy that you decided to stay in and cook.

INGREDIENTS | SERVES 6–8

1 pound ground beef
½ pound ground pork
⅓ cup dry breadcrumbs
4 minced garlic cloves
2 eggs
2 minced green onions
1 minced small yellow onion
3 tablespoons grated Parmesan cheese
3 tablespoons grated Romano cheese
3 tablespoons minced fresh parsley
3 tablespoons minced fresh basil
Salt and pepper, to taste
1 cup olive oil

1. Preheat oven to 400°F.
2. Combine all ingredients except olive oil in a large bowl.
3. Roll the mixture into 1½" balls.
4. Pour olive oil on a 2" × 13" × 9" baking pan and place meatballs on top. Swirl pan around to coat meatballs in oil.
5. Bake the meatballs in the oven for 25–30 minutes, until golden brown.
6. Remove the meatballs from the oil, drain on paper towels, and stir into your favorite pasta sauce.

Carrabba's Pasta Weesie

Pasta Weesie is a nice Alfredo seafood recipe.

INGREDIENTS | SERVES 2

8 jumbo shrimp
Pinch minced garlic
1 tablespoon sliced green onions
¼ cup sautéed mushrooms
¼ cup lemon butter
½ cup Alfredo sauce
Half a 16-ounce box of cooked fettuccine
½ cup grated Romano cheese

1. In a saucepan over medium heat, sauté the shrimp for 3–4 minutes until they turn pink.
2. Add the garlic, onions, and mushrooms. Sauté for 2–3 minutes. Finish with the lemon butter.
3. In a separate pan, warm the Alfredo to a simmer.
4. Add the fettuccine and cheese.
5. Plate the pasta and top with shrimp mixture.

Origin of Alfredo Sauce

Alfredo sauce was invented in Rome in the early 1900s and contained only fresh noodles, butter, and Parmigiano-Reggiano cheese. The Americans added heavy cream to the recipe to make the Alfredo sauce you see in restaurants today.

Carrabba's Mussels in Wine Sauce

If you like restaurant-quality mussels, you will enjoy this recipe from Carrabba's.

INGREDIENTS | SERVES 4

4 cups mussels
2 tablespoons extra-virgin olive oil
2 tablespoons chopped yellow onion
2 cloves minced garlic
1–2 tablespoons chopped fresh basil
Juice of ½ lemon
¾ cup lemon butter sauce (recipe follows)

Lemon Butter Sauce

2 tablespoons clarified butter
2 tablespoons finely chopped yellow onion
2 tablespoons finely chopped garlic
6 tablespoons fresh lemon juice
2 tablespoons dry white wine
Salt, to taste
White pepper, to taste
2 tablespoons cold butter

1. Soak mussels in cold water for several minutes, then scrub with a stiff brush and remove any little tuft of fibers protruding from the shell, either with a sharp knife or by pulling on it with a damp cloth. Rinse mussels again in cold water.

2. Heat olive oil in a 10" skillet and add mussels. Cover with another 10" skillet or lid and cook until shells begin to open, about 2 minutes.

3. Remove top, add onion and garlic, and toss. Cover pan again and cook for 1 minute.

4. To clarify the butter: Melt ½ stick butter over low heat. When melted, remove from heat and set aside for several minutes to allow the milk solids to settle to the bottom. Skim the clear butter from the top and discard sediment.

5. Remove top and add basil, lemon juice, and lemon butter sauce. Return to flame for 30–45 seconds with top off skillet. Discard any mussels that did not open. Serve in a deep bowl.

Little Caesars Crazy Sauce

This sauce can be used over pasta or for dipping bread sticks.

INGREDIENTS | **YIELDS 1½ CUPS**

1 (15-ounce) can tomato paste
½ teaspoon salt
¼ teaspoon pepper
¼ teaspoon garlic powder
¼ teaspoon dried basil
¼ teaspoon dried marjoram
¼ teaspoon dried oregano
¼ teaspoon ground thyme

1. Combine all the ingredients in an uncovered saucepan over medium heat.
2. When the sauce begins to bubble, reduce the heat.
3. Simmer for 30 minutes, stirring often.
4. Remove the sauce from the heat and let it cool.

Olive Garden Capellini Pomodoro

This simple recipe uses traditional Italian ingredients to make a chunky red sauce that is served over angel hair pasta.

INGREDIENTS | SERVES 2

⅓ cup extra-virgin olive oil
2 cloves minced garlic
2 pounds seeded and diced plum tomatoes
¼ teaspoon pepper
12 ounces cooked dry angel hair pasta
2 tablespoons minced fresh basil leaves
½ cup Parmesan cheese

1. Heat olive oil in a skillet over medium heat. Add garlic and cook for 2–3 minutes until the garlic turns white.

2. Add tomatoes and pepper. Heat the dish for about 2–3 minutes. Tomatoes should not lose their shape.

3. Remove from heat. Transfer hot pasta to large bowl. Toss pasta gently with tomato mixture, basil, and half of Parmesan.

4. Serve immediately with the remaining Parmesan.

Grating Cheese and Storing Sauces

To prevent the cheese from sticking to the grater, spray the grater with cooking spray. Most homemade Italian sauces can be refrigerated for about 1 week in a covered container and last up to 6 months in the freezer.

Olive Garden Chicken Milanese

Olive Garden serves this dish with a creamy spinach sauce over pasta.

INGREDIENTS | SERVES 4

4 boneless, skinless chicken breasts
3 large eggs
¼ cup milk
1 cup Panko breadcrumbs
½ cup grated Parmesan cheese
3 teaspoons chopped fresh parsley
1½ teaspoons Italian seasoning
¼ teaspoon black pepper
1 tablespoon chopped garlic
½ cup flour
½ cup unsalted butter
4 cloves garlic, minced
¼ cup flour
1 cup white wine
1 cup chicken broth
1 cup heavy cream
1 cup grated Parmesan cheese
¼ teaspoon black pepper, to taste
½ teaspoon salt
8 halved cherry tomatoes
¼ cup chopped spinach
4 tablespoons extra-virgin olive oil
1 (20-ounce) package cooked tortelloni or tortellini
4 lemon wedges
8 roasted garlic cloves
Chopped parsley, for garnish

1. Flatten the chicken breasts between 2 sheets of plastic wrap by pounding gently until chicken is approximately ½" thick.

2. In a flat-bottom bowl, whisk the eggs and milk together.

3. Mix breadcrumbs, cheese, parsley, Italian seasoning, and pepper. Transfer to a flat plate.

4. Dredge the chicken in flour, coating both sides. Dip chicken pieces in egg mixture, coating both sides. Dredge in breadcrumb mixture, coating completely on both sides. Set aside.

5. Melt the butter in sauce pan over medium heat. Add minced garlic and sauté for 1 minute. Add flour and stir well until blended.

6. Add the wine, broth, cream, and cheese and bring to a boil. Reduce heat and simmer for 5 minutes until mixture starts to thicken. Add roasted garlic, pepper, and salt. Stir until well blended.

7. Add tomatoes and spinach to sauce and allow to simmer over low heat for about 5 minutes, stirring frequently.

8. Heat olive oil in a frying pan over medium-high heat. Add the breaded chicken to the pan and cook for 3–4 minutes per side until both sides are golden brown.

9. Add pasta to sauce and blend well.

10. Transfer chicken to a large platter and garnish with the parsley and lemon wedges. Serve with the pasta.

Olive Garden Chicken Scampi

Scampi refers to meat or seafood that is grilled or sautéed in oil or butter and garlic.

INGREDIENTS | SERVES 4

White Sauce
1 tablespoon butter
2 tablespoons flour
¾ cup milk

Scampi Sauce
3 tablespoons butter
2 tablespoons crushed garlic
2 teaspoons Italian seasoning
½ teaspoon crushed red pepper
Black pepper, to taste
¾ cup white wine
1 cup chicken broth

Other
2 sliced chicken breasts
Olive oil
1 green pepper, thinly sliced
1 red onion, thinly sliced
10 cloves roasted garlic (see below)
½ package cooked angel hair pasta

1. To create the white sauce, heat butter in a sauce pan and add the flour. Cook for 2 minutes on medium heat, stirring constantly. Slowly add the milk and cook for 3–4 minutes. Set aside.

2. To create the scampi sauce, heat butter over low heat. Add the garlic, Italian seasoning, red pepper, and black pepper. Cook for about 2 minutes on low heat. Add the wine and chicken broth and stir until combined.

3. Add ¼ cup of the white sauce to the scampi sauce and cook for 5 minutes until slightly thickened.

4. Sauté the chicken in a large skillet with a little olive oil. Add the peppers and onions. Sauté for 3–4 minutes until the chicken is done.

5. Add the sauce and sauté until everything is warmed. Add the roasted garlic cloves.

6. Serve over hot pasta.

Roasting Garlic

For the roasted garlic, separate the head of the garlic into individual cloves still in the paper. Toss in olive oil, wrap tightly in aluminum foil, and bake in a 350°F oven for 45 minutes. When the garlic has cooled to the touch, you should be able to squeeze it out of the paper shell of the individual cloves.

Olive Garden Penne Romana

The penne alla romana is a lovely dish of pasta and green beans in a light broth-based sauce.

INGREDIENTS | SERVES 4

½ cup extra-virgin olive oil
¾ cup diced yellow onion
½ teaspoon crushed red pepper
1 tablespoon minced fresh garlic
2 cups white wine
2 teaspoons chopped fresh rosemary
1 tablespoon chopped fresh parsley
½ teaspoon salt
1½ tablespoons cornstarch
2 cups chicken broth
2 cups blanched green beans
1 cup diced tomato
4 cups cooked penne pasta
3 tablespoons grated fresh Romano cheese
3 tablespoons grated fresh Parmesan cheese

1. Heat the oil in a small saucepan over medium-high heat.
2. Add onions and red pepper. Cook until soft, about 5 minutes, stirring frequently.
3. Add minced garlic and cook for 1 minute. Whisk in wine, rosemary, parsley, and salt.
4. In separate bowl, whisk cornstarch and chicken broth.
5. Add mixture to sauce and stir well. Bring to a boil and set aside.
6. Heat a sauté pan over medium-high heat. Add green beans and tomato and cook for 1 minute.
7. Add the sauce and pasta. Add the cheeses. Stir well with a spoon, making sure the pasta is well coated.

Olive Garden Tuscan Garlic Chicken

This is one of Olive Garden's most popular dishes and was inspired by recipes from the heart of Italy.

INGREDIENTS | SERVES 4

1½ cups flour plus 1 tablespoon
1 tablespoon salt
2 teaspoons black pepper
2 teaspoons Italian seasoning
4 (4-ounce) boneless, skinless chicken breasts
5 divided tablespoons olive oil
1 tablespoon chopped garlic
1 julienned red pepper
½ cup white wine
½ pound stemmed whole-leaf spinach
2 cups heavy cream
1 cup divided grated Parmesan cheese
1 pound fettuccine pasta

1. Mix the 1½ cups flour, salt, pepper, and Italian seasoning in a shallow dish. Dredge chicken in the mixture, shaking off any excess.

2. Heat 3 tablespoons of oil in a large skillet. Cook chicken breasts 2 at a time over medium-high heat for about 2–3 minutes, until golden brown and crisp. Add more oil for each batch as necessary.

3. Place cooked chicken breasts on a baking sheet and transfer to a 350°F oven. Cook for 10–15 minutes, or until internal temperature reaches 165°F.

4. Heat 2 tablespoons of oil in a saucepan. Add garlic and red pepper and cook for approximately 1 minute.

5. Stir in 1 tablespoon flour, wine, spinach, and cream and bring to a boil. Sauce is done when spinach becomes wilted (about 1–2 minutes). Complete by stirring in Parmesan cheese.

6. Coat the pasta with sauce, then top with chicken and remaining sauce. Garnish with extra Parmesan cheese.

Olive Garden Venetian Apricot Chicken

Olive Garden is known for their seasonal menus, and this is one of their most recent additions to the menu.

INGREDIENTS | SERVES 4

- 3 teaspoons garlic pepper
- 1 teaspoon Italian seasoning
- ½ cup chicken broth
- ½ cup apricot preserves
- Salt and pepper, to taste
- ½ pound Roma tomatoes, cut into 1" pieces
- 6 basil leaves, cut into ½" pieces
- 1 teaspoon garlic pepper
- Salt, to taste
- 1 bunch asparagus, bottom 1" of stems removed
- ½ pound broccoli florets
- 1 tablespoon extra-virgin olive oil
- 4 boneless, skinless chicken breasts
- Chopped parsley, to garnish

1. Combine garlic pepper and Italian seasoning in a small mixing bowl and set aside.

2. In a saucepan, blend chicken broth and apricot preserves. Add salt and pepper to taste. Bring to a boil and remove from heat.

3. In another mixing bowl, combine tomatoes, basil, garlic pepper, and salt and set aside.

4. In a pot of salted boiling water, blanch asparagus and broccoli for 1 minute. Transfer immediately to ice bath to stop cooking.

5. Coat a sauté pan with 1 tablespoon olive oil. While keeping ingredients separated in pan, heat cooled asparagus, broccoli, and tomato mixture until hot, about 2–3 minutes. Do not overcook.

6. Grill the chicken 5 minutes per side until done.

7. Place the grilled chicken on a platter next to the broccoli and asparagus. Sprinkle the garlic seasoning mixture on the broccoli. Pour the tomato mixture on top of the vegetables.

8. Top the chicken breasts with apricot sauce and garnish with chopped parsley.

Papa John's Garlic Sauce

If you love dipping your pizza crust in Papa John's garlic sauce, then you will love this easy recipe to recreate at home.

INGREDIENTS | YIELDS ½ CUP

½ stick margarine
¼ teaspoon salt
½ teaspoon garlic powder

1. Melt margarine in the microwave for about 30 seconds.
2. Add salt and garlic powder to taste.
3. Microwave the mixture for 5 seconds longer.

Pizza Hut Cavatini

Cavatini has been off the menu at Pizza Hut for a long time, so the only way to get this dish is to make it yourself.

INGREDIENTS | SERVES 4

½ stick margarine
1 diced large onion
1 diced large green bell pepper
1 teaspoon garlic powder
1 pound assorted pasta (wheels, shells, spirals, ziti)
1 (16-ounce) jar meat-flavored spaghetti sauce
½ pound browned hamburger
½ pound browned Italian sausage
½ pound thinly sliced pepperoni
1 cup shredded mozzarella cheese

1. Preheat oven to 350°F.
2. In a skillet, melt the margarine over medium-high heat. Add onions, peppers, and garlic powder and sauté for about 4 minutes. Meanwhile, cook pasta according to box directions.
3. Heat sauce and combine with hamburger and sausage.
4. Use cooking spray to lightly grease a 13" × 11" casserole dish. Place ½ of the cooked pasta in the dish, followed by ½ the vegetables, ½ of the pepperoni, and ½ the sauce. Repeat with another layer.
5. Spread mozzarella cheese over the top and bake for about 45 minutes, or until cheese has melted.

Pizza Hut Stuffed Crust Pizza

Here is a quick and easy way to make stuffed crust pizza like Pizza Hut, using ready-made refrigerated pizza dough and string cheese.

INGREDIENTS | SERVES 4–6

1 (13.8-ounce) can of refrigerated pizza dough
7 pieces of string cheese
Olive oil, for brushing
½ cup marinara sauce
2 cups shredded pizza cheese
24 slices pepperoni

1. Preheat the oven to 425°F.
2. Roll out the dough on a floured surface until it's 18" across. Put on a greased pan.
3. Poke the dough several times with a fork to prevent bubbling.
4. Place a ring of string cheese end to end all the way around the edge of the dough.
5. Fold the dough over the cheese and press firmly. Brush the top of the folded dough with olive oil.
6. Cover with sauce, cheese, and pepperoni.
7. Bake for 12–16 minutes, until the crust turns brown and the cheese has melted.

Romano's Macaroni Grill Carmela's Chicken

Carmela's chicken features rigatoni pasta with a Parmesan cream sauce.

INGREDIENTS | SERVES 4

6 ounces butter-flavored oil
8 ounces mushrooms
12 ounces grilled chicken
2 teaspoons basil
¾ cup caramelized onions
Salt and pepper, to taste
¾ cup cooking wine
1 (16-ounce) container heavy cream
1 (16-ounce) box rigatoni pasta
¼ cup Parmesan cheese
Parsley, for garnish

1. In a hot sauté pan, add butter-flavored oil, mushrooms, chicken, basil, onions, salt, and pepper and sauté for approximately 60–90 seconds.

2. Add the wine and sauté for 60 seconds. Add the cream and bring to a boil over high heat.

3. Dip precooked pasta in boiling water for 10 seconds and drain thoroughly.

4. Add the pasta to the sauté pan and sauté for 3–4 minutes until well incorporated. Toss briefly over the fire, add Parmesan cheese, and continue to toss until cheese is completely incorporated.

5. Transfer to a plate and garnish with parsley.

Romano's Macaroni Grill Penne Rustica

This is a wonderful dish combining 3 meats and pasta in a savory cream sauce. Serve with a salad and bread sticks.

INGREDIENTS | SERVES 4–6

Granita Sauce
2 tablespoons butter
2 tablespoons chopped garlic
1 teaspoon chopped rosemary
1 cup Marsala wine
1 tablespoon Dijon mustard
1 teaspoon salt
¼ teaspoon cayenne pepper
8 cups heavy cream

Penne Rustica
1 ounce pancetta or bacon
¾ cup butter
1 tablespoon chopped shallots
18 peeled and deveined shrimp
12 ounces sliced grilled chicken breast
Pinch of salt and pepper
4½ cups of Granita Sauce
1 cup Parmesan cheese
48 ounces penne pasta, precooked
3 tablespoons pimentos
½ teaspoon paprika
4–6 sprigs fresh rosemary, for garnish

1. To make the Granita Sauce, sauté butter, garlic, and rosemary for 2–3 minutes until garlic begins to brown.

2. Add the wine and reduce by one-third (about 5 minutes).

3. Add the remaining ingredients and cook for 5 minutes until mixture has reduced by half of original volume. Set aside.

4. Preheat oven to 475°F.

5. Sauté pancetta for 6 minutes until it begins to brown. Add butter, shallots, and shrimp. Cook until shrimp are evenly pink but still translucent, about 3–4 minutes.

6. Add the chicken, salt, and pepper and mix thoroughly. Add Granita Sauce and ½ cup of Parmesan cheese and simmer for 5 minutes until sauce thickens.

7. In a large bowl, combine shrimp and chicken mixture with pasta. Place onto single serving dishes or one large casserole dish.

8. Top with remaining cheese and pimentos and sprinkle with paprika. Bake in the oven for 10–15 minutes.

9. Remove and garnish with fresh rosemary sprigs.

Romano's Macaroni Grill Shrimp Portofino

This is a quick recipe that can be served over rice or pasta.

INGREDIENTS | SERVES 4

16 medium mushrooms
2 teaspoons chopped garlic
½ cup melted butter
16 large cleaned shrimp
½ teaspoon pepper
¼ cup fresh lemon juice
1 (7.5-ounce) jar marinated artichoke hearts
4 slices lemon
2 tablespoons parsley

1. Sauté the mushrooms and garlic in butter for 2–3 minutes until tender. Add shrimp and sauté about 3 minutes.

2. Add the remaining ingredients except lemon and parsley and heat for 5 minutes.

3. Garnish with lemon slices and parsley.

CHAPTER 12

Family Style

Boston Market
Creamed Spinach
210

Boston Market Dill
Potato Wedges
210

Boston Market Macaroni
and Cheese
211

Boston Market Meatloaf
212

Boston Market Squash Casserole
213

Boston Market Stuffing
214

Boston Market
Sweet Potato Casserole
215

Boston Market Whole
Rotisserie Chicken
216

Cheesecake Factory Crab Cakes
217

Dave and Buster's
Cheeseburger Pizza
218

Hometown Buffet
Spinach Casserole
219

KFC Barbecue Baked Beans
220

KFC Corn
220

KFC Coleslaw
221

KFC Macaroni Salad
221

KFC Mashed Potatoes
and Gravy
222

KFC Potato Salad
223

KFC Potato Wedges
223

Shoney's Broccoli Casserole
224

Shoney's Pot Roast
225

Boston Market Creamed Spinach

This is a great side dish—even people who hate spinach love this recipe.

INGREDIENTS | SERVES 6

2 (10-ounce) boxes frozen chopped spinach
1 (10-ounce) can cream of celery soup
1 tablespoon flour
4 tablespoons butter
½ teaspoon garlic salt
Salt and pepper, to taste
1 small diced onion

1. Cook the spinach in the microwave on high for 5 minutes. Drain and pat dry.

2. In a saucepan on medium heat, stir together the soup, flour, butter, garlic salt, salt, and pepper until smooth and hot (about 5 minutes).

3. Add the spinach and onion and heat for 5–7 minutes.

Boston Market Dill Potato Wedges

Spring is the perfect time to make this dish since it uses new red potatoes.

INGREDIENTS | SERVES 8

7 or 8 new red potatoes
¼ pound butter
2 cloves minced garlic
½ teaspoon salt
½ teaspoon black pepper
½ teaspoon celery salt
2 teaspoons dried dill weed

1. Wash potatoes well and boil for 8–10 minutes until barely soft.

2. Drain and cut in wedges.

3. Melt the butter in a large frying pan and sauté garlic for about 1 minute.

4. Add the potatoes and the rest of the seasonings.

5. Fry the potatoes for 5 minutes until they are lightly brown.

Boston Market Macaroni and Cheese

Macaroni and cheese is always a family favorite, sure to please the little ones in your family.

INGREDIENTS | SERVES 4–6

6 ounces dry spiral pasta
4 tablespoons butter
1 tablespoon minced onion
¼ cup flour
2 cups milk
1 cup Velveeta cheese
1 teaspoon salt
Dash pepper
¼ teaspoon dry mustard

1. Preheat oven to 400°F.
2. Cook pasta according to instructions, drain, and set aside.
3. To make the cheese sauce, melt butter in a saucepan and add onion and flour. Allow this to cook for about 5 minutes and when thickened, slowly add the milk. When all the milk is added, add the cheese.
4. Add salt, pepper, and dry mustard. When the cheese melts, add pasta.
5. Lightly butter a casserole dish and add pasta mixture. Bake for 20 minutes.

Boston Market Meatloaf

This is an easy recipe for a classic comfort food. Serve with mashed potatoes and some country green beans for a full meal.

INGREDIENTS | SERVES 8

1 cup tomato sauce
1½ tablespoons barbecue sauce
1 tablespoon sugar
1½ pounds ground beef
6 tablespoons flour
¾ teaspoon salt
½ teaspoon onion powder
¼ teaspoon ground black pepper
Dash garlic powder

Leftover Meatloaf

If you don't enjoy eating the same meal more than once and you find yourself with too much meatloaf, you can turn it into another dish by adding it into chili, shepherd's pie, casseroles, sloppy joes, patty melts, tacos, or spaghetti sauce.

1. Preheat oven to 400°F.
2. In a small saucepan over medium heat, combine the tomato sauce, barbecue sauce, and sugar. Heat for 5 minutes until it begins to bubble, stirring often. Remove from heat.
3. In a large bowl, add all but 2 tablespoons of the tomato sauce to the meat.
4. Combine the remaining ingredients with the ground beef. Use a wooden spoon or your hands to work the spices and sauce into the meat.
5. Place the meat into a loaf pan. Wrap foil over the pan and bake for 30 minutes.
6. After 30 minutes, take the meatloaf from the oven, remove the foil, and drain the fat.
7. Slice the meatloaf all the way through into 8 slices while it is still in the pan. This will help to cook the center of the meatloaf.
8. Pour the remaining 2 tablespoons of sauce over the top of the meatloaf in a stream down the center. Don't spread the sauce.
9. Place the meatloaf back into the oven, uncovered, for 25–30 minutes.

Boston Market Squash Casserole

Tender squash and gooey cheese make this a memorable side dish or a hearty main course.

INGREDIENTS | SERVES 6–8

1 (8.5-ounce) box Jiffy corn muffin mix
4½ cups diced zucchini
4½ cups diced yellow squash
1½ sticks butter
1½ cups chopped sweet onion
3 chicken bouillon cubes
1 teaspoon minced garlic
1 teaspoon salt
½ teaspoon ground pepper
½ teaspoon thyme
1 tablespoon chopped parsley
8 ounces diced Velveeta cheese

1. Preheat oven to 350°F.
2. Prepare Jiffy mix as directed and set aside to cool.
3. Place zucchini and squash in a large sauce pan and add just enough water to cover. Cook on medium-low heat for 5–7 minutes till tender. Remove from heat. Drain and reserve 1 cup of water for casserole.
4. In a large saucepan over medium-low heat, melt the butter and sauté the onion for 2–3 minutes until it turns clear.
5. Add bouillon cubes and garlic to onion and stir. Add squash, salt, pepper, thyme, parsley and cheese. Stir again.
6. Crumble corn bread into squash, add the reserved cup of water, and mix well. Place mixture in a 9" × 13" baking pan that has been sprayed with nonstick spray.
7. Cover the casserole and bake for 50–60 minutes. Remove cover the last 20 minutes of baking time.

Boston Market Stuffing

This is a basic bread stuffing recipe that would go well as a side dish with rotisserie chicken.

INGREDIENTS | SERVES 6–8

1 (10-ounce) can sliced carrots
1 (4-ounce) can sliced mushrooms
1 (14-ounce) can chicken broth
2 thickly chopped celery ribs
1 tablespoon sage
12 teaspoons poultry seasoning
1 tablespoon chicken bouillon powder
3 tablespoons melted margarine
3 English muffins
1 (8-ounce) bag unseasoned croutons
1 tablespoon parsley
2 tablespoons minced onion

1. Preheat the oven to 350°F.

2. When you open the can of carrots, run the blade of a small knife through them right in the can so that you've reduced them to tiny bits without mashing them. Empty the carrots and mushrooms with their juices into a Dutch oven.

3. Empty the can of broth into a blender and add the celery, sage, poultry seasoning, bouillon powder, and margarine. Blend a few seconds on high speed, only until celery is finely minced.

4. Slice the English muffin into cubes. Add the cubes, croutons, parsley, and onion to the Dutch oven. Pour the blender mixture over and stir to combine until completely moist.

5. Cover with a lid and bake 45 minutes to 1 hour, or until hot.

Boston Market Sweet Potato Casserole

This scrumptious sweet potato casserole gets its fabulous flavor from a sweet crunchy topping.

INGREDIENTS | SERVES 4–6

Potatoes
3 large sweet potatoes
1 cup sugar
2 eggs
1 stick butter, softened

Crunch Topping
1 teaspoon vanilla extract
⅓ cup melted butter
⅓ cup flour
1 cup brown sugar
1 cup chopped pecans
1 tablespoon cinnamon

1. Preheat the oven to 350°F.
2. Boil potatoes for 12–15 minutes until tender. Remove skins when cooled. Put into a large bowl.
3. Add the sugar, eggs, and butter and whip until fluffy.
4. Pour the mixture into a greased casserole dish.
5. In a separate bowl, combine all the ingredients for the crunch topping. Add to the top of the casserole.
6. Bake for 45 minutes.

Boston Market Whole Rotisserie Chicken

Ever wish you could get that restaurant-style rotisserie chicken at home? Now you can with this recipe.

INGREDIENTS | SERVES 6–8

1 (3½ pound) whole chicken
4–6 unpeeled apple wedges
4–6 onion chunks
10 chunks celery
¼ cup vegetable oil
1 tablespoon honey
1 tablespoon lime juice
¼ teaspoon paprika
Seasoned salt, to taste

1. Preheat oven to 350°F.

2. Fill the cavity of the chicken with apple, onions, and celery. Place in a roasting pan deep enough that it can later be sealed with foil without the foil touching the skin of the chicken.

3. Mix vegetable oil, honey, lime juice, paprika, and seasoned salt in a saucepan and warm just enough to melt the honey. Brush the sauce on the skin of the chicken.

4. Bake for 1 hour plus 15–30 minutes, depending on the size of the chicken, basting chicken without turning 3 or 4 times during baking, or until nicely browned.

5. Seal baking dish tightly in foil immediately upon removing from oven and let stand 15–20 minutes before serving.

Cheesecake Factory Crab Cakes

These delicious crab cakes are easy to prepare and will be a hit with family and guests. They are great as a main dish or appetizer.

INGREDIENTS | SERVES 6

½ pound lump crabmeat
3 tablespoons plain breadcrumbs
2 tablespoons mayonnaise
2 tablespoons minced green onions
2 tablespoons minced red bell peppers
½ beaten egg
1 teaspoon minced fresh parsley
1 teaspoon Old Bay Seasoning
½ teaspoon prepared yellow mustard
¼ cup Panko bread crumbs
Vegetable oil for frying

1. In a large bowl, add all the ingredients except the breadcrumbs and vegetable oil. Carefully fold the ingredients together. Be sure not to overstir or the lumps of crab will fall apart.

2. Use your hands or a spoon to fill 6 cups of a clean muffin tin with equal amounts of the crab mixture. Press down a bit on each so the top is flat. Don't press too hard or the crab cakes will be hard to get out of the pan.

3. Cover the muffin tin with plastic wrap and put in the refrigerator for a couple of hours. This will help the cakes stay together when they're browned in the oil.

4. After the crab cakes have chilled through, in a large skillet over medium-low, heat about ¼" of vegetable oil.

5. Fill a shallow bowl with the breadcrumbs. Carefully turn the crab cakes out onto a plate. Gently roll each cake around in the breadcrumbs.

6. Test the oil by dropping a pinch of breadcrumbs into the pan. It should sizzle.

7. Sauté the crab cakes in the hot oil for 1½–3 minutes on each side, or until the cakes are golden brown.

8. Drain on paper towels.

Dave and Buster's Cheeseburger Pizza

The cheeseburger pizza is a strange yet very popular hybrid of a cheeseburger and a pizza.

INGREDIENTS | YIELDS 1 PIZZA

1 (13.8-ounce) can of refrigerated pizza dough
1 tablespoon cornmeal
2 tablespoons olive oil
3 tablespoons ketchup
3 tablespoons mustard
¾ cup shredded Cheddar cheese
2 diced grilled hamburgers
2 tablespoons julienned kosher pickle slices
2 tablespoons sliced red onions
½ cup shredded mozzarella cheese

Toppings

1 tablespoon spicy ketchup
1 tablespoon real crispy bacon bits
½ cup shredded lettuce
2 slices tomatoes
2 tablespoons diced onions

1. Preheat the oven to 450°F.
2. Dip the pizza dough in flour and roll out to form a 10"–11" circle. Place on a pan that has been lightly dusted with cornmeal.
3. Brush the top of the pizza with olive oil.
4. In a small bowl, mix the ketchup and mustard together. Spread the mixture over the dough almost to the edges. Place the Cheddar cheese evenly over the pizza.
5. Add the burger, pickles, red onions, and mozzarella.
6. Bake for about 12–15 minutes.
7. When the pizza is done, remove from the oven. Place the spicy ketchup, bacon bits, lettuce, tomatoes, and onions evenly over the pizza.

Dave and Buster's

Dave and Buster's is a full-service restaurant with a midway full of carnival games, high-tech entertainment, and old, popular video arcade games. Their motto is "Escape to play," and they offer an "eat and play" deal for around $16.

Hometown Buffet Spinach Casserole

If you can't get your family to eat their spinach, try this creamy and cheesy casserole recipe.

INGREDIENTS | SERVES 4–6

1 (10-ounce) package frozen chopped spinach
4 eggs
¼ teaspoon salt
⅛ teaspoon pepper
2¾ cups heavy cream
2 cups shredded mild Cheddar cheese
1 cup fine dry breadcrumbs
1–2 teaspoons paprika
2 tablespoons butter

1. Preheat oven to 375°F.
2. Grease a medium-size casserole dish.
3. Thaw and drain the spinach.
4. In a mixing bowl, beat the eggs. Add salt, pepper, and cream. Stir in the spinach and cheese.
5. Pour into dish. Top with ¼–1 cup of the breadcrumbs and sprinkle generously with paprika. Dot the top butter.
6. Bake for 35–40 minutes.

Hometown Buffet

Hometown Buffet operates over 150 restaurants with other names like Country Buffet and Old Country Buffet. The menu on any given day contains over 100 items, including desserts and a large variety of side dishes made in small batches for every meal.

KFC Barbecue Baked Beans

This recipe gives a wonderful old-fashioned flavor to the beans.

INGREDIENTS | SERVES 6–8

2 (15-ounce) cans small white beans
2 tablespoons water
1 tablespoon cornstarch
½ cup ketchup
½ cup dark brown sugar
2 teaspoons white vinegar
4 teaspoons minced fresh onion
2 pieces cooked bacon
½ teaspoon dry mustard
¼ teaspoon salt
Dash pepper
Dash garlic powder

1. Preheat the oven to 350°F.
2. Pour the beans, including juices, into a covered casserole dish.
3. In a small bowl, combine the water with the cornstarch until the cornstarch dissolves. Stir mixture into the beans.
4. Stir the remaining ingredients into the beans and cover the dish.
5. Bake for 90 minutes, until the sauce thickens, stirring every 30 minutes. Let the beans sit for 5–10 minutes before serving.

KFC Corn

Learn how to cook corn on the cob with this simple recipe that is a terrific side dish.

INGREDIENTS | SERVES 6

1 (12-count) package of frozen corn on the cob
Stick of butter
½ teaspoon salt
½ teaspoon sugar
¼ teaspoon pepper

1. Cook the corn in hot salted water with a dash of milk until tender, about 10 minutes.
2. When it is done, roll the corn in butter and sprinkle with the seasonings.

KFC Coleslaw

What is it about KFC coleslaw that makes you want to go back for more? Now you can make it at home with this recipe.

INGREDIENTS | SERVES 10–12

⅓ cup sugar
½ teaspoon salt
⅛ teaspoon pepper
¼ cup milk
½ cup mayonnaise
¼ cup buttermilk
1½ tablespoons white vinegar
2½ tablespoons lemon juice
1 head finely chopped cabbage
1 finely chopped medium carrot
2 tablespoons minced onion

1. In a large bowl, combine the sugar, salt, pepper, milk, mayonnaise, buttermilk, vinegar, and lemon juice and beat until smooth.

2. Add the cabbage, carrot, and onion and mix well.

3. Cover and refrigerate for at least 2 hours before serving.

KFC Macaroni Salad

This is a salad that everyone seems to love. You can double or triple this recipe to make enough for a crowd.

INGREDIENTS | SERVES 6–8

8 ounces cooked elbow macaroni
2 stalks finely minced celery
1 tablespoon dry minced onion
⅓ cup diced sweet pickles
1½ cups Miracle Whip
½ cup mayonnaise
¼ teaspoon black pepper
¼ teaspoon dry mustard
1 teaspoon sugar
Salt, to taste

1. Combine all the ingredients into a large mixing bowl with a lid.

2. Refrigerate salad tightly covered several hours before serving.

KFC Mashed Potatoes and Gravy

Gravy is another immensely popular item in the KFC menu. It has a distinct taste and is liked by many people around the world.

INGREDIENTS | SERVES 4–6

Potatoes
2½ cups hot water
2 tablespoons butter
½ cup margarine
1 teaspoon salt
2½ cups Idaho potato flakes
¾ cup milk

Gravy
1½ tablespoons melted shortening
3 tablespoons bread flour
2 tablespoons all-purpose flour
1 (10-ounce) can condensed chicken stock
1 (10-ounce) can-full of water
¼ teaspoon salt
⅛ teaspoon Accent seasoning
⅛ teaspoon ground black pepper
2 chicken bouillon cubes
1 (10-ounce) jar Franco-American beef gravy
Pinch ground sage

1. Heat the water for the potatoes. Add the butter and margarine.

2. Add the salt and cook for 2 minutes. Add the potato flakes and mix till it looks like regular potatoes. Add milk to get the proper consistency.

3. For the gravy, prepare a roux with the shortening and 1½ tablespoons bread flour. Cook this over low heat for about 5 minutes until the roux browns in color to resemble a nice milk chocolate color.

4. Once the mixture turns brown, remove it from the heat and add the remaining flour, then slowly add the liquids and other ingredients so no lumps form.

5. Bring to a boil and boil for 2 minutes. Reduce the heat and allow the mixture to thicken. Serve gravy over mashed potatoes.

KFC

Colonel Sanders founded Kentucky Fried Chicken in 1952 with his secret recipe of 11 herbs and spices used to flavor the fried chicken. Under pressure from a lawsuit, the company stopped using trans fats in the cooking oil and now offers lower-calorie grilled chicken.

KFC Potato Salad

Here's a simple clone for the potato salad that is purchased as a side dish from America's largest fast food chicken chain.

INGREDIENTS | SERVES 8

2 pounds russet potatoes
1 cup mayonnaise
4 teaspoons sweet pickle relish
4 teaspoons sugar
2 teaspoons minced white onion
2 teaspoons prepared mustard
1 teaspoon vinegar
1 teaspoon minced celery
1 teaspoon diced pimentos
½ teaspoon shredded carrot
¼ teaspoon dried parsley
¼ teaspoon pepper
Dash salt

1. Peel the potatoes and chop them into bite-size pieces. Boil in 6 cups of salted water for 7–10 minutes. The chunks should be tender, yet slightly tough in the middle when done. Drain and rinse with cold water.

2. In a medium bowl, combine remaining ingredients and whisk until smooth.

3. Put potatoes in a large bowl. Pour the dressing over the potatoes and mix until well combined.

4. Cover and chill for at least 4 hours; overnight is best.

KFC Potato Wedges

KFC lightly batters their potato wedges and seasons them with savory herbs and spices for a full flavor.

INGREDIENTS | SERVES 4–6

Oil, for frying
5 baking potatoes
1 egg
1 cup milk
1 cup flour
2 tablespoons salt
1 teaspoon pepper
¼ teaspoon paprika
Dash garlic powder

1. Preheat oil in a deep fryer to 375°F.

2. Cut the potatoes into 16–18 equal-size wedges.

3. In a large bowl, mix the egg and milk until well blended. In another large bowl, mix the dry ingredients.

4. Put some of the potato wedges in the milk and egg then into the flour mixture until well coated.

5. Fry for 3 minutes, remove from the oil, allow them to sit for 1 minute, then cook them again for 5 minutes. Do not overcrowd the potatoes; fry in small batches.

Shoney's Broccoli Casserole

This dish is favorite vegetable and cheese combination that can be made in 30 minutes.

INGREDIENTS | SERVES 6–8

2 eggs
6 cups coarsely chopped broccoli florets
3 cups cooked rice
½ teaspoon salt
½ teaspoon black pepper
1¼ pounds Velveeta cheese
3 cups half-and-half
1 cup crushed Ritz crackers
1 cup shredded Cheddar cheese

Shoney's

Shoney's is a restaurant chain operating mostly in the southern states, with a fairly basic dinner menu for the budget-conscience family. One of the most popular features is that they serve breakfast all day and put out a large breakfast buffet.

1. Preheat oven to 350°F.

2. Place eggs in mixing bowl and lightly whip for approximately 20 seconds.

3. Add broccoli, rice, salt, and pepper. Mix well to incorporate ingredients.

4. Dice Velveeta into ¼" pieces. Place cheese and half-and-half in microwave-safe container, cover, and microwave for 2 minutes, or until cheese is melted. Add to ingredients in bowl. Blend well to mix all ingredients.

5. Spray a medium baking dish with cooking spray.

6. Pour casserole mixture into the pan and bake for 30 minutes.

7. Top the casserole with Ritz crackers and Cheddar cheese and cook for 5 minutes more, or until cheese melts and crackers brown.

Shoney's Pot Roast

Shoney's makes a wonderful pot roast, and the leftovers are great for sandwiches.

INGREDIENTS | SERVES 8–10

3 pounds trimmed rump roast
2 tablespoons butter or margarine
2 stalks chopped celery
1 large chopped onion
3 cloves minced garlic
½ teaspoon dried parsley
½ tablespoon dried thyme
2 cups beef broth
20 whole peppercorns
1 whole bay leaf
½ tablespoon salt
2 sliced carrots
2 peeled and cubed potatoes
½ teaspoon salt
⅓ cup flour

1. Preheat oven to 325°F.
2. Brown roast in butter in Dutch oven and remove.
3. Sauté celery, onion, garlic, parsley, and thyme in Dutch oven for 5 minutes, then return meat to Dutch oven.
4. Add the broth, peppercorns, bay leaf, and salt. Bake with the lid on for 4 hours, basting every ½ hour. Remove the roast from the Dutch oven.
5. Strain stock into a bowl. Discard the vegetables and spices. Using 2 forks, shred the roast into bite-size pieces. Pour reserved stock over beef in Dutch oven.
6. Add carrots, potatoes, and salt to the Dutch oven and bake for 45 minutes.
7. Drain stock from the Dutch oven and add enough beef broth to make 3 cups. Whisk stock and flour together in a saucepan and simmer until thick.
8. Pour the gravy over the meat and vegetables.

CHAPTER 13

Southern Style

Boston Market Corn Bread
228

Cheesecake Factory
Jambalaya Pasta
229

Cracker Barrel Baby Carrots
230

Cracker Barrel Corn
Bread Dressing
230

Cracker Barrel Country
Green Beans
231

Cracker Barrel Grilled
Chicken Tenders
231

Popeye's Biscuits
232

Popeye's Cajun Gravy
233

Popeye's Dirty Rice
234

Popeye's Fried Chicken
235

Popeye's Red Beans and Rice
236

Ruby Tuesday
New Orleans Seafood
237

Tony Roma's Carolina
Barbecue Sauce
237

Tony Roma's
Corn Fritter Casserole
238

Tony Roma's Maple
Sweet Potatoes
239

Tony Roma's Red Hot
Barbecue Sauce
240

Boston Market Corn Bread

*You'll wonder if this is a corn bread or cake recipe.
This tastes exactly like the dish served at Boston Market*

INGREDIENTS | SERVES 8–10

1 (9-ounce) box corn muffin mix
1 (9-ounce) box yellow cake mix

Boston Market

Boston Market has over 500 restaurants, with a great number of them in the northeastern part of the United States. When it was founded in 1985 it was known as Boston Chicken. The restaurants specialize in rotisserie chickens and a variety of side dishes available to eat in or take out. Their frozen meals can be found in supermarkets nationwide.

1. Preheat the oven to 350°F.
2. In a large mixing bowl, prepare the corn muffin mix according to the directions on the box.
3. In another large mixing bowl, prepare the cake mix according to the directions on the box.
4. Pour the cake mix into the corn muffin mix and stir well.
5. Pour the mixture into a greased 9" × 12" × 2" pan and bake for 30–35 minutes, until a toothpick inserted in the middle comes out clean.

Cheesecake Factory Jambalaya Pasta

This is one of the most popular pasta dishes served at the restaurant chain.

INGREDIENTS | SERVES 4

1 green bell pepper
1 red bell pepper
½ red onion
1 pound boneless, skinless chicken breasts
1 stick of butter
2 teaspoons Cajun spice mix
1 pound linguini pasta
½ cup clam juice
½ pound peeled fresh medium shrimp
½ cup diced tomatoes

1. Slice the peppers and onions into thin strips and cut the chicken into small pieces.

2. Place the butter in a sauté pan and allow it to melt slightly. Add the spice mix and stir together with the butter.

3. Add the chicken and continue to cook for 4 minutes until the chicken is about half done.

4. While the chicken is cooking, cook the pasta until al dente.

5. Pour the clam juice into the pan and add the peppers and onions. Cook for another minute, making sure the vegetables are heated through and the chicken is almost done.

6. Add the shrimp and toss the ingredients together. Continue to cook for 3 minutes until the shrimp are almost done.

7. Add the tomatoes and continue to cook for 5 more minutes until both the shrimp and chicken are thoroughly cooked.

8. Place some pasta into each bowl. Spoon equal portions of the jambalaya mixture over the pasta.

Cracker Barrel Baby Carrots

These glazed carrots make a nice side dish for almost any meal.

INGREDIENTS | SERVES 4

¼ cup butter
1 (1-pound) package washed baby carrots
2 tablespoons water
2 tablespoons brown sugar
¼ teaspoon salt

1. Melt the butter in a saucepan over medium heat.
2. Add the remaining ingredients.
3. Cover and cook on medium-low for 35–40 minutes, stirring twice.

Cracker Barrel Corn Bread Dressing

This southern stuffing is sure to be a hit at your holiday table.

INGREDIENTS | SERVES 16

⅔ cup chopped onion
2 cups chopped celery
8 cups day-old grated corn bread
4 cups day-old grated biscuits
¼ cup dried parsley flakes
2 teaspoons poultry seasoning
2 teaspoons ground sage
1 teaspoon coarse-ground pepper
1 stick melted butter
1 quart plus 1 (14-ounce) can chicken broth

1. Preheat the oven to 400°F.
2. In a large mixing bowl, mix the onion, celery, corn bread, biscuits, parsley, poultry seasoning, sage, and pepper. Add the butter and blend well.
3. Add chicken broth to dry ingredients and mix well. The dressing should have a wet but not soupy consistency, like a quick-bread batter.
4. Divide the mixture evenly into two 8" pans sprayed with nonstick spray. Bake uncovered for 1 hour, or until lightly brown on the top.

Cracker Barrel Country Green Beans

These country-style beans are flavored just the way you like them at Cracker Barrel.

INGREDIENTS | SERVES 8

¼ pound sliced bacon
3 (14½-ounce) cans whole green beans
½ teaspoon salt
1 teaspoon sugar
½ teaspoon black pepper
¼ diced yellow onion

1. In a 2-quart saucepan over medium heat, cook the bacon for 10–12 minutes until lightly brown but not crisp.
2. When the bacon has browned, add the green beans and liquid from the cans. Add salt, sugar, and pepper and mix well.
3. Place onions on top of the green beans. Cover the saucepan with a lid and bring to a light boil.
4. Turn the heat down to low and simmer for 45 minutes.

Cracker Barrel Grilled Chicken Tenders

This is such an easy recipe for one of Cracker Barrel's popular menu items.

INGREDIENTS | SERVES 4

½ cup Italian dressing
1 teaspoon fresh lime juice
1½ teaspoons honey
1 pound chicken breast tenders

1. Mix the dressing, lime juice, and honey together.
2. Pour the mixture over the chicken tenders, making sure all the chicken is covered. Marinate for 1 hour in the refrigerator.
3. Grill the chicken to a lightly golden color, about 2 minutes per side.

Popeye's Biscuits

Any good southern meal should include some biscuits, and this recipe makes a big batch that can be frozen.

INGREDIENTS | YIELDS 18

4 cups Bisquick
8 ounces sour cream
¾ cup club soda
½ stick butter

Popeye's
The Popeye's franchise began in Louisiana in the early 1970s. They serve chicken products in mild and spicy flavors and offer sides such as Cajun fries, mashed potatoes with Cajun gravy, and Cajun rice.

1. Preheat the oven to 400°F.
2. In a large bowl, mix together the Bisquick, sour cream, and club soda. Turn the dough out onto lightly floured wax paper and pat it out flat with your hand. Cut with a biscuit cutter.
3. Place the biscuits in a baking pan.
4. Melt butter in the microwave and pour ½ the butter over the biscuits before you bake them.
5. Bake the biscuits for 15–20 minutes.
6. Brush the remainder of the butter over the biscuits as soon as they come out of the oven.

Popeye's Cajun Gravy

This spicy gravy is so good that you will want to put it on everything from mashed potatoes for dinner to eggs and biscuits in the morning.

INGREDIENTS | SERVES 6–8

1 tablespoon vegetable oil
1 chicken gizzard
¼ cup ground beef
¼ cup ground pork
2 tablespoons minced green bell pepper
2 cups water
1 (14-ounce) can beef broth
2 tablespoons cornstarch
1 tablespoon flour
2 teaspoons milk
2 teaspoons distilled white vinegar
1 teaspoon sugar
1 teaspoon salt
½ teaspoon coarse-ground black pepper
¼ teaspoon cayenne pepper
⅛ teaspoon garlic powder
⅛ teaspoon onion powder
Dash dried parsley flakes

1. Heat the vegetable oil in a large saucepan over medium heat. Sauté the chicken gizzard for 4–5 minutes, until cooked. Remove the gizzard from the pan and let cool. Finely mince the gizzard after it has cooled.

2. In a medium bowl, combine the beef and pork. Mix well with your hands.

3. Add the bell pepper to the saucepan and sauté it for 1 minute. Add the beef and pork to the pan and cook for 6–8 minutes until brown. Mash the meat into tiny pieces as it browns.

4. Add water and beef broth to the saucepan, and immediately whisk in the cornstarch and flour.

5. Add the remaining ingredients and bring to a boil. Reduce the heat and simmer for 30–35 minutes, until the gravy is thick.

Popeye's Dirty Rice

Dirty rice is a traditional Cajun dish that you can enjoy at home with this easy recipe.

INGREDIENTS | SERVES 4

1 pound spicy bulk breakfast sausage
1 (14-ounce) can clear chicken broth
½ cup long-grain rice
1 teaspoon dry minced onion

1. Brown the sausage in a skillet for 6–8 minutes until the pink color disappears, crumbling with a fork.

2. Stir in the broth, rice, and onion.

3. Simmer gently, covered, for 18–20 minutes, or until the rice is tender and most of the broth is absorbed.

Popeye's Fried Chicken

Popeye's is a leading quick-service restaurant chain popular for its spicy fried chicken.

INGREDIENTS | SERVES 6–8

3 cups flour
1 cup cornstarch
3 tablespoons seasoned salt
2 tablespoons paprika
1 teaspoon baking soda
1 (.7-ounce) package dry Italian salad dressing mix
1 (1.25-ounce) package dry onion soup mix
1 (1.37-ounce) package dry spaghetti sauce mix
3 tablespoons sugar
3 cups crushed corn flakes
2 eggs
¼ cup cold water
Oil, for frying
4 pounds chicken, cut into bite-sized pieces

1. In a large bowl, combine flour, cornstarch, seasoned salt, paprika, baking soda, Italian dressing mix, onion soup mix, spaghetti sauce mix, and sugar.

2. In another bowl, put the cornflakes.

3. In a third bowl, beat the eggs and water.

4. Put enough oil in a heavy skillet to fill it 1" deep and heat on medium-high.

5. Grease a 9" × 12" × 2" baking pan and set aside. Preheat the oven to 350°F.

6. Dip the chicken pieces 1 piece at a time first into the dry coating mix, then the egg and water mix, then the corn flakes, and briefly back into the dry mix.

7. Drop the chicken into hot oil, skin-side-down, and brown 3–4 minutes on medium-high. Turn and brown other side of each piece. Don't crowd the pieces during frying.

8. Place in the prepared pan in single layer, skin-side up. Seal in foil, leaving 1 side loose for steam to escape.

9. Bake for 35–40 minutes, then remove the foil to test the tenderness of the chicken.

10. Bake uncovered 5 minutes longer to crisp the coating.

Popeye's Red Beans and Rice

Red beans and rice is a popular southern dish and this is a very easy version to create at home.

INGREDIENTS | SERVES 4

1 (16-ounce) can red chili beans in chili gravy
1 teaspoon chili powder
¼ teaspoon cumin
Dash garlic salt
2 cups cooked long-grain rice

1. In a saucepan, heat the beans without letting them boil.
2. Stir in chili powder, cumin, and garlic salt.
3. When the beans are hot, add the warm rice and gently mix.

Red Beans and Rice

Red beans and rice originated in Louisiana, and was traditionally made on Mondays, which was wash day. Leftover meat from Sunday dinner such as pork, ham, or sausage was added to a big pot of beans along with vegetables and spices and slow cooked. This allowed the women to do the laundry and still have dinner ready to serve over rice.

Ruby Tuesday New Orleans Seafood

This spicy fish and shrimp dish has an Italian twist in the ingredients.

INGREDIENTS | SERVES 6–8

2½ pounds tilapia fillets
3 tablespoons olive oil
2 tablespoons Creole seasoning
1 cup Alfredo sauce
4 tablespoons butter
2 finely minced garlic cloves
¾ pound shelled shrimp
Parmesan cheese, for garnish

1. Preheat the oven to 425°F. Wash and dry the tilapia fillets and spread olive oil and Creole seasoning on them, to taste.

2. Place in a well-oiled baking pan and bake for 8–10 minutes, until just white. While the fish is baking, warm the Alfredo sauce in a small pan.

3. In a fry pan, melt 4 tablespoons of butter. Add the garlic and shrimp and sauté for about 5 minutes.

4. Remove fish from oven. Carefully place the fillets onto plates and top with cooked shrimp and ¼ cup of Alfredo sauce. Sprinkle with grated Parmesan cheese and a dusting more of Creole seasoning.

Tony Roma's Carolina Barbecue Sauce

Tony Roma's restaurants make a wonderful rack of pork ribs, and this sauce can be used on beef, pork, or chicken.

INGREDIENTS | SERVES 4

1 cup ketchup
1 cup red wine vinegar
½ cup brown sugar
¼ cup molasses
1½ teaspoons liquid smoke
½ teaspoon salt
¼ teaspoon black pepper
¼ teaspoon garlic powder
¼ teaspoon onion powder

1. Combine all the ingredients in a medium saucepan over high heat and whisk until smooth.

2. Bring the sauce to a boil. Reduce heat and simmer uncovered for 30–40 minutes, or until the sauce has thickened.

Tony Roma's

This company claims that they pioneered the baby back ribs, which are popular on the menu at many restaurants. Their barbecue sauce is available on supermarket shelves nationwide, and their precooked ribs with sauce can be found in the frozen foods aisle.

Tony Roma's Corn Fritter Casserole

This moist, sweet, and savory side dish is a cross between corn bread and corn pudding.

INGREDIENTS | SERVES 6–8

2 (8.5-ounce) boxes Jiffy corn bread mix
1 (15-ounce) can drained whole kernel corn
2 eggs
⅔ cup milk
Salt and pepper, to taste
2 tablespoons butter
½ cup finely diced onions
½ cup finely diced green bell pepper
3 chicken bouillon cubes
1⅓ cups warm water
3 tablespoons melted butter

1. Preheat the oven to 350°F.

2. Mix together the corn bread mix, corn, eggs, milk, salt and pepper.

3. Coat the bottom of a nonstick skillet with vegetable oil. Heat the skillet to medium-high. Drop a spoonful of corn fritter mix into skillet. Cook on each side until lightly golden. Place on a paper towel to drain. Add more oil as needed to complete frying all the corn fritters.

4. Melt 2 tablespoons butter in a skillet over medium-low heat. Sauté the onions and bell pepper for 2–3 minutes until the onions are transparent. Remove the skillet from the heat.

5. Place the bouillon cubes in the water and dissolve.

6. Crumble the corn fritters into a large bowl. Add the sautéed onions and bell pepper. Add 3 tablespoons of melted butter. Pour the dissolved chicken bouillon and water mixture over the corn and vegetables and mix well.

7. Place the mixture in a well-greased 8" square baking pan and cover with aluminum foil. Bake for 20–25 minutes. Remove the foil and return to oven for 10–15 minutes.

Tony Roma's Maple Sweet Potatoes

This recipe calls for roasting sweet potatoes, which is easier than boiling and mashing them.

INGREDIENTS | SERVES 2

1 large yam
1 tablespoon butter
½ cup chopped onion
3 tablespoons finely chopped pecans
3 tablespoons maple syrup
¼ teaspoon cinnamon

1. Bake the yam in the oven for 40–45 minutes at 400°F.

2. Remove the yam from oven and allow it to cool enough so that you can handle it. Remove the skin and slice into 1" pieces.

3. In a large skillet, melt the butter and sauté the onion and pecans for approximately 2 minutes, until the onion pieces begin to turn brown.

4. Add the yam slices, maple syrup, and cinnamon and sauté for 3–5 minutes, stirring often, until the yam pieces are hot and tender.

Tony Roma's Red Hot Barbecue Sauce

A southern cook needs a good homemade barbecue sauce for chicken, beef, and pork.

INGREDIENTS | SERVES 4

1 cup ketchup
1 cup vinegar
½ cup dark corn syrup
2 tablespoons molasses
½ teaspoon finely diced red bell pepper
2 teaspoons sugar
1 teaspoon liquid smoke
½ teaspoon salt
½ teaspoon crushed red pepper flakes
½ teaspoon Tabasco
¼ teaspoon cayenne pepper
¼ teaspoon black pepper
¼ teaspoon garlic powder
¼ teaspoon onion powder

1. Combine all of the ingredients in a saucepan over high heat. Use a whisk to blend the ingredients until smooth.

2. When the mixture comes to a boil, reduce the heat and simmer uncovered for 30–45 minutes, until the mixture thickens.

3. Remove it from the heat. If you want a thicker sauce, cook it longer. If you make the sauce too thick; thin it with more vinegar.

CHAPTER 14

Desserts

Applebee's Blondie Brownies
243

Applebee's Strawberry
Dessert Shooters
244

Arby's Apple Turnovers
245

Bennigan's Death by
Chocolate Cake
246

Bob Evans Peanut Butter Pie
246

Cheesecake Factory
Oreo Cheesecake
247

Cheesecake Factory
Pumpkin Cheesecake
248

Chili's Chocolate Chip
Paradise Pie
249

Chili's Mighty Ice Cream Pie
250

Chili's Molten Lava Cake
251

Cracker Barrel Banana Pudding
252

Cracker Barrel Carrot Cake
253

Cracker Barrel Cherry
Chocolate Cobbler
254

Golden Corral Bread Pudding
255

Olive Garden Apple Carmelina
256

Olive Garden
Strawberries Romano
257

Outback Steakhouse
Key Lime Pie
257

Pizza Hut Dessert Pizza
258

Desserts

(continued)

Starbucks Black
Bottom Cupcakes
259

Starbucks Oatmeal Cookies
260

Subway White Chocolate
Macadamia Nut Cookies
261

Taco Bell Caramel
Apple Empanadas
262

The Melting Pot Dark Chocolate
Raspberry Fondue
263

The Melting Pot Flaming
Turtle Fondue
264

Applebee's Blondie Brownies

Everyone has a sweet tooth, and nothing is better than a warm brownie with ice cream.

INGREDIENTS | SERVES 12

1 cup flour
½ teaspoon baking powder
Pinch baking soda
Pinch salt
½ cup chopped walnuts
⅓ cup melted unsalted butter
1⅓ cups packed brown sugar
1 egg
1 tablespoon vanilla extract
½ cup vanilla baking chips
¼ cup unsalted butter
¼ cup maple syrup
1 (8-ounce) package softened cream cheese
½ teaspoon maple extract

1. Preheat the oven to 350°F.
2. Sift together the flour, baking powder, baking soda, and salt. Stir in the nuts. Set aside.
3. Use an electric mixer to beat together the butter and 1 cup brown sugar. Beat in egg and vanilla.
4. Slowly beat dry mixture in to wet mixture. Stir in vanilla baking chips by hand.
5. Spread batter into a greased 9" × 9" × 2" baking pan. Bake for 20–25 minutes, or until a toothpick inserted in the center comes out clean. Set aside to cool.
6. In a saucepan over low heat, melt ¼ cup butter and maple syrup. Stir remaining ⅓ cup brown sugar into saucepan until it has dissolved.
7. Remove the saucepan from the heat and beat in cream cheese and maple extract until smooth. Return saucepan to low heat and simmer for about 5 minutes until the consistency of peanut butter and then spread the mixture over the top of the cooled brownies.

Applebee's Strawberry Dessert Shooters

These cute little dessert parfaits are as much fun to make as they are to eat.

INGREDIENTS | SERVES 4

1½ (8-ounce) packages cream cheese
2 eggs
⅓ cup sugar
2 tablespoons sour cream
½ teaspoon vanilla extract
½ cup graham cracker crumbs
2 tablespoons melted butter
½ cup thawed frozen sliced strawberries in syrup
Whipped cream, for garnish

Dessert Shots

Dessert shots are all the rage in a lot of restaurants right now. Small sweet treats are a trend that's found its way onto dessert carts all over America. Mini parfaits, sundaes, and layered cakes in shot glasses are being served for $2–$3. It is a brilliant idea for diners to indulge in a waist-friendly dessert without guilt, and can easily be adapted for the home cook.

1. To make the cheesecake filling, in a large bowl, using a mixer on high, blend the cream cheese, eggs, sugar, sour cream, and vanilla until smooth.

2. Pour the mixture into a large saucepan and cook over medium-high heat, stirring often, for 8–10 minutes, or until mixture begins to thicken. Pour into a covered container and chill for several hours, until cold.

3. To prepare each serving, combine butter with graham cracker crumbs.

4. Spoon 2 tablespoons of graham cracker crumbs into a 6-ounce glass and top with ⅓ cup of the cheesecake filling.

5. Spoon 2 tablespoons of strawberries and syrup on top of cheesecake filling and top off with whipped cream.

Arby's Apple Turnovers

This recipe is easier than apple pie, and you get the same great taste without all the work.

INGREDIENTS | SERVES 8

4 large cooking apples
½ cup sugar
1 tablespoon cornstarch
1 teaspoon lemon juice
¼ teaspoon ground cinnamon
1 (17.3-ounce) package puff pastry sheets
½ cup confectioner's sugar
1 tablespoon water

1. Peel, core, and slice apples. In a medium saucepan over low heat, cook apples with sugar, cornstarch, lemon juice, and cinnamon, stirring frequently, for 6–8 minutes until apples are tender. Refrigerate until cool.

2. Thaw the pastry sheets at room temperature 20 minutes.

3. Preheat the oven to 400°F.

4. Unfold the pastry on lightly floured surface. Roll each sheet into a 12" square, then cut into four 6" squares. Place ¼ cup of apple mixture in center of each square. Brush the edges with water. Fold to form triangles and seal edges firmly with a fork.

5. Place on baking sheets and bake for 25 minutes, or until golden. Cool on wire rack.

6. For the sugar drizzle, mix together the confectioners' sugar and water in a small bowl. With a spoon, drizzle over the turnovers and allow to set before serving.

Bennigan's Death by Chocolate Cake

When you are craving chocolate, you cannot go wrong with this recipe.

INGREDIENTS | SERVES 6–8

1 (18.25-ounce) box chocolate cake mix
1 cup Kahlúa
4 (3.9-ounce) boxes Jell-O chocolate pudding mix
3 (8-ounce) containers Cool Whip
6 Skor candy bars

1. Bake the cake according to package directions for a 9" × 13" cake. Prick the top of the baked cake with a fork and pour the Kahlúa over the cake. Let this soak in. It can be left this way overnight.

2. Make the chocolate pudding according to the package directions.

3. To assemble the cake, crumble up half of the cake and place it on the bottom of a large glass bowl. Layer half of the pudding, then half of the Cool Whip, then half of the Skor candy bars, broken into small pieces. Repeat.

Bob Evans Peanut Butter Pie

This no-bake pie is a winner for peanut better lovers.

INGREDIENTS | YIELDS 1 PIE

1 (5-ounce) package Jell-O instant vanilla pudding
2 cups cold milk
½ cup whipped cream
1¼ cups creamy peanut butter
1 prebaked pie shell
1 (8-ounce) container Cool Whip
Chocolate syrup, for garnish
Crushed peanuts, for garnish

1. Whisk together pudding mix and milk in bowl until creamy. Add the whipped cream and peanut butter and whisk until completely blended.

2. Pour into pie shell and cover with a generous layer of Cool Whip. Put in the freezer for 1 hour, until set.

3. Remove from freezer and drizzle with your favorite chocolate syrup and crushed peanuts.

4. Cover and chill for 2 hours.

Cheesecake Factory Oreo Cheesecake

Oreos and cheesecake are truly a match made in heaven.

INGREDIENTS | YIELDS 1 PIE

2 tablespoons melted butter
1½ cups Oreo cookie crumbs
1½ pounds room-temperature cream cheese
1 cup sugar
5 room-temperature eggs
1 cup room-temperature sour cream
¼ cup flour
2 teaspoons vanilla extract
¼ teaspoon salt
15 divided coarsely chopped Oreo cookies

1. Preheat the oven to 375°F.
2. Combine the butter and cookie crumbs and press evenly into the bottom of a greased 10" pie pan. Set aside.
3. Beat cream cheese with an electric mixer until light and fluffy. Add in the sugar, then the eggs. Stir in the sour cream, flour, vanilla, and salt. Gently stir in 5 chopped cookies.
4. Pour the mixture into the pan and top with remaining chopped cookies. Bake on the top rack for 75 minutes.
5. Turn off the oven, prop the door open several inches, and allow the cake to rest in oven for 1 hour.
6. Refrigerate overnight.

Cheesecake Factory Pumpkin Cheesecake

This restaurant is famous for its cheesecakes, and this one is a real holiday treat.

INGREDIENTS | YIELDS 1 PIE

1½ cups graham cracker crumbs
5 tablespoons melted butter
1 cup plus 1 tablespoon sugar
3 (8-ounce) softened packages cream cheese
1 teaspoon vanilla
1 cup canned pumpkin
3 eggs
½ teaspoon cinnamon
¼ teaspoon nutmeg
¼ teaspoon allspice
Whipped cream, for garnish

The Cheesecake Factory
The Cheesecake Factory has over 150 restaurants and boasts more than 200 items on the menu. There are over forty different cheesecake varieties on their website, which can be shipped nationwide.

1. Preheat the oven to 350°F.
2. In a medium bowl, combine the graham cracker crumbs, butter, and 1 tablespoon sugar. Stir well enough to coat all of the crumbs with the butter.
3. Press the crumbs onto the bottom and about two-thirds of the way up the sides of a 9" pie pan. Bake the crust for 5 minutes. Set aside.
4. In a large mixing bowl, combine the cream cheese, 1 cup sugar, and the vanilla. Mix with an electric mixer until smooth.
5. Add the pumpkin, eggs, cinnamon, nutmeg, and allspice and continue to beat until smooth and creamy.
6. Pour the filling into the pan. Bake for 60–70 minutes. The top will turn a bit darker at this point. Remove from the oven and allow the cheesecake to cool.
7. When the cheesecake has come to room temperature, put it into the refrigerator.
8. Serve with a generous portion of whipped cream on top.

Chili's Chocolate Chip Paradise Pie

You know it. You love it. Chili's Chocolate Chip Paradise Pie is one of the most incredible desserts available at any restaurant chain.

INGREDIENTS | YIELDS 1 PIE

Crust
3 tablespoons butter
⅓ cup graham cracker crumbs
3 tablespoons sugar
⅓ cup chocolate chips

Filling
½ cup flour
¼ cup sugar
¾ teaspoon baking powder
⅓ cup milk
1 tablespoon oil
1 teaspoon vanilla extract
⅓ cup semisweet or milk chocolate chips
¼ cup shredded coconut
¼ cup crushed walnuts or almonds
2 tablespoons butter per slice of pie
Dash of cinnamon

Toppings
Ice cream
Hot fudge and caramel toppings

1. Preheat the oven to 350°F.

2. Melt the butter and combine with the graham cracker crumbs and sugar. Press into bottom of a 1-quart casserole dish. Top evenly with chocolate chips and bake for 5 minutes, until the chocolate is melted. Spread the melted chips out evenly over the crust.

3. In a large mixing bowl, combine the dry ingredients. Add the milk, oil, and vanilla and stir until smooth. Stir in the chocolate chips, coconut, and nuts.

4. Pour into the crust and bake, uncovered, for 35–40 minutes, until a toothpick inserted into the center comes out clean.

5. To serve, place 2 tablespoons of butter on an ovenproof serving plate, then sprinkle with cinnamon. Place in a warm oven until the butter melts. Remove the plate from oven and place a large piece of warm pie directly onto the melted butter. Top the pie with ice cream and drizzle with hot fudge and caramel toppings.

Chili's Mighty Ice Cream Pie

Ice cream and Oreo cookies are another combination that will please your taste buds.

INGREDIENTS | YIELDS 1 PIE

1 Oreo cookie crust
1 (6-ounce) package Heath Bits
1 cup semisweet chocolate chips
½ gallon vanilla ice cream
⅓ cup chocolate fudge topping
⅓ cup caramel topping

1. Freeze the pie crust, Heath bits, and chips separately. When Heath bits and chips are frozen, chop them in the food processor until fine. Put the pieces back in freezer.

2. Soften the ice cream just until it's workable so that the bits can be stirred in without the ice cream melting.

3. Place the lightly thawed ice cream in a chilled mixing bowl and add Heath bits and chocolate chips that have been processed. Stir and mix well.

4. Place ice cream in frozen pie shell and refreeze for 2–3 hours. Place ⅓ cup of chocolate fudge topping and ⅓ cup of the caramel sauce in two separate bowls and melt both bowls in the microwave on medium heat for 1–2 minutes until slightly melted.

5. Remove the pie from freezer and stream chocolate and caramel sauce on top of the pie and place it back in the freezer. Freeze for 2–3 hours before serving.

Chili's Molten Lava Cake

Chili's serves this cake topped with vanilla ice cream and a crunchy chocolate shell, which can be made with Smucker's Magic Shell.

INGREDIENTS | SERVES 4

5 tablespoons butter
3.5 ounces dark chocolate
2 extra-large eggs
1 extra-large egg yolk
3 teaspoons sugar
1 teaspoon vanilla extract
3 tablespoons flour
2 teaspoons cocoa powder
1 teaspoon salt

Origins of the Lava Cake

Legend has it that this chocolate lava cake was the result of a major culinary disaster. The dessert was meant to be individual chocolate cakes, but a cook took them out of the ovens too soon, and the centers where still liquefied. Since there was no time to cook them further, the chef simply introduced the dessert as a chocolate lava cake.

1. Preheat the oven to 425°F.

2. Melt the butter and chocolate together in the microwave for 2–3 minutes on medium heat. Stir to combine.

3. In a large mixing bowl, whisk together the eggs, sugar and vanilla until the mixture is light yellow in color and the sugar is dissolved.

4. Stir the warm chocolate mixture into the egg mixture and whisk until combined. Sift in the flour, cocoa, and salt. Fold in with a spatula until combined.

5. Spoon into 4 buttered 5-ounce ramekins, and tap on the table to settle any air bubbles. Refrigerate for 30 minutes.

6. Place the ramekins in a baking dish and add water to the dish until it is halfway up the sides. Bake for 15 minutes.

Cracker Barrel Banana Pudding

Banana pudding is a classic southern dish, and nobody makes it better than Cracker Barrel. You will need a food thermometer for this recipe.

INGREDIENTS | SERVES 6–8

1½ quarts milk
1¼ cups liquid egg substitute
1⅛ cups flour
¼ cup vanilla extract
1¼ cups sugar
12 ounces vanilla wafers
1¾ peeled bananas
1 (8-ounce) container Cool Whip

1. Heat the milk in a saucepan to 170°F.
2. In a bowl, mix the eggs, flour, vanilla, and sugar.
3. Add the sugar mixture to the milk in the pan.
4. Cook for 10–12 minutes until it becomes custard like, stirring constantly.
5. Spread the wafers on the bottom of the baking pan.
6. Slice the bananas and place over the wafers.
7. Pour the custard over the wafers and bananas.
8. Let cool and add Cool Whip to the top.

Cracker Barrel Carrot Cake

Cracker Barrel makes this cake special by adding several ingredients you wouldn't find in an ordinary carrot cake.

INGREDIENTS | YIELDS 1 SHEET CAKE

3 cups flour
2 teaspoons baking powder
2 teaspoons baking soda
½ teaspoon salt
2 teaspoons ground cinnamon
1 teaspoon ground nutmeg
½ teaspoon ground cloves
1¼ cups vegetable oil
1½ cups sugar
½ cup brown sugar
2 teaspoons vanilla
3 eggs
1 cup crushed pineapple
¾ cup finely chopped walnuts
½ cup shredded coconut
2 cups shredded carrots
½ cup raisins

Cream Cheese Frosting
8 ounces cream cheese
½ cup room-temperature butter
1 teaspoon vanilla
2 cups powdered sugar
½ cup chopped pecans, for garnish

1. Preheat the oven to 350°F.

2. Mix together flour, baking powder, baking soda, salt, cinnamon, nutmeg, and cloves. Set aside.

3. In a large bowl, using a beater, mix the oil, sugars, vanilla, and eggs until smooth and fluffy. Add the pineapple, walnuts, coconut, carrots, and raisins and blend well. Gradually add the flour mixture half at a time until blended through.

4. Pour the batter into a greased and floured 9" × 13" pan and bake for about 40–50 minutes. Test with toothpick for doneness.

5. To make the frosting, blend the cream cheese and butter until it is light and fluffy. Add the vanilla and a little powdered sugar at a time until all has been well blended. Turn the mixer on high and beat until frosting is light and fluffy.

6. Spread the frosting over the cooled cake and sprinkle with pecans

Cracker Barrel Cherry Chocolate Cobbler

The Cracker Barrel Cherry Chocolate Cobbler is a seasonal favorite and very easy to make.

INGREDIENTS | SERVES 6

1½ cups flour
½ cup sugar
2 teaspoons baking powder
½ teaspoon salt
¼ cup butter
6 ounces semisweet chocolate morsels
¼ cup milk
1 egg
1 (21-ounce) can cherry pie filling
½ cup finely chopped peanuts

1. Preheat the oven to 350°F.
2. In a large bowl, combine flour, sugar, baking powder, salt, and butter. Cut with a pastry blender until the crumbs are the size of large peas.
3. Melt the chocolate morsels in the microwave for 2–3 minutes on medium. Add the milk and egg and mix well.
4. Blend the chocolate into the flour mixture.
5. Spread the cherry pie filling in the bottom of a 2-quart casserole.
6. Drop the chocolate batter randomly over the cherries and sprinkle the top with chopped nuts.
7. Bake in the oven for 40–45 minutes.

Golden Corral Bread Pudding

This recipe is a great way to use bread that has lost its freshness.

INGREDIENTS | SERVES 4–6

Bread Pudding
2 cups milk
½ cup butter
2 eggs
⅓ cup brown sugar
¼ teaspoon salt
1 teaspoon cinnamon
3 cups cubed French bread

White Sauce
1 cup milk
2 tablespoons butter
½ cup sugar
1 teaspoon vanilla
1 tablespoon flour
Dash of salt

1. Preheat the oven to 350°F.
2. In a saucepan over medium, heat the milk and butter together. Remove and set aside.
3. In a large mixing bowl, beat the eggs and add the brown sugar, salt and cinnamon. Let the milk cool for 30 minutes then add it to the egg mixture, making sure that the egg mixture does not curdle.
4. Add the bread cubes and stir carefully; do not beat.
5. Place the mixture in an 8" × 11" well-oiled pan and bake for about 40 minutes, until a toothpick inserted into the middle comes out clean. Set aside.
6. Mix all the sauce ingredients together and bring to a boil in a pan for 3–4 minutes, stirring constantly. Pour about ½ the mixture on the warm bread pudding and place the remainder of the sauce in a serving bowl for those who desire a little extra.

Olive Garden Apple Carmelina

Serve these baked apples topped with your favorite vanilla ice cream and a drizzle of caramel sauce.

INGREDIENTS | SERVES 6–8

Filling
2 (20-ounce) cans drained sliced apples
½ cup sugar
½ teaspoon apple pie spice
¼ cup brown sugar
¼ cup flour
¼ teaspoon salt

Topping
¾ cup flour
¼ teaspoon salt
½ cup light brown sugar
¼ cup sugar
5 tablespoons softened butter

1. Preheat the oven to 350°F.

2. Mix all the ingredients for the filling together in a bowl and stir well.

3. Pour the mixture into a lightly buttered 8" × 8" baking dish.

4. Create the topping in a separate bowl by adding the flour, salt, and sugars and blending well. Work in the butter. Mixture should look like coarse meal.

5. Sprinkle over the apples and bake for 30–35 minutes.

Olive Garden Strawberries Romano

This seasonal recipe gives strawberries an Italian twist sure to please the palate.

INGREDIENTS | SERVES 4

1 cup mascarpone cheese
⅓ cup brown sugar
Juice of 1 orange
1 tablespoon triple sec
1 cup whipped cream
2 quarts quartered strawberries
Fresh mint sprig

1. In a mixing bowl, combine the cheese, brown sugar, orange juice, and triple sec and mix thoroughly. Fold in whipped cream.

2. Place the berries in a dessert dish or wine glass. Top with cream mixture.

3. Garnish with a sprig of mint and chill until ready to serve.

Outback Steakhouse Key Lime Pie

This sweet and tangy no-bake pie is best served topped with Cool Whip.

INGREDIENTS | YIELDS 1 PIE

Crust
1 stick butter
1 cup graham cracker crumbs

Filling
1 cup water
3 cups sugar
1 package unflavored gelatin
1 teaspoon salt
Juice of 3 limes
1 cup condensed milk

1. To prepare the crust, melt the butter in a pan. Mix in the crumbs. Press into a 9" pie pan.

2. To prepare the filling, heat the water, sugar, gelatin, salt, and lime juice in a pot. Add the condensed milk and heat for 5–7 minutes without boiling.

3. Pour the filling into the crust and let the pie cool. Cool in the refrigerator for 4 hours.

Pizza Hut Dessert Pizza

The folks at Pizza Hut came up with a creative way to make dessert with pizza dough.

INGREDIENTS | SERVES 8

1 (13.8-ounce) can of refrigerated pizza dough
1 (21-ounce) can cherry, blueberry, or apple pie filling
½ cup flour
½ cup brown sugar
½ cup quick oats
½ cup cold butter
1 teaspoon cinnamon
2 cups powdered sugar
3 tablespoons milk
1 tablespoon butter
1 teaspoon vanilla

1. Preheat the oven to 400°F.
2. Roll the dough on a floured surface until it is the diameter for your pizza pan. Place in the pan and form the dough to the edge.
3. Brush with vegetable oil and prick with a fork.
4. Prebake the dough for 3 minutes. Remove from the oven.
5. Spread the pie filling over the dough.
6. Mix the flour, brown sugar, quick oats, cold butter, and cinnamon with a fork or pastry blender and spoon over the pie the filling.
7. Return the pizza to the oven and continue to bake for 10–15 minutes, or until crust is light golden brown. Remove from oven.
8. Create the vanilla drizzle by combining powdered sugar, milk, butter, and vanilla. Drizzle glaze over pizza.

Dessert Pizzas

Dessert pizzas have become a very hot item on many restaurant menus. They come in many variations depending on the seasons and the local flavor. You can make your own crust from scratch of course, but this calls for a ready-made store-bought crust found at any grocery store.

Starbucks Black Bottom Cupcakes

These soft and gooey cupcakes are fun to make no matter how old you are.

INGREDIENTS | YIELDS 36 CUPCAKES

1 (8-ounce) package softened cream cheese
⅓ cup sugar
1 large egg
Pinch salt
2 cups semisweet mini chocolate chips
3 cups flour
2 cups sugar
⅔ cup sifted unsweetened baking cocoa
2 teaspoons baking soda
½ teaspoon salt
2 cups water
⅔ cup oil
2 tablespoons white vinegar
3 teaspoons vanilla

1. Preheat the oven to 350°F. Line 36 regular-size muffin tins with paper liners.

2. In a bowl, beat the cream cheese, sugar, egg, and salt until fluffy and well combined. Add in the chocolate chips and mix to combine. Set aside.

3. For the cake batter, in a bowl, sift together flour, sugar, cocoa, baking soda, and salt.

4. In a small bowl, whisk together water, oil, vinegar, and vanilla. Beat well until thoroughly combined. Combine the wet ingredients with the dry ingredients.

5. Fill the liners ¾ full with chocolate batter and drop about 1 teaspoon of the cream cheese mixture on top and in the middle of each chocolate batter.

6. Bake for about 20 minutes, or until the cupcakes test done.

Starbucks Oatmeal Cookies

Cookies are the ultimate portable dessert, and this recipe from Starbucks is loaded with flavor.

INGREDIENTS | **YIELDS 36 COOKIES**

1½ cups old-fashioned oats
½ cup flour
¼ cup dark raisins
¼ cup golden raisins
¼ cup dried cranberries
¼ teaspoon baking powder
¼ teaspoon baking soda
½ teaspoon salt
6 tablespoons room-temperature butter
½ cup packed dark brown sugar
¼ cup sugar
1 large egg
½ teaspoon ground cinnamon
1 teaspoon vanilla
4 tablespoons dark raisins, for topping
4 tablespoons golden raisins, for topping

1. Preheat oven to 350°F.
2. Blend the oats, flour, raisins, cranberries, baking powder, baking soda, and salt. Set aside.
3. Beat the butter and sugars together until light and fluffy. Add egg, cinnamon, and vanilla and beat until combined.
4. Gradually add the oat mixture to the butter mixture. Beat until combined.
5. Combine the raisins for the topping in a separate bowl and set aside.
6. Drop the dough by rounded tablespoons, 2" apart, onto 2 lightly greased baking sheets.
7. Place 1 mounded teaspoon of raisins on top of the dough.
8. Bake about 12–16 minutes, until cookies are golden brown but still soft.
9. Cool on sheets before serving.

Subway White Chocolate Macadamia Nut Cookies

These cookies are a big seller at Subway, and sure to be at hit in your home as well.

INGREDIENTS | YIELDS 24 COOKIES

½ cup butter
¾ cup sugar
1 egg
1 teaspoon vanilla extract
1¼ cups flour
½ teaspoon baking soda
½ teaspoon salt
8 ounces chopped white chocolate
1 (6.5-ounce) jar chopped macadamia nuts

1. Preheat the oven to 375°F.
2. In a medium bowl, cream together the butter and sugar. Stir in the egg and vanilla.
3. Combine the flour, baking soda, and salt and stir into the creamed mixture. Stir in the chocolate and nuts.
4. Drop the cookies by heaping teaspoonfuls onto an ungreased cookie sheet, about 2" apart.
5. Bake for 8–10 minutes, until lightly browned.
6. Cool on wire racks. When cool, store in an airtight container.

Taco Bell Caramel Apple Empanadas

Taco Bell makes these Mexican treats and now you can make them too.

INGREDIENTS | SERVES 12

1 (12-ounce) package Stouffer's frozen harvest apples
1 tablespoon flour
¼ cup butter
¼ cup firmly packed light brown sugar
¼ teaspoon ground allspice
3½ cups baking mix
1 cup whipping cream
2 tablespoons melted butter

Empanadas

Empanadas are a very popular street food in South America. An empanada is a crescent-shaped pastry with a filling. They can be fried or baked, and may use a variety of fillings from cheese to seafood.

1. Preheat the oven to 400°F.

2. Thaw the apples in the microwave at half power for 6–7 minutes. Let them stand for 3 minutes. Stir together with the flour.

3. Melt the ¼ cup of butter in a medium skillet over medium heat. Add the apple mixture, brown sugar, and allspice. Cook, stirring constantly, for 4 minutes, or until thickened. Remove from heat.

4. Coarsely mash the apple mixture and set aside.

5. Stir together the baking mix and whipping cream with a fork until moistened. Turn the dough out onto a lightly floured surface and knead 3–4 times.

6. Roll the dough to ½" thickness and cut into 12 (5") squares.

7. Divide the apple mixture into 12 servings and place 1 serving in the center of each square.

8. Fold 1 side of square over, pressing edges with a fork to seal. Place on a lightly greased baking sheet. Brush the tops with melted butter and bake for 18–20 minutes, or until golden brown.

The Melting Pot Dark Chocolate Raspberry Fondue

A meal at the Melting Pot can be quite pricey, so here is an easy and inexpensive version of their delicious dessert to make at home.

INGREDIENTS | SERVES 2–4

12 ounces finely chopped dark chocolate
¼ cup heavy cream
3 tablespoons raspberry liqueur

The Melting Pot

The Melting Pot motto states: "Dipping is something different!" and this restaurant is a different place to go to treat yourself on a special occasion. Eating out is always a party at the Melting Pot. It is an experience meant to be shared, and an experience like no other. The Big Night Out is a 4-course meal consisting of a cheese fondue, salad, entrée, and dessert fondue. Expect to spend at least 2 hours or more, and the cost can range $30–$60 per person.

1. Combine the chocolate and cream in a microwave-safe bowl.

2. Heat in the microwave on medium heat for 2–3 minutes stopping to stir every 30 seconds. Be careful not to let the chocolate burn.

3. Pour into a warm crock or fondue pot.

4. Drizzle with the liqueur. Suggested dippers include graham crackers, fruit, and marshmallows.

The Melting Pot Flaming Turtle Fondue

Serve dippers such as rice crispy treats, pound cake, brownie bites, strawberries, raspberries, bananas, cheesecake, and marshmallows for the true restaurant experience.

INGREDIENTS | SERVES 2–4

2 ounces melted milk chocolate
2 ounces caramel sundae syrup
Whole milk for thinning, if necessary
⅓ ounce 151 rum
1 ounce chopped pecans

1. Heat the chocolate and caramel in a saucepan on low heat, stirring frequently.
2. If the mixture seems too thick, slowly add whole milk to reach the desired consistency. (The consistency should be like honey and suitable for dipping but not so runny that it won't stick to the dippers.)
3. Slowly add the rum to the pot.
4. Using a long match, carefully ignite the liquor by touching the flame to the edge of the pot.
5. Once the flame burns out, add the nuts to the pot and stir.

CHAPTER 15

Signature Cocktails and Drinks

Applebee's Bananaberry Freeze
267

Bennigan's Candy Bar Drink
267

Chili's Calypso Cooler
268

Chili's Electric Lemonade
268

Chili's Presidente Margarita
269

Outback Steakhouse Wallaby Darned
269

T.G.I. Friday's Chocolate Monkey
270

T.G.I. Friday's Dreamsicle
271

T.G.I. Friday's Flying Grasshopper
271

T.G.I. Friday's Long Island Iced Tea
272

T.G.I. Friday's Midnight Meltdown
272

Tommy Bahama Blue Hawaiian
273

Tommy Bahama Calypso Sun
273

Tommy Bahama Crazy Cuban
274

Tommy Bahama Millionaire Mojito
274

Cinnabon Mochalatte Chill
275

Cinnabon Orange Icescape
275

Dairy Queen Moolatte
276

Dunkin Donuts Iced Coffee
276

Houlihan's Houli Fruit Fizz
277

Signature Cocktails and Drinks
(continued)

Jack in the Box Oreo Shake
277

McDonald's Caramel Frappe
278

McDonald's Vanilla Iced Coffee
278

Orange Julius
279

Red Lobster Boston Tea
279

Sonic Cherry Limeade
280

Starbucks Coffee Frappe
280

Starbucks Mocha Frappucino
281

Wendy's Frosty
281

Applebee's Bananaberry Freeze

This fruity cocktail from Applebee's will quench your thirst.

INGREDIENTS | SERVES 2

2 cups ice
1 peeled ripe banana
¾ cup strawberry daiquiri mix
¼ cup piña colada mix
Whipped cream, for garnish
Strawberry slices, for garnish
Banana slices, for garnish

1. Purée ice, banana, daiquiri, and colada mixes in a blender on high until the mixture is smooth.
2. Pour into 2 wine glasses.
3. Garnish with whipped cream, strawberries, and bananas.

Bennigan's Candy Bar Drink

Chocolate syrup and coconut give this cocktail its unique flavor.

INGREDIENTS | SERVES 1

1¼ ounces Frangelico
2 ounces chocolate syrup
2 ounces Coco Lopez
2 ounces finely shredded coconut
2 ounces ice milk

1. Combine all the ingredients in a blender.
2. Serve in a champagne or other small glass.

Bennigan's

Bennigan's Grill and Tavern is a casual dining restaurant chain that serves American dishes with an Irish twist. Restaurants also feature a full bar with many varieties of beer.

Chili's Calypso Cooler

This cocktail is really pretty and very easy to make.

INGREDIENTS | SERVES 1

1½ ounces Captain Morgan spiced rum
½ ounce peach schnapps
4 ounces orange juice
Splash lime juice
½ ounce grenadine
Orange wedge, for garnish
Maraschino cherry, for garnish

1. Fill a 16-ounce glass with ice.
2. Pour all of the ingredients over ice in the order listed. Do not stir.
3. Garnish the drink with an orange wedge and a cherry on a toothpick.

Chili's Electric Lemonade

Spiked lemonade is a popular cocktail on the menu at many restaurants.

INGREDIENTS | SERVES 1

1¼ ounces Bacardi Limon vodka
½ ounce Blue Curacao
2 ounces sweet and sour mix
Splash of 7-Up
Lemon wedge, for garnish

1. Put vodka, Blue Curacao, and sweet and sour mix in a shaker with a lid. Mix well. Pour into a glass.
2. Add a splash of 7-Up and garnish with a lemon squeeze.

Chili's Presidente Margarita

Chili's Presidente Margarita is quite possibly one of the best margaritas of all time.

INGREDIENTS | SERVES 1

1¼ ounces Sauza Commemorativo Tequila
½ ounce Presidente brandy
½ ounce Cointreau
4 ounces sour mix
Splash of lime juice

Mix all ingredients together and serve in a salt-rimmed glass filled with ice.

Outback Steakhouse Wallaby Darned

This cocktail recipe is Outback's version of the fuzzy navel.

INGREDIENTS | SERVES 2

8 ounces frozen sliced peaches
½ cup Bacardi Fuzzy Navel mix
½ cup ice
½ cup champagne
3 ounces water
1½ ounces peach schnapps
1½ ounces vodka
1 tablespoon sugar

1. Place all the drink ingredients into a blender. Blend until smooth.
2. Pour into 2 (10-ounce) glasses and serve immediately.

T.G.I. Friday's Chocolate Monkey

T.G.I. Friday's created this banana split drink, which is more like a dessert than a cocktail.

INGREDIENTS | SERVES 1

½ ripe banana
2 scoops vanilla ice cream
1 scoop crushed ice
1 ounce banana liqueur
½ ounce chocolate syrup
Whipped cream, for garnish
Banana slices, for garnish
Cherry, for garnish

1. Place all the drink ingredients into a blender. Blend until thick and creamy.

2. Serve in a tall wine glass with a straw. Top with whipped cream. Garnish with banana slices and a cherry.

T.G.I. Friday's Happy Hour

T.G.I. Friday's offers great food and innovative drinks. Friday's has an engaging atmosphere with its popular happy hour. It is famous for its flashy bartenders, who compete annually for the title of the World's Greatest T.G.I. Friday's Bartender.

T.G.I. Friday's Dreamsicle

This cocktail reminds you of the childhood treat, but of course, it has an adult kick.

INGREDIENTS | YIELDS 4 CUPS

1½ cups Bailey's Irish Cream
3½ cups Orange Juice

1. Place all ingredients into a large pitcher and stir.
2. Serve the drinks in low-ball glasses.

T.G.I. Friday's Flying Grasshopper

The grasshopper drink is a well-known cocktail that was first concocted in New Orleans.

INGREDIENTS | SERVES 1

¾ ounce green Crème de Menthe
¾ ounce white Crème de Cacao
¾ ounce vodka
2 scoops vanilla ice cream
½ scoop crushed ice

1. Combine all the ingredients in a blender. Blend until smooth.
2. Serve in a tall specialty glass.

T.G.I. Friday's Long Island Iced Tea

Friday's claims they invented this famous cocktail. Be careful with this recipe, it is powerful.

INGREDIENTS | SERVES 1

½ ounce gin
½ ounce vodka
½ ounce rum
½ ounce Triple Sec
2 ounces sweet and sour mix
Splash of cola

1. Mix all the ingredients in a shaker.
2. Pour over ice and top with cola.

Long Island Iced Tea
This drink was first served in the mid-1970s at a bar in Long Island, New York, thus the name. The drink has a much higher alcohol concentration than most cocktails.

T.G.I. Friday's Midnight Meltdown

This is another Friday's original cocktail recipe.

INGREDIENTS | SERVES 1

Chocolate syrup
1 ounce Finlandia
1 ounce Kahlúa
1 ounce half-and-half
Cherry, for garnish
Coke, for garnish

1. Swirl a chilled cocktail glass with chocolate syrup.
2. Pour Finlandia, Kahlúa and half-and-half into a mixing tin over ice. Shake well and strain into the cocktail glass.
3. Spear cherries onto a sword toothpick.
4. Hang it on the rim of the glass and drizzle chocolate over the cherries into the drink.
5. Garnish with splash of Coke and 2 cherries.

Tommy Bahama Blue Hawaiian

The Blue Hawaiian is a tropical cocktail made of rum, pineapple juice, blue Curacao, sweet and sour mix, and sometimes vodka.

INGREDIENTS | SERVES 1

1 part (1 shot) Tommy Bahama White Sand Rum
1 part Blue Curacao
2 parts pineapple juice
1 part coconut cream
Crushed ice
Pineapple slice, for garnish
Maraschino cherry, for garnish

1. Pour rum, Blue Curacao, pineapple juice, and coconut cream into a blender with a scoop of crushed ice. Blend until smooth. Pour into a glass.
2. Garnish with a slice of fresh pineapple and a maraschino cherry.

Tommy Bahama Calypso Sun

This tropical drink is full of fruity flavor.

INGREDIENTS | SERVES 1

2 ounces Tommy Bahama Golden Sun Rum
2 ounces pineapple juice
1 ounce fresh orange juice
1 ounce Coco Lopez

Mix all ingredients over ice in a hurricane glass.

Tommy Bahama Crazy Cuban

This island-inspired cocktail features rum and tropical juices.

INGREDIENTS | SERVES 1

1 ounce Tommy Bahama White Sand Rum
½ ounce Tommy Bahama Golden Sand Rum
1 ounce coconut rum
½ ounce 99 Bananas
3 ounces pineapple juice
Pineapple, for garnish
Cherry, for garnish

1. Mix all the ingredients over ice in a hurricane glass.
2. Garnish the drink with a pineapple and a cherry.

Tommy Bahama Millionaire Mojito

Sugar is used in this popular cocktail from Tommy Bahama.

INGREDIENTS | SERVES 1

2 parts Tommy Bahama White Sand Rum
1 teaspoon superfine sugar
Juice of 1 lime
Crushed ice
Dash of sparkling soda
1 bunch fresh mint

1. Mix the rum, sugar, and lime juice in a shaker. Add ice.
2. Shake well and pour into a chilled glass.
3. Add sparkling soda.
4. Garnish with a mint sprig.

Cinnabon Mochalatte Chill

A Cinnabon Mochalatta Chill is a really sweet treat.

INGREDIENTS | SERVES 2

1 cup cold strong coffee
1 cup half-and-half
½ cup chocolate syrup
Whipped cream, for garnish

1. Make double-strength coffee in your coffee maker by adding half the water suggested by the manufacturer.
2. Allow the brewed coffee to chill in the refrigerator for at least an hour.
3. Combine all ingredients in a small pitcher and stir well.
4. Pour over ice in 2 (16-ounce) glasses
5. Top with whipped cream.

Cinnabon Orange Icescape

This orange drink is similar in flavor to the Orange Julius served in malls throughout the United States.

INGREDIENTS | SERVES 2

3 cups crushed ice
1 cup water
⅔ cup orange juice
½ cup half-and-half
3 tablespoons Tang orange drink mix

1. Pour all the ingredients in a blender.
2. Mix on high speed until smooth and creamy.
3. Serve in 2 (16-ounce) glasses.

Dairy Queen Moolatte

You will enjoy this coffee and ice cream drink from Dairy Queen

INGREDIENTS | SERVES 2

⅓ cup sugar
1 cup strong coffee
3 cups ice
2 cups vanilla ice cream
¼ cup milk
Whipped cream, for garnish

1. Dissolve the sugar in the coffee and chill until cold.
2. Combine all the ingredients in a blender.
3. Blend until the ice is crushed and the drink is smooth.
4. Pour into 2 (16-ounce) glasses and top with whipped cream.

Dunkin Donuts Iced Coffee

Iced coffee is a popular item at all the fast food chains. This one is very easy to make.

INGREDIENTS | SERVES 1

1 tablespoon sugar
4 ice cubes
⅔ cup cold coffee
⅔ cup milk

1. Put the sugar in a large glass.
2. Drop in ice cubes.
3. Pour the coffee over the ice and add milk.
4. Stir until the sugar has dissolved.

Houlihan's Houli Fruit Fizz

This is a refreshing fruit drink recipe for a hot summer day.

INGREDIENTS | SERVES 2

1 (12-ounce) can cold Sprite
½ cup cold pineapple juice
¼ cup cold orange juice
1 cup cold cranberry juice

1. Combine all of the ingredients in a pitcher.
2. Pour into 2 glasses over ice.

Jack in the Box Oreo Shake

The children in your family will enjoy this sweet treat.

INGREDIENTS | SERVES 2

3 cups vanilla ice cream
1½ cups milk
8 Oreo cookies

1. Combine the ice cream and milk in a blender. Mix on low speed until smooth.
2. Break Oreo cookies and add them to the blender.
3. Mix on low speed for 5–10 seconds, until cookies are mostly puréed into the shake but a few larger pieces remain.
4. Stir with a spoon to help combine the cookies.
5. Pour the shakes into 2 (12-ounce) glasses.

McDonald's Caramel Frappe

According to McDonald's, you deserve a break today with this sweet coffee drink.

INGREDIENTS | SERVES 2

2 cups ice
½ cup milk
½ cup strong coffee
2 tablespoons sugar
2 tablespoons caramel syrup
⅓ cup whipped cream, for garnish
Drizzle of caramel syrup, for garnish

1. Add all the drink ingredients into a blender. Mix well.
2. Divide into 2 tall glasses.
3. Garnish with whipped cream and drizzle with caramel syrup.

McDonald's Vanilla Iced Coffee

McDonald's is cashing in on the coffee craze with this iced coffee recipe.

INGREDIENTS | SERVES 6

6 tablespoons ground coffee
6⅓ cups cold water
14 ounces sweetened condensed milk
2 tablespoons vanilla extract
Ice cubes

1. Brew the coffee in a coffee maker. After it's done brewing, set aside to cool.
2. Combine brewed coffee and sweetened condensed milk in a large pitcher. Stir thoroughly until coffee and condensed milk are blended together.
3. Stir in the vanilla extract.
4. Refrigerate until the coffee is chilled.
5. Serve in glasses filled with ice.

Orange Julius

You know it and you love it, and now you can make it at home.

INGREDIENTS | SERVES 1

6 ounces frozen orange juice concentrate
1 cup milk
1 cup water
¼ cup sugar
1 teaspoon vanilla
8 ice cubes

1. Combine all the ingredients except the ice cubes in a blender.
2. Blend 1–2 minutes.
3. Add ice cubes one at a time, until smooth.

Orange Julius
The Orange Julius grew out of a California orange juice stand in the late 1920s. The stand was run by a man named Julius Freed, and the creamy texture of the drink recipe was developed to make the acid in the orange juice less bothersome to the stomach.

Red Lobster Boston Tea

New Englander's love their cranberry juice, and this tea is full of it.

INGREDIENTS | SERVES 1

1 cup brewed tea
1 cup cranberry juice

1. Mix equal parts tea and cranberry juice.
2. Serve in a tall glass over ice.

Sonic Cherry Limeade

No need to run to the mall when you crave this signature drink.

INGREDIENTS | SERVES 1

1 (12-ounce) can of Sprite
Juice of 3 lime wedges
¼ cup cherry juice

1. Fill a 16-ounce glass ⅔ full with ice.
2. Pour the Sprite over the ice.
3. Squeeze the lime juice into the drink and drop the wedges in.
4. Add the cherry juice.
5. Serve with a straw.

Starbucks Coffee Frappe

Learn how easy it is to make a copycat of Starbucks iced coffee.

INGREDIENTS | SERVES 2

18–22 crushed ice cubes
7 ounces chilled double-strength coffee
2 tablespoons granulated sugar
2 tablespoons flavored syrup of choice
Whipped cream, for garnish

1. Place the ice, coffee, sugar, and syrup in a blender. Blend until smooth.
2. Pour into a large, tall glass. Garnish with whipped cream.

Starbucks Mocha Frappucino

This is a recipe for the frosty chocolate goodness that you crave.

INGREDIENTS | SERVES 4

6 cups double-strength brewed dark roast coffee
⅔ cup unsweetened cocoa powder
2 cups nonfat milk
Cocoa powder, for garnish

1. Fill ice-cube trays with half of the brewed coffee and place in the freezer.
2. In a bowl, combine the remaining brewed coffee, cocoa powder, and milk and stir well to dissolve.
3. Cover and chill.
4. When the ice cubes have frozen, transfer them to a zip-top bag and crush them.
5. Fill 4 glasses with the crushed ice and divide the coffee-cocoa mixture evenly among them. Dust the top of each glass with cocoa powder.

Wendy's Frosty

This is the original recipe for the cool and refreshing ice cream drink.

INGREDIENTS | SERVES 2–4

¾ cup milk
¼ cup Hershey chocolate powder
4 cups vanilla ice cream

1. Combine all of the drink ingredients in a blender.
2. Blend on medium speed until creamy and thick. Stir if necessary.
3. If too thin, freeze the mixture in the serving cups until thicker.

APPENDIX A
Recipe List by Restaurant Name

A

Applebee's Baby Back Ribs
Applebee's Bananaberry Breeze
Applebee's Blondie Brownies
Applebee's Bourbon Street Steak
Applebee's Cheese Chicken Tortilla Soup
Applebee's Garlic and Peppercorn Fried Shrimp
Applebee's Garlic Mashed Potatoes
Applebee's Oriental Chicken Salad
Applebee's Pico de Gallo
Applebee's Strawberry Dessert Shooters
Applebee's Southwest Steak
Applebee's Spinach and Artichoke Dip
Applebee's Tequila Lime Chicken
Applebee's Veggie Patch Pizza
Arby's Apple Turnovers
Arby's Barbecue Sauce
Arby's Roast Beef Sandwich
Auntie Anne's Soft Pretzels
A&W Coney Island Sauce

B

Bahama Breeze Calypso Shrimp Pasta
Bahama Breeze Jamaican Marinade
Bahama Breeze Vegetable Sauté
Benihana Fried Rice
Benihana Hibachi Meat Marinade
Benihana Sesame Chicken
Bennigan's Chicken and Shrimp Skewers
Bennigan's Broccoli Bites
Bennigan's Candy Bar Drink
Bennigan's Death by Chocolate Cake
Bob Evans Peanut Butter Pie
Bob Evans Sausage Gravy
Boston Market Corn Bread
Boston Market Creamed Spinach
Boston Market Dill Potato Wedges
Boston Market Macaroni and Cheese
Boston Market Meatloaf
Boston Market Squash Casserole
Boston Market Stuffing
Boston Market Sweet Potato Casserole
Boston Market Whole Rotisserie Chicken
Buca di Beppo Chicken Limone
Buca di Beppo Chicken Marsala
Buca di Beppo Penne Cardinale
Buca di Beppo Chicken Saltimbocca
Burger King Chicken Fries

C

California Pizza Kitchen Pea and Barley Soup
California Pizza Kitchen Waldorf Chicken Salad
California Pizza Kitchen Wedge Salad
Carino's Angel Hair with Artichokes
Carino's Five Meat Tuscan Pasta
Carino's Grilled Chicken Bowtie Festival
Carino's Spicy Shrimp and Chicken
Carl's Jr. Six Dollar Burger
Carl's Jr. Western Bacon Cheeseburger
Carrabba's Bread Dipping Mix
Carrabba's Linguine Pescatore
Carrabba's Meatballs
Carrabba's Mussels in Wine Sauce
Carrabba's Pasta Weesie
Cheesecake Factory Crab Cakes
Cheesecake Factory Jambalaya Pasta
Cheesecake Factory Oreo Cheesecake

Cheesecake Factory Pumpkin Cheesecake
Chevys Fresh Mex Fuego Spice Mix
Chevys Fresh Mex San Antonio Veggies
Chevys Fresh Mex Habanero Steak Fajitas
Chi-Chi's Baked Chicken Chimichangas
Chi-Chi's Margarita Marinade
Chi-Chi's Seafood Enchiladas
Chi-Chi's Seafood Nachos
Chili's Black Bean Soup
Chili's Boneless Buffalo Wings
Chili's Cajun Chicken Pasta
Chili's Calypso Cooler
Chili's Chicken Enchilada Soup
Chili's Chicken Mushroom Soup
Chili's Chicken Fajita Nachos
Chili's Chocolate Chip Paradise Pie
Chili's Electric Lemonade
Chili's Grilled Caribbean Chicken Salad
Chili's Margarita Grilled Chicken
Chili's Mighty Ice Cream Pie
Chili's Molten Lava Cake
Chili's Monterey Chicken
Chili's Presidente Margarita
Chili's Skillet Queso
Chili's Southwest Chicken Chili
Chili's Southwestern Egg Rolls
Chili's Texas Cheese Fries
Chipotle Cilantro Lime Rice
Chipotle Marinated Chicken
Chipotle Pork Carnitas
Chipotle Steak Barbacoa

Cinnabon Cinnamon Rolls
Cinnabon Mochalatte Chill
Cinnabon Orange Icescape
Cracker Barrel Apple Streusel French Toast
Cracker Barrel Baby Carrots
Cracker Barrel Banana Pudding
Cracker Barrel Carrot Cake
Cracker Barrel Cherry Chocolate Cobbler
Cracker Barrel Corn Bread Dressing
Cracker Barrel Country Green Beans
Cracker Barrel Fried Apples
Cracker Barrel Grilled Chicken Tenders
Cracker Barrel Ham and Red Eye Gravy
Cracker Barrel Hash Brown Casserole

D

Dairy Queen Moolatte
Dave and Buster's Philly Steak Rolls
Dave and Buster's Cheeseburger Pizza
Dave and Buster's Muffaletta Salad
Denny's Country Fried Steak
Denny's Country Gravy
Denny's Pancake Puppies
Domino's Cinna Stix
Dunkin Donuts Iced Coffee

E

El Pollo Loco Chicken
El Torito Guacamole
El Torito Veggie Mix

G

Golden Corral Bread Pudding
Golden Corral Seafood Salad

H

Hardee's Mushroom Swiss Burger
Hometown Buffet Spinach Casserole
Hooters Hot Wings
Hooters Hot Wing Sauce
Houlihan's Houli Fruit Fizz
Houston's Hawaiian Steak Marinade

I

IHOP Chicken Fajita Omelette
IHOP Colorado Omelette
IHOP Harvest Grain and Nut Pancakes
IHOP Loaded Country Hash Brown Potatoes
IHOP New York Cheesecake Pancakes
IHOP Stuffed French Toast
In-n-Out Double-Double Burger

J

Jack in the Box Mini Buffalo Chicken Sandwich
Jack in the Box Oreo Shake
Joe's Crab Shack Crab Dip
Joe's Crab Shack Crab Nachos
Johnny Carino's Italian Nachos

K

KFC Barbecue Baked Beans
KFC Bean Salad
KFC Coleslaw
KFC Corn
KFC Crispy Strips
KFC Macaroni Salad

APPENDIX A **RECIPE LIST BY RESTAURANT NAME**

KFC Mashed Potatoes and Gravy
KFC Pepper Mayonnaise Sauce
KFC Potato Salad
KFC Potato Wedges
KFC Twister

L

Little Caesars Crazy Sauce
Long John Silver's Baja Sauce
Long John Silver's Beer-Battered Fish
Long John Silver's Fish Tacos
LongHorn Steakhouse Steak Marinade
Lone Star Steakhouse Steak Sauce

M

McDonald's Breakfast Burrito
McDonald's Caramel Frappe
McDonald's Fillet of Fish
McDonald's Steak, Egg, and Cheese Bagel Sandwich
McDonald's Vanilla Iced Coffee
McDonald's Yogurt Parfait
Morton's Garlic Green Beans
Mrs. Fields Chocolate Chip Cookies

O

O'Charley's Black and Blue Steak Salad
O'Charley's Loaded Potato Soup
Olive Garden Angel Hair and Three Onion Soup
Olive Garden Apple Carmelina
Olive Garden Bread Sticks
Olive Garden Capellini Pomodoro
Olive Garden Chicken and Gnocchi Soup
Olive Garden Chicken Milanese
Olive Garden Chicken Scampi
Olive Garden Fried Mozzarella
Olive Garden House Salad
Olive Garden Salad Dressing
Olive Garden Italian Sausage Soup
Olive Garden Minestrone Soup
Olive Garden Pasta e Fagioli Soup
Olive Garden Pasta Roma Soup
Olive Garden Penne Romana
Olive Garden Seafood Pasta Chowder
Olive Garden Smoked Mozzarella Fondue
Olive Garden Steak Tuscano
Olive Garden Strawberries Romano
Olive Garden Stuffed Mushrooms
Olive Garden Toasted Ravioli
Olive Garden Tomato Basil Crostini
Olive Garden Tuscan Garlic Chicken
Olive Garden Venetian Apricot Chicken
Olive Garden Zuppa Toscana Soup
Orange Julius
Outback Steakhouse Aussie Fries
Outback Steakhouse Bloomin' Onion
Outback Steakhouse Bloomin' Onion Dipping Sauce
Outback Steakhouse Coconut Shrimp
Outback Steakhouse Key Lime Pie
Outback Steakhouse Creole Marmalade Dipping Sauce
Outback Steakhouse Sautéed Mushrooms
Outback Steakhouse Shrimp on the Barbie
Outback Steakhouse Steak Seasoning
Outback Steakhouse Sweet Potato
Outback Steakhouse Wallaby Darned

P

Panda Express Beijing Beef
Panda Express Chow Mein
Panda Express Kung Pao Chicken, Shrimp, or Beef
Panda Express Mandarin Chicken
Panda Express Orange Chicken
Panda Express Spicy Chicken
Panera Bread Company Tomato Mozzarella Salad
Papa John's Garlic Sauce
P.F. Chang's Chicken Lettuce Wraps
P.F. Chang's Coconut Curry Vegetables
P.F. Chang's Dan Dan Noodles
P.F. Chang's Firecracker Shrimp
P.F. Chang's Lemon Pepper Shrimp
P.F. Chang's Mongolian Beef
P.F. Chang's Singapore Street Noodles
P.F. Chang's Spare Ribs
P.F. Chang's Spicy Eggplant
P.F. Chang's Szechuan Chicken Chow Fun
P.F. Chang's Wonton Soup
P.F. Chang's Zodiac Noodles
Pizza Hut Cavatini
Pizza Hut Dessert Pizza
Pizza Hut Stuffed Crust Pizza
Ponderosa Steak Sauce
Popeye's Biscuits
Popeye's Cajun Gravy

Popeye's Dirty Rice
Popeye's Fried Chicken
Popeye's Red Beans and Rice

Q

Qdoba Mango Salsa
Quiznos Steakhouse Dip Submarine

R

Red Lobster Boston Tea
Red Lobster Cheddar Bay Biscuits
Red Lobster Clam Chowder
Romano's Macaroni Carmela's Chicken
Romano's Macaroni Grill Penne Rustica
Romano's Macaroni Grill Shrimp Portofino
Ruby Tuesday Chicken Quesadillas
Ruby Tuesday New Orleans Seafood
Ruby Tuesday Sonora Chicken Pasta
Ruby Tuesday White Chicken Chili

S

Shoney's Broccoli Casserole
Shoney's Pot Roast
Sizzler Cheese Toast
Sonic Cherry Limeade
Sonic Fritos Chili Cheese Wrap
Sonic Hickory Burger
Starbucks Black Bottom Cupcakes
Starbucks Bran Muffins
Starbucks Coffee Frappe
Starbucks Mocha Frappucino
Starbucks Oatmeal Cookies
Starbucks Tarragon Chicken Salad
Steak & Ale Burgundy Mushrooms
Steak 'n Shake Chili

Steak 'n Shake Frisco Melt
Subway Orchard Chicken Salad
Subway Sweet Onion Chicken Teriyaki Sandwich
Subway Veggie Delite Wrap
Subway White Chocolate Macadamia Nut Cookies

T

Taco Bell Caramel Apple Empanadas
Taco Bell Crispitos
Taco Bell Enchiritos
Taco Bell Fiesta Bowls
Taco Bell Fire Border Sauce
Taco Bell Mexican Pizza
Taco Bell Santa Fe Gorditas
Texas Roadhouse Honey Cinnamon Butter
Texas Roadhouse Steak Rub
T.G.I. Friday's Baked Potato Skins
T.G.I. Friday's Broccoli Cheese Soup
T.G.I. Friday's Chocolate Monkey
T.G.I. Friday's Dragonfire Chicken
T.G.I. Friday's Dreamsicle
T.G.I. Friday's Flying Grasshopper
T.G.I. Friday's French Onion Soup
T.G.I. Friday's Jack Daniels Grilling Sauce
T.G.I. Friday's Long Island Iced Tea
T.G.I. Friday's Midnight Meltdown
T.G.I. Friday's Nine Layer Dip
T.G.I. Friday's Sizzling Chicken and Cheese
T.G.I. Friday's Spicy Cajun Chicken Pasta

T.G.I. Friday's Strawberry Fields Salad
The Melting Pot Dark Chocolate Raspberry Fondue
The Melting Pot Flaming Turtle Fondue
Tommy Bahama Blue Hawaiian
Tommy Bahama Calypso Sun
Tommy Bahama Crab Cakes
Tommy Bahama Crazy Cuban
Tommy Bahama Millionaire Mojito
Tony Roma's Carolina Barbecue Sauce
Tony Roma's Corn Fritter Casserole
Tony Roma's Maple Sweet Potatoes
Tony Roma's Red Hot Barbecue Sauce

W

Wendy's Frosty
Wendy's Spicy Chicken Sandwich
White Castle Sliders

APPENDIX B

Restaurant and Copycat Recipe Websites

Restaurant Websites

Applebee's
www.applebees.com

Bahama Breeze
www.bahamabreeze.com

Benihana
www.benihana.com

Bennigans
www.bennigans.com

Bob Evans
www.bobevans.com

Boston Market
www.bostonmarket.com

Buca di Beppo
www.bucadibeppo.com

Burger King
www.bk.com

California Pizza Kitchen
www.cpk.com

Carino's
www.carinos.com

Carl's Jr.
www.carlsjr.com

Carrabba's Italian Grill
www.carrabbas.com

Cheesecake Factory
www.thecheesecakefactory.com

Chevy's Fresh Mex
www.chevys.com

Chi Chi's
www.chichissalsa.com

Chili's
www.chilis.com

Chipotle Mexican Grill
www.chipotle.com

Cinnabon
www.cinnabon.com

Cracker Barrel
www.crackerbarrel.com

Dairy Queen
www.dairyqueen.com

Dave and Buster's
www.daveandbusters.com

Denny's
www.dennys.com

Dominos
www.dominos.com

Dunkin Donuts
www.dunkindonuts.com

El Pollo Loco
www.elpolloloco.com

El Torito's
www.eltorito.com

Golden Corral
www.goldencorral.com

Hardee's
www.hardees.com

Hometown Buffet
www.oldcountrybuffet.com

Hooters
www.hooters.com

Houlihan's
www.houlihans.com

IHOP
www.ihop.com

In-n-Out
www.in-n-out.com

Jack in the Box
www.jackinthebox.com

Joe's Crab Shack
www.joescrabshack.com

KFC
www.kfc.com

Little Caesar's
www.littlecaesars.com

Long John Silver
www.longjohnsilvers.com

McDonald's
www.mcdonalds.com

The Melting Pot
www.meltingpot.com

Morton's
www.mortons.com

Mrs. Fields
www.mrsfields.com

O'Charley's
www.ocharleys.com

Olive Garden
www.olivegarden.com

Orange Julius
www.orangejulius.com

Outback Steakhouse
www.outback.com

Panda Express
www.pandaexpress.com

Panera Bread Company
www.panerabread.com

Papa John
www.papajohns.com

P.F. Chang's China Bistro
www.pfchangs.com

Pizza Hut
www.pizzahut.com

Ponderosa
www.ponderosasteakhouses.com

Popeye's
www.popeyes.com

Qdoba
www.qdoba.com

Red Lobster
www.redlobster.com

Romano's Macaroni Grill
www.macaronigrill.com

Ruby Tuesday's
www.rubytuesday.com

Shoneys
www.shoneys.com

Sizzler
www.sizzler.com

Sonic Drive In
www.sonicdrivein.com

Starbucks
www.starbucks.com

Steak 'n Shake
www.steaknshake.com

Subway
www.subway.com

Taco Bell
www.tacobell.com

Texas Roadhouse
www.texasroadhouse.com

T.G.I. Friday's
www.tgifridays.com

Tommy Bahama
www.tommybahama.com

Tony Roma's
www.tonyromas.com

Wendy's
www.wendys.com

White Castle
www.whitecastle.com

Copycat Websites

CD Kitchen *(www.cdkitchen.com/copycat/)*

Every Last Recipe *(www.everylastrecipe.com)*

Food.com *(www.food.com)*

Kitchen Link *(www.kitchenlink.com/copycat.html)*

Recipe Goldmine *(www.recipegoldmine.com)*

Recipe Lion *(www.recipelion.com)*

Recipe Secrets *(www.recipesecrets.net)*

Top Secret Recipes *(www.topsecretrecipes.com)*

APPENDIX C
Healthier Substitutions and Conversions

Bacon	Canadian bacon, turkey bacon, smoked turkey, or lean prosciutto (Italian ham)
White bread	Whole-wheat bread
White bread crumbs	Rolled oats, whole-wheat panko crumbs, or crushed bran cereal
Butter, margarine, shortening or oil to prevent sticking	Cooking spray or nonstick pans
Cream cheese	Fat-free or low-fat cream cheese, fat-free ricotta cheese
Cheese	Low-fat or fat-free cheese
Eggs	Two egg whites or 1/4 cup egg substitute for each whole egg
White flour	Whole-wheat flour for half of the called-for all-purpose flour
Ground beef	Extra-lean or lean ground beef, chicken or turkey breast
Iceberg lettuce	Arugula, chicory, collard greens, dandelion greens, kale, mustard greens, spinach or watercress
Whole milk	Evaporated skim milk, reduced-fat or fat-free milk
Pasta	Whole-wheat pasta
White rice	Brown rice, wild rice, bulgur, or pearl barley
Salad dressing	Fat-free or reduced-calorie dressing or flavored vinegars
Salt	Herbs, spices, fruit juices or salt-free seasoning mixes or herb blends
Sour cream	Fat-free or low-fat sour cream, plain fat-free or low-fat yogurt
Soy sauce	Sweet-and-sour sauce, hot mustard sauce or low-sodium soy sauce
Syrup	Pureed fruit, such as applesauce, or low-calorie, sugar-free syrup

Standard U.S./Metric Measurement Conversions

VOLUME CONVERSIONS

U.S. Volume Measure	Metric Equivalent
⅛ teaspoon	0.5 milliliters
¼ teaspoon	1 milliliters
½ teaspoon	2 milliliters
1 teaspoon	5 milliliters
½ tablespoon	7 milliliters
1 tablespoon (3 teaspoons)	15 milliliters
2 tablespoons (1 fluid ounce)	30 milliliters
¼ cup (4 tablespoons)	60 milliliters
⅓ cup	90 milliliters
½ cup (4 fluid ounces)	125 milliliters
⅔ cup	160 milliliters
¾ cup (6 fluid ounces)	180 milliliters
1 cup (16 tablespoons)	250 milliliters
1 pint (2 cups)	500 milliliters
1 quart (4 cups)	1 liter (about)

WEIGHT CONVERSIONS

U.S. Weight Measure	Metric Equivalent
½ ounce	15 grams
1 ounce	30 grams
2 ounces	60 grams
3 ounces	85 grams
¼ pound (4 ounces)	115 grams
½ pound (8 ounces)	225 grams
¾ pound (12 ounces)	340 grams
1 pound (16 ounces)	454 grams

OVEN TEMPERATURE CONVERSIONS

Degrees Fahrenheit	Degrees Celsius
200 degrees F	100 degrees C
250 degrees F	120 degrees C
275 degrees F	140 degrees C
300 degrees F	150 degrees C
325 degrees F	160 degrees C
350 degrees F	180 degrees C
375 degrees F	190 degrees C
400 degrees F	200 degrees C
425 degrees F	220 degrees C
450 degrees F	230 degrees C

BAKING PAN SIZES

American	Metric
8 x 1½ inch round baking pan	20 x 4 cm cake tin
9 x 1½ inch round baking pan	23 x 3.5 cm cake tin
1 x 7 x 1½ inch baking pan	28 x 18 x 4 cm baking tin
13 x 9 x 2 inch baking pan	30 x 20 x 5 cm baking tin
2 quart rectangular baking dish	30 x 20 x 3 cm baking tin
15 x 10 x 2 inch baking pan	30 x 25 x 2 cm baking tin (Swiss roll tin)
9 inch pie plate	22 x 4 or 23 x 4 cm pie plate
7 or 8 inch springform pan	18 or 20 cm springform or loose bottom cake tin
9 x 5 x 3 inch loaf pan	23 x 13 x 7 cm or 2 lb narrow loaf or pate tin
1½ quart casserole	1.5 litre casserole
2 quart casserole	2 litre casserole

Index

Note: Page numbers in **bold** indicate recipe category lists.

A&W Coney Island Sauce, 95
Appetizers, **32–33**, 34–54
Applebee's
   about, 127
   Baby Back Ribs, 126
   Bananaberry Freeze, 267
   Blondie Brownies, 243
   Bourbon Street Steak, 112
   Cheese Chicken Tortilla Soup, 56
   Garlic and Peppercorn Fried Shrimp, 127
   Garlic Mashed Potatoes, 128
   Oriental Chicken Salad, 76
   Pico de Gallo, 34
   Southwest Steak, 113
   Spinach and Artichoke Dip, 34
   Strawberry Dessert Shooters, 244
   Tequila Lime Chicken, 129
   Veggie Patch Pizza, 130
Apples
   Arby's Apple Turnovers, 245
   Cracker Barrel Apple Streusel French Toast, 18
   Cracker Barrel Fried Apples, 19
   Olive Garden Apple Carmelina, 256
   Taco Bell Caramel Apple Empanadas, 262
Appliances and cookware, 2–4
Arby's
   Apple Turnovers, 245
   Barbecue Sauce, 77
   Roast Beef Sandwich, 77
Artichokes
   Applebee's Spinach and Artichoke Dip, 34
   Carino's Angel Hair with Artichokes, 190
Asian food, **163**–83. *See also specific restaurants*
Asparagus, buying, 10
Aunt Annie's Soft Pretzels, 94
Avocado, in El Torito Guacamole, 156

Bahama Breeze
   about, 132
   Calypso Shrimp Pasta, 131
   Jamaican Marinade, 132
   Vegetable Sauté, 133
Baking items, 6–7
Bananas
   Applebee's Bananaberry Breeze, 267

Cracker Barrel Banana Pudding, 252
Bar food, **125**–44
Basting, 12
Beans and legumes. *See also* Green beans
   about: buying, 10, 11
   California Pizza Kitchen Pea and Barley Soup, 57
   Chili's Black Bean Soup, 58
   Chili's Southwestern Eggrolls, 40
   KFC Barbecue Baked Beans, 220
   KFC Bean Salad, 82
   Olive Garden Minestrone Soup, 66
   Olive Garden Pasta e Fagioli Soup, 67
   Olive Garden Pasta Roma Soup, 68
   Popeye's Red Beans and Rice, 236
   Ruby Tuesday White Chicken Chili, 72
   Steak 'n Shake Chili, 73
   Taco Bell Fiesta Bowls, 159
   Taco Bell Santa Fe Gorditas, 161
Beef. *See also* Sandwiches
   about: beans and rice, 236; buying and storing, 8, 9; history of chicken fried steak, 21; leftover meatloaf, 212; slicing, 167
   Applebee's Bourbon Street Steak, 112
   Applebee's Southwest Steak, 113
   Boston Market Meatloaf, 212
   Carrabba's Meatballs, 194
   Chevys Fresh Mex Habanero Steak Fajitas, 147
   Chipotle Steak Barbacoa, 154
   Dave and Buster's Cheeseburger Pizza, 218
   Dave and Buster's Philly Steak Rolls, 42
   Denny's Country Fried Steak, 21
   McDonald's Steak, Egg, and Cheese Bagel Sandwich, 30
   O'Charley's Black and Blue Steak Salad, 116
   Olive Garden Pasta e Fagioli Soup, 67
   Olive Garden Steak Tuscano, 117
   Outback Steakhouse Steak Seasoning, 120
   Panda Express Beijing Beef, 167
   Panda Express Kung Pao Beef, 169
   P.F. Chang's Mongolian Beef, 178
   sauces and marinades. *See* Sauces, dressings, and dips
   Shoney's Pot Roast, 225

Steak 'n Shake Chili, 73
Taco Bell Enchiritos, 158
Benihana
   about, 165
   Fried Rice, 164
   Hibachi Meat Marinade, 164
   Sesame Chicken, 165
Bennigan's
   about, 267
   Bamboo Chicken and Shrimp Skewers, 166
   Broccoli Bites, 35
   Candy Bar Drink, 267
   Death by Chocolate Cake, 246
   Honey-Mustard Dipping Sauce, 35
Berries
   Applebee's Strawberry Dessert Shooters, 244
   Olive Garden Strawberries Romano, 257
   T.G.I. Friday's Strawberry Fields Salad, 90
Blanching, 12
Bob Evans
   about: in the supermarket, 16
   Peanut Butter Pie, 246
   Sausage Gravy, 16
Boston Market
   about, 228
   Corn Bread, 228
   Creamed Spinach, 210
   Dill Potato Wedges, 210
   Macaroni and Cheese, 211
   Meatloaf, 212
   Squash Casserole, 213
   Stuffing, 214
   Sweet Potato Casserole, 215
   Whole Rotisserie Chicken, 216
Boyardee, Chef, 191
Braising, 12
Breads. *See also* Pancakes, waffles, and French toast; Pizzas
   Boston Market Corn Bread, 228
   Cinnabon Cinnamon Rolls, 17
   Olive Garden Bread Sticks, 45
   Olive Garden Tomato Basil Crostini, 50
   Popeye's Biscuits, 232
   Red Lobster Cheddar Bay Biscuits, 53
   Sizzler Cheese Toast, 121
   Starbucks Bran Muffins, 31
   Tony Roma's Corn Fritter Casserole, 238
Breakfast and brunch, **15**–31
Brining, 12

Broccoli
   about: buying, 10
   Bennigan's Broccoli Bites, 35
   P.F. Chang's Coconut Curry Vegetables, 174
   Shoney's Broccoli Casserole, 224
   T.G.I. Friday's Broccoli Cheese Soup, 74
Broiling, 12
Buca di Beppo
   about, 187
   Chicken Limone, 186
   Chicken Marsala, 187
   Chicken Saltimbocca, 189
   Penne Cardinale, 188
Burger King Chicken Fries, 96
Butterflying, 12

Cabbage
   about: buying, 10
   KFC Coleslaw, 221
   Panda Express Chow Mein, 168
California Pizza Kitchen
   about, 78
   Pea and Barley Soup, 57
   Waldorf Chicken Salad, 79
   Wedge Salad, 78
Carino's
   Angel Hair with Artichokes, 190
   Five Meat Tuscan Pasta, 191
   Grilled Chicken Bowtie Festival, 192
   Spicy Shrimp and Chicken, 193
Carl's Jr.
   Six Dollar Burger, 97
   Western Bacon Cheeseburger, 98
Carrabba's
   Bread Dipping Mix, 36
   Linguine Pescatore, 193
   Meatballs, 194
   Mussels in Wine Sauce, 196
   Pasta Weesie, 195
Carrots
   Cracker Barrel Baby Carrots, 230
   Cracker Barrel Carrot Cake, 253
Cauliflower, buying, 10
Celery, buying, 10
Cheese
   about: grating, 198
   Applebee's Cheese Chicken Tortilla Soup, 56
   Boston Market Macaroni and Cheese, 211
   Cheesecake Factory Oreo Cheesecake, 247
   Cheesecake Factory Pumpkin

Cheesecake, 248
Chili's Skillet Queso, 39
Cream Cheese Frosting, 253
IHOP New York Cheesecake Pancakes, 27
Olive Garden Fried Mozzarella, 46
Olive Garden Smoked Mozzarella Fondue, 47
Olive Garden Strawberries Romano, 257
Taco Bell Fiesta Bowls, 159
Cheesecake Factory
 about, 248
 Crab Cakes, 217
 Jambalaya Pasta, 229
 Oreo Cheesecake, 247
 Pumpkin Cheesecake, 248
Cherries
 Cracker Barrel Cherry Chocolate Cobbler, 254
 Sonic Cherry Limeade, 280
Chevys Fresh Mex
 about, 146
 Fuego Spice Mix, 146
 Habanero Steak Fajitas, 147
 San Antonio Veggies, 146
Chi-Chi's
 about, 148
 Baked Chicken Chimichangas, 148
 Margarita Marinade, 149
 Seafood Enchiladas, 150
 Seafood Nachos, 36
Chicken
 about: buying and preparing, 8–9, 59; history of hot wings, 136; rotisserie, 59
 Applebee's Cheese Chicken Tortilla Soup, 56
 Applebee's Oriental Chicken Salad, 76
 Applebee's Tequila Lime Chicken, 129
 Benihana Sesame Chicken, 165
 Bennigan's Bamboo Chicken and Shrimp Skewers, 166
 Boston Market Whole Rotisserie Chicken, 216
 Buca di Beppo Chicken Limone, 186
 Buca di Beppo Chicken Marsala, 187
 Buca di Beppo Chicken Saltimbocca, 189
 Buca di Beppo Penne Cardinale, 188
 Burger King Chicken Fries, 96
 California Pizza Kitchen Waldorf Chicken Salad, 79
 Carino's Grilled Chicken Bowtie Festival, 192
 Carino's Spicy Shrimp and Chicken, 193
 Cheesecake Factory Jambalaya Pasta, 229
 Chi-Chi's Baked Chicken Chimichangas, 148
 Chili's Boneless Buffalo Wings, 37
 Chili's Cajun Chicken Pasta, 134
 Chili's Chicken Enchilada Soup, 59
 Chili's Chicken Fajita Nachos, 38
 Chili's Chicken Mushroom Soup, 60
 Chili's Grilled Caribbean Chicken Salad, 80
 Chili's Margarita Grilled Chicken, 134
 Chili's Monterey Chicken, 135
 Chili's Southwest Chicken Chili, 61
 Chipotle Marinated Chicken, 152
 Cracker Barrel Grilled Chicken Tenders, 231
 El Pollo Loco Chicken, 155
 Hooters Hot Wings and Sauce, 136–37
 IHOP Chicken Fajita Omelet, 24
 Jack in the Box Mini Buffalo Chicken Sandwiches, 101
 Johnny Carino's Italian Nachos, 44
 KFC Crispy Strips, 102
 KFC Twister, 103
 Olive Garden Chicken and Gnocchi Soup, 64
 Olive Garden Chicken Milanese, 199
 Olive Garden Chicken Scampi, 200
 Olive Garden Tuscan Garlic Chicken, 202
 Olive Garden Venetian Apricot Chicken, 203
 Panda Express Kung Pao Chicken, 169
 Panda Express Mandarin Chicken, 170
 Panda Express Orange Chicken, 171
 Panda Express Spicy Chicken, 172
 P.F. Chang's Chicken Lettuce Wraps, 173
 P.F. Chang's Singapore Street Noodles, 179
 P.F. Chang's Szechuan Chicken Chow Fun, 182
 P.F. Chang's Wonton Soup, 71
 Popeye's Fried Chicken, 235
 Romano's Macaroni Grill Carmela's Chicken, 206
 Ruby Tuesday Chicken Quesadillas, 138
 Ruby Tuesday Sonora Chicken Pasta, 139
 Ruby Tuesday White Chicken Chili, 72
 Starbucks Tarragon Chicken Salad, 86
 Subway Orchard Chicken Salad, 88
 Subway Sweet Onion Chicken Teriyaki Sandwich, 89
 Taco Bell Santa Fe Gorditas, 161
 T.G.I. Friday's Dragonfire Chicken, 140
 T.G.I. Friday's Sizzling Chicken and Cheese, 142
 T.G.I. Friday's Spicy Cajun Chicken Pasta, 143
 Wendy's Spicy Chicken Sandwich, 91
Chili's
 about, 134; appetizer/dessert promotions, 39
 Black Bean Soup, 58
 Boneless Buffalo Wings, 37
 Cajun Chicken Pasta, 134
 Calypso Cooler, 268
 Chicken Enchilada Soup, 59
 Chicken Fajita Nachos, 38
 Chicken Mushroom Soup, 60
 Chocolate Chip Paradise Pie, 249
 Electric Lemonade, 268
 Grilled Caribbean Chicken Salad, 80
 Margarita Grilled Chicken, 134
 Mighty Ice Cream Pie, 250
 Molten Lava Cake, 251
 Monterey Chicken, 135
 Presidente Margarita, 269
 Skillet Queso, 39
 Southwest Chicken Chili, 61
 Southwestern Eggrolls, 40
 Texas Cheese Fries, 41
Chipotle
 about, 152
 Cilantro Lime Rice, 151
 Marinated Chicken, 152
 Pork Carnitas, 153
 Steak Barbacoa, 154
Chocolate
 about: lava cake origins, 251
 Bennigan's Death by Chocolate Cake, 246
 Cheesecake Factory Oreo Cheesecake, 247
 Chili's Chocolate Chip Paradise Pie, 249
 Chili's Mighty Ice Cream Pie, 250
 Chili's Molten Lava Cake, 251
 Cinnabon Mochalatte Chill, 275
 Cracker Barrel Cherry Chocolate Cobbler, 254
 Jack in the Box Oreo Shake, 277
 Mrs. Fields Chocolate Chip Cookies, 107
 Starbucks Black Bottom Cupcakes, 259
 Starbucks Mocha Frappucino, 281
 Subway White Chocolate Macadamia Nut Cookies, 261
 T.G.I. Friday's Chocolate Monkey, 270
 The Melting Pot Dark Chocolate Raspberry Fondue, 263
 The Melting Pot Flaming Turtle Fondue, 264
 Wendy's Frosty, 281
Chopping, 11
Cinnabon
 Cinnamon Rolls, 17
 Mochalatte Chill, 275
 Orange Icescape, 275
Citrus
 Chili's Electric Lemonade, 268
 Cinnabon Orange Icescape, 275
 Lemon Butter Sauce, 196
 Orange Julius, 279
 Outback Steakhouse Key Lime Pie, 257
 Sonic Cherry Limeade, 280
 T.G.I. Friday's Dreamsicle, 271
Cocktails and drinks, **265–66**, 267–81
Coffee drinks
 Cinnabon Mochalatte Chill, 275
 Dairy Queen Moolatte, 276
 Dunkin Donuts Iced Coffee, 276
 McDonald's Caramel Frappe, 278
 McDonald's Vanilla Iced Coffee, 278
 Starbucks Coffee Frappe, 280
 Starbucks Mocha Frappucino, 281
Cooking terms and techniques, 11–13
Cookware and bakeware, 4
Copycat websites, 287
Corn
 Boston Market Corn Bread, 228
 Chili's Southwestern Eggrolls, 40
 Cracker Barrel Corn Bread Dressing, 230
 KFC Corn, 220
 Taco Bell Santa Fe Gorditas, 161
 Tony Roma's Corn Fritter Casserole, 238
Cracker Barrel
 about: anniversary menu, 18; restaurant chain, 20
 Apple Streusel French Toast, 18
 Baby Carrots, 230
 Banana Pudding, 252
 Carrot Cake, 253
 Cherry Chocolate Cobbler, 254
 Corn Bread Dressing, 230
 Country Green Beans, 231
 Fried Apples, 19
 Grilled Chicken Tenders, 231
 Ham and Red Eye Gravy, 19
 Hash Brown Casserole, 20

Cucumbers, buying, 10

Dairy Queen Moolatte, 276
Dave and Buster's
   about, 218
   Cheeseburger Pizza, 218
   Muffaletta Salad, 81
   Philly Steak Rolls, 42
Deep frying, 12
Denny's
   Country Fried Steak, 21
   Country Gravy, 22
   Pancake Puppies, 23
Desserts, **241–42**, 243–64. *See also* Chocolate; Fast food and treats
   about: dessert shots, 244; pantry items, 7; presenting, 14
   Applebee's Blondie Brownies, 243
   Applebee's Strawberry Dessert Shooters, 244
   Arby's Apple Turnovers, 245
   Bob Evans Peanut Butter Pie, 246
   Cheesecake Factory Pumpkin Cheesecake, 248
   Cracker Barrel Banana Pudding, 252
   Cracker Barrel Carrot Cake, 253
   Cream Cheese Frosting, 253
   Golden Corral Bread Pudding, 255
   Olive Garden Apple Carmelina, 256
   Outback Steakhouse Key Lime Pie, 257
   Pizza Hut Dessert Pizza, 258
   Starbucks Oatmeal Cookies, 260
   Subway White Chocolate Macadamia Nut Cookies, 261
   Taco Bell Caramel Apple Empanadas, 262
Dicing, 11
Domino's Cinna Stix, 99
Drinks and cocktails, **265–66**, 267–81
Dunkin Donuts Iced Coffee, 276

Eggplant, in P.F. Chang's Spicy Eggplant, 181
Eggs
   Cracker Barrel Apple Streusel French Toast, 18
   IHOP Chicken Fajita Omelet, 24
   IHOP Colorado Omelet, 24
   IHOP Stuffed French Toast, 28
   McDonald's Breakfast Burrito, 29
   McDonald's Steak, Egg, and Cheese Bagel Sandwich, 30
El Pollo Loco Chicken, 155
El Torito Guacamole, and Veggie Mix, 156
Empanadas, 262

Family-style foods, **209**–25

Fast food and treats, 93–110. *See also specific restaurants*
Fish and seafood
   about: buying, 10
   Applebee's Garlic and Peppercorn Fried Shrimp, 127
   Bahama Breeze Calypso Shrimp Pasta, 131
   Bennigan's Bamboo Chicken and Shrimp Skewers, 166
   Carino's Spicy Shrimp and Chicken, 193
   Carrabba's Linguine Pescatore, 193
   Carrabba's Mussels in Wine Sauce, 196
   Carrabba's Pasta Weesie, 195
   Cheesecake Factory Crab Cakes, 217
   Chi-Chi's Seafood Enchiladas, 150
   Chi-Chi's Seafood Nachos, 36
   Golden Corral Seafood Salad, 82
   Joe's Crab Shack Crab Nachos, 43
   Long John Silver's Beer-Battered Fish, 104
   Long John Silver's Fish Tacos, 105
   McDonald's Fillet of Fish, 106
   Olive Garden Seafood Pasta Chowder, 69
   Outback Steakhouse Coconut Shrimp, 52
   Outback Steakhouse Shrimp on the Barbie, 119
   Panda Express Kung Pao Shrimp, 169
   P.F. Chang's Firecracker Shrimp, 176
   P.F. Chang's Lemon Pepper Shrimp, 177
   Red Lobster Clam Chowder, 72
   Romano's Macaroni Grill Shrimp Portofino, 208
   Ruby Tuesday New Orleans Seafood, 237
   Tommy Bahama Crab Cakes, 144
Freezer items, 7–8
Fruits
   about. *See also specific fruits*: buying, 10; in drinks. *See* Cocktails and drinks
   Houlihan's Houli Fruit Fizz, 277

Gadgets, appliances, and tools, 2–4
Garlic
   about: roasting, 200
   Papa John's Garlic Sauce, 204
Garnishes, 13
Golden Corral
   Bread Pudding, 255
   Seafood Salad, 82
Grating, 11, 198
Green beans
   Cracker Barrel Country Green Beans, 231
   KFC Bean Salad, 82
   Morton's Garlic Green Beans, 115
   Olive Garden Penne Romana, 201

Hardee's Mushroom Swiss Burger, 100
Herbs and spices, 4–5, 120, 146
Hometown Buffet Spinach Casserole, 219
Hooters Hot Wings and Sauce, 136–37
Houlihan's Houli Fruit Fizz, 277
Houston's Hawaiian Steak Marinade, 114

IHOP
   about: potato variations, 26
   Chicken Fajita Omelet, 24
   Colorado Omelet, 24
   Harvest Grain and Nut Pancakes, 25
   Loaded Country Hash Brown Potatoes, 26
   New York Cheesecake Pancakes, 27
   Stuffed French Toast, 28
Ingredients, choosing, 8–11
In-n-Out Double-Double Burger, 100
Italian food, **184–85**, 186–208. *See also specific restaurants*

Jack in the Box
   Mini Buffalo Chicken Sandwiches, 101
   Oreo Shake, 277
Joe's Crab Shack
   Crab Dip, 43
   Crab Nachos, 43
Johnny Carino's Italian Nachos, 44
Julienne, 12

KFC
   about, 222
   Barbecue Baked Beans, 220
   Bean Salad, 82
   Coleslaw, 221
   Corn, 220
   Crispy Strips, 102
   Macaroni Salad, 221
   Mashed Potatoes and Gravy, 222
   Pepper Mayonnaise Sauce, 103
   Potato Salad, 223
   Potato Wedges, 223
   Twister, 103

Little Caesars Crazy Sauce, 197
Lone Star Steakhouse Steak Sauce, 115
LongHorn Steakhouse Steak Marinade, 114
Long John Silver's
   Baja Sauce, 105

Beer-Battered Fish, 104
   Fish Tacos, 105

Macaroni Grill. *See* Romano's Macaroni Grill
Marinades and rubs. *See* Sauces, dressings, and dips
Marinating, 12
McDonald's
   about, 29, 106
   Breakfast Burrito, 29
   Caramel Frappe, 278
   Fillet of Fish, 106
   Steak, Egg, and Cheese Bagel Sandwich, 30
   Vanilla Iced Coffee, 278
   Yogurt Parfait, 29
Measurement conversion charts, 288
Mexican food, **145–61**. *See also specific restaurants*
Mincing, 11
Morton's Garlic Green Beans, 115
Mrs. Fields Chocolate Chip Cookies, 107
Mushrooms
   about: buying, 11
   Chili's Chicken Mushroom Soup, 60
   Olive Garden Stuffed Mushrooms, 48
   Outback Steakhouse Sautéed Mushrooms, 118
   Romano's Macaroni Grill Shrimp Portofino, 208
   Steak & Ale Burgundy Mushrooms, 122

O'Charley's
   about, 62, 116
   Black and Blue Steak Salad, 116
   Loaded Potato Soup, 62
Olive Garden
   about: Culinary Institute of Tuscany, 65; dipping sauces, 45
   Angel Hair and Three Onion Soup, 63
   Apple Carmelina, 256
   Bread Sticks, 45
   Capellini Pomodoro, 198
   Chicken and Gnocchi Soup, 64
   Chicken Milanese, 199
   Chicken Scampi, 200
   Fried Mozzarella, 46
   House Salad and Dressing, 83
   Italian Sausage Soup, 65
   Minestrone Soup, 66
   Pasta e Fagioli Soup, 67
   Pasta Roma Soup, 68
   Penne Romana, 201
   Seafood Pasta Chowder, 69
   Smoked Mozzarella Fondue, 47

Steak Tuscano, 117
Strawberries Romano, 257
Stuffed Mushrooms, 48
Toasted Ravioli, 49
Tomato Basil Crostini, 50
Tuscan Garlic Chicken, 202
Venetian Apricot Chicken, 203
Zuppa Toscana Soup, 70
Onions
　Olive Garden Angel Hair and Three Onion Soup, 63
　Outback Steakhouse Blooming Onion Dipping Sauce, 52
　Outback Steakhouse Blooming Onions, 51
　T.G.I. Friday's French Onion Soup, 74
Orange Julius, 279
Outback Steakhouse
　Aussie Fries, 118
　Blooming Onion Dipping Sauce, 52
　Blooming Onions, 51
　Coconut Shrimp, 52
　Creole Marmalade Dipping Sauce, 53
　Key Lime Pie, 257
　Sautéed Mushrooms, 118
　Shrimp on the Barbie, 119
　Steak Seasoning, 120
　Sweet Potato, 120
　Wallaby Darned, 269

Pancakes, waffles, and French toast
　Cracker Barrel Apple Streusel French Toast, 18
　Denny's Pancake Puppies, 23
　IHOP Harvest Grain and Nut Pancakes, 25
　IHOP New York Cheesecake Pancakes, 27
　IHOP Stuffed French Toast, 28
Panda Express
　about, 171
　Beijing Beef, 167
　Chow Mein, 168
　Kung Pao Chicken, Shrimp, or Beef, 169
　Mandarin Chicken, 170
　Orange Chicken, 171
　Spicy Chicken, 172
Panera Bread Company Tomato Mozzarella Salad, 84
Pantry, stocking, 4–8
Papa John's Garlic Sauce, 204
Pasta
　about: al dente, 12; gnocchi, 64
　Bahama Breeze Calypso Shrimp Pasta, 131
　Boston Market Macaroni and Cheese, 211

Buca di Beppo Penne Cardinale, 188
Carino's Angel Hair with Artichokes, 190
Carino's Five Meat Tuscan Pasta, 191
Carino's Grilled Chicken Bowtie Festival, 192
Carrabba's Linguine Pescatore, 193
Carrabba's Pasta Weesie, 195
Cheesecake Factory Jambalaya Pasta, 229
Chili's Cajun Chicken Pasta, 134
Dave and Buster's Muffaletta Salad, 81
KFC Macaroni Salad, 221
Olive Garden Angel Hair and Three Onion Soup, 63
Olive Garden Capellini Pomodoro, 198
Olive Garden Chicken and Gnocchi Soup, 64
Olive Garden Pasta e Fagioli Soup, 67
Olive Garden Pasta Roma Soup, 68
Olive Garden Penne Romana, 201
Olive Garden Seafood Pasta Chowder, 69
Olive Garden Toasted Ravioli, 49
Panda Express Chow Mein, 168
P.F. Chang's Dan Dan Noodles, 175
P.F. Chang's Singapore Street Noodles, 179
P.F. Chang's Szechuan Chicken Chow Fun, 182
P.F. Chang's Zodiac Noodles, 183
Pizza Hut Cavatini, 204
Romano's Macaroni Grill Penne Rustica, 207
Ruby Tuesday Sonora Chicken Pasta, 139
T.G.I. Friday's Spicy Cajun Chicken Pasta, 143
Peanut butter
　Bob Evans Peanut Butter Pie, 246
　Peanut Sauce, 166
Peas. See Beans and legumes
Peppers
　about: buying, 11
　Bahama Breeze Vegetable Sauté, 133
　Cheesecake Factory Jambalaya Pasta, 229
P.F. Chang's
　about, 174
　Chicken Lettuce Wraps, 173
　Coconut Curry Vegetables, 174
　Dan Dan Noodles, 175
　Firecracker Shrimp, 176
　Lemon Pepper Shrimp, 177
　Mongolian Beef, 178

Singapore Street Noodles, 179
Spare Ribs, 180
Spicy Eggplant, 181
Szechuan Chicken Chow Fun, 182
Wonton Soup, 71
Zodiac Noodles, 183
Pizza Hut
　Cavatini, 204
　Dessert Pizza, 258
　Stuffed Crust Pizza, 205
Pizzas
　about: dessert, 258
　Applebee's Veggie Patch Pizza, 130
　Dave and Buster's Cheeseburger Pizza, 218
　Pizza Hut Dessert Pizza, 258
　Pizza Hut Stuffed Crust Pizza, 205
　Taco Bell Mexican Pizza, 160
Plating food, 13–14
Poaching, 12
Ponderosa Steak Sauce, 121
Popeye's
　about, 232
　Biscuits, 232
　Cajun Gravy, 233
　Dirty Rice, 234
　Fried Chicken, 235
　Red Beans and Rice, 236
Pork
　about: buying and storing, 8, 9
　Applebee's Baby Back Ribs, 126
　Bob Evans Sausage Gravy, 16
　Chipotle Pork Carnitas, 153
　Cracker Barrel Ham and Red Eye Gravy, 19
　Johnny Carino's Italian Nachos, 44
　McDonald's Breakfast Burrito, 29
　Olive Garden Italian Sausage Soup, 65
　Olive Garden Zuppa Toscana Soup, 70
　P.F. Chang's Spare Ribs, 180
Potatoes
　Applebee's Garlic Mashed Potatoes, 128
　Boston Market Dill Potato Wedges, 210
　Chili's Texas Cheese Fries, 41
　Cracker Barrel Hash Brown Casserole, 20
　IHOP Loaded Country Hash Brown Potatoes, 26
　KFC Mashed Potatoes and Gravy, 222
　KFC Potato Salad, 223
　KFC Potato Wedges, 223
　O'Charley's Loaded Potato Soup, 62
　Olive Garden Zuppa Toscana Soup, 70

Outback Steakhouse Aussie Fries, 118
T.G.I. Friday's Baked Potato Skins, 54
Presentation of food, 13–14

Qdoba Mango Salsa, 157
Quiznos Steakhouse Dip Submarine, 85

Red Lobster
　Boston Tea, 279
　Cheddar Bay Biscuits, 53
　Clam Chowder, 72
Refrigerator items, 7
Restaurant feel at home, 1–14
　appliances and cookware, 2–4
　choosing ingredients, 8–11
　cooking terms and techniques, 11–13
　copycat recipe creation, 2
　food presentation, 13–14
　measurement conversion charts, 288
　stocking pantry, 4–8
Restaurant websites, 286–87
Rice
　about: beans and, 236
　Benihana Fried Rice, 164
　Chipotle Cilantro Lime Rice, 151
　Popeye's Dirty Rice, 234
　Popeye's Red Beans and Rice, 236
　Taco Bell Fiesta Bowls, 159
Roasting, 12, 200
Romano's Macaroni Grill
　Carmela's Chicken, 206
　Penne Rustica, 207
　Shrimp Portofino, 208
Ruby Tuesday
　about, 138
　Chicken Quesadillas, 138
　New Orleans Seafood, 237
　Sonora Chicken Pasta, 139
　White Chicken Chili, 72

Salads, 75
　Applebee's Oriental Chicken Salad, 76
　California Pizza Kitchen Waldorf Chicken Salad, 79
　California Pizza Kitchen Wedge Salad, 78
　Chili's Grilled Caribbean Chicken Salad, 80
　Dave and Buster's Muffaletta Salad, 81
　Golden Corral Seafood Salad, 82
　KFC Bean Salad, 82
　KFC Coleslaw, 221
　KFC Macaroni Salad, 221
　KFC Potato Salad, 223

INDEX　293

Salads—*continued*
   O'Charley's Black and Blue Steak Salad, 116
   Olive Garden House Salad and Dressing, 83
   Panera Bread Company Tomato Mozzarella Salad, 84
   Starbucks Tarragon Chicken Salad, 86
   Subway Orchard Chicken Salad, 88
   T.G.I. Friday's Strawberry Fields Salad, 90
Sandwiches, 75
   about: muffaletta origins, 81; toasted submarines, 85
   Arby's Roast Beef Sandwich, 77
   Carl's Jr. Six Dollar Burger, 97
   Carl's Jr. Western Bacon Cheeseburger, 98
   Dave and Buster's Muffaletta Salad, 81
   Hardee's Mushroom Swiss Burger, 100
   In-n-Out Double-Double Burger, 100
   Jack in the Box Mini Buffalo Chicken Sandwiches, 101
   Quiznos Steakhouse Dip Submarine, 85
   Sonic Fritos Chili Cheese Wraps, 108
   Sonic Hickory Burger, 108
   Steak 'n Shake Frisco Melt, 87
   Subway Sweet Onion Chicken Teriyaki Sandwich, 89
   Subway Veggie Delite Wrap, 88
   Wendy's Spicy Chicken Sandwich, 91
   White Castle Sliders, 110
Sauces, dressings, and dips
   A&W Coney Island Sauce, 95
   about: Alfredo sauce origin, 195; marinades and rubs, 123; Olive Garden dipping sauces, 45; pantry items, 5; storing sauces, 198
   Applebee's Pico de Gallo, 34
   Arby's Barbecue Sauce, 77
   Bahama Breeze Jamaican Marinade, 132
   Benihana Hibachi Meat Marinade, 164
   Bob Evans Sausage Gravy, 16
   Carrabba's Bread Dipping Mix, 36
   Chi-Chi's Margarita Marinade, 149
   Chili's Skillet Queso, 39
   Coconut Curry Sauce, 174
   Denny's Country Gravy, 22
   El Torito Guacamole, 156
   Granita Sauce, 207
   Honey-Mustard Dipping Sauce, 35
   Hooters Hot Wing Sauce, 137
   Houston's Hawaiian Steak Marinade, 114
   Joe's Crab Shack Crab Dip, 43
   KFC Gravy, 222
   KFC Pepper Mayonnaise Sauce, 103
   Lemon Butter Sauce, 196
   Little Caesars Crazy Sauce, 197
   Lone Star Steakhouse Steak Sauce, 115
   LongHorn Steakhouse Steak Marinade, 114
   Long John Silver's Baja Sauce, 105
   Olive Garden Salad Dressing, 83
   Outback Steakhouse Blooming Onion Dipping Sauce, 52
   Outback Steakhouse Creole Marmalade Dipping Sauce, 53
   Peanut Sauce, 166
   Ponderosa Steak Sauce, 121
   Popeye's Cajun Gravy, 233
   Qdoba Mango Salsa, 157
   Singapore Sauce, 179
   Spicy Sauce, 181
   Taco Bell Fire Border Sauce, 159
   Texas Roadhouse Honey Cinnamon Butter, 123
   Texas Roadhouse Steak Rub, 123
   T.G.I. Friday's Jack Daniels Grilling Sauce, 141
   T.G.I. Friday's Nine Layer Dip, 54
   Tony Roma's Carolina Barbecue Sauce, 237
   Tony Roma's Red Hot Barbecue Sauce, 240
Sautéing, 13
Searing, 13
Shoney's
   about, 224
   Broccoli Casserole, 224
   Pot Roast, 225
Simmering, 13
Sizzler Cheese Toast, 121
Slicing, 12
Sonic
   Cherry Limeade, 280
   Fritos Chili Cheese Wraps, 108
   Hickory Burger, 108
Soups, stews, and chilis, **55**–74
Southern-style food, **227**–40
Spinach
   about: buying, 11
   Applebee's Spinach and Artichoke Dip, 34
   Boston Market Creamed Spinach, 210
   Chili's Southwestern Eggrolls, 40
   Hometown Buffet Spinach Casserole, 219

Squash, in Boston Market Squash Casserole, 213
Starbucks
   about, 31
   Black Bottom Cupcakes, 259
   Bran Muffins, 31
   Coffee Frappe, 280
   Mocha Frappucino, 281
   Oatmeal Cookies, 260
   Tarragon Chicken Salad, 86
Steak & Ale Burgundy Mushrooms, 122
Steakhouse favorites, **111**–23
Steak 'n Shake
   Chili, 73
   Frisco Melt, 87
Steaming, 13
Stewing, 13
Stir-frying, 13
Stuffings, 48, 214, 230
Subway
   Orchard Chicken Salad, 88
   Sweet Onion Chicken Teriyaki Sandwich, 89
   Veggie Delite Wrap, 88
   White Chocolate Macadamia Nut Cookies, 261
Sweet potatoes
   Boston Market Sweet Potato Casserole, 215
   Outback Steakhouse Sweet Potato, 120
   Tony Roma's Maple Sweet Potatoes, 239

Taco Bell
   Caramel Apple Empanadas, 262
   Crispitos, 109
   Enchiritos, 158
   Fiesta Bowls, 159
   Fire Border Sauce, 159
   Mexican Pizza, 160
   Santa Fe Gorditas, 161
Terms and techniques, 11–13
Texas Roadhouse
   Honey Cinnamon Butter, 123
   Steak Rub, 123
T.G.I. Friday's
   about, 54; happy hour, 270; salads, 90
   Baked Potato Skins, 54
   Broccoli Cheese Soup, 74
   Chocolate Monkey, 270
   Dragonfire Chicken, 140
   Dreamsicle, 271
   Flying Grasshopper, 271
   French Onion Soup, 74
   Jack Daniels Grilling Sauce, 141
   Long Island Iced Tea, 272
   Midnight Meltdown, 272
   Nine Layer Dip, 54

Sizzling Chicken and Cheese, 142
Spicy Cajun Chicken Pasta, 143
Strawberry Fields Salad, 90
The Melting Pot
   about, 263
   Dark Chocolate Raspberry Fondue, 263
   Flaming Turtle Fondue, 264
Tomatoes
   Olive Garden Tomato Basil Crostini, 50
   in sauces. *See* Sauces, dressings, and dips
Tommy Bahama
   Blue Hawaiian, 273
   Calypso Sun, 273
   Crab Cakes, 144
   Crazy Cuban, 274
   Millionaire Mojito, 274
Tony Roma's
   about, 237
   Carolina Barbecue Sauce, 237
   Corn Fritter Casserole, 238
   Maple Sweet Potatoes, 239
   Red Hot Barbecue Sauce, 240

Vegetables. *See also specific vegetables*
   about: buying, 10–11
   Bahama Breeze Vegetable Sauté, 133
   Chevys Fresh Mex San Antonio Veggies, 146
   El Torito Veggie Mix, 156
   Olive Garden Minestrone Soup, 66
   Panda Express Chow Mein, 168

Websites, 286–87
Wendy's
   Frosty, 281
   Spicy Chicken Sandwich, 91
White Castle Sliders, 110
Wontons, homemade, 71

Yogurt, in McDonald's Yogurt Parfait, 29

Zesting, 12